Inside Networks

Inside Networks

A Process View on Multi-organisational
Partnerships, Alliances and Networks

Edited by

Tobias Gössling, Leon Oerlemans and Rob Jansen

Tilburg University
The Netherlands

Edward Elgar
Cheltenham, UK • Northampton, MA, USA

Published by
Edward Elgar Publishing Limited
Glensanda House
Montpellier Parade
Cheltenham
Glos GL50 1UA
UK

Edward Elgar Publishing, Inc.
William Pratt House
9 Dewey Court
Northampton
Massachusetts 01060
USA

A catalogue record for this book
is available from the British Library

Library of Congress Cataloguing in Publication Data

Inside networks : a process view on multi-organisational partnerships, alliances and networks / edited by Tobias Gössling, Leon Oerlemans, Rob Jansen.
    p. cm.
  Includes bibliographical references and index.
1. Business networks. 2. Organisational behaviour. I. Gössling, Tobias.
II. Oerlemans, L. A. G. III. Jansen, Rob.
  HD69 S8I55 2007
  338.8'7–dc22
                 2007001392

ISBN 978 1 84542 784 9

Printed and bound in Great Britain by MPG Books Ltd, Bodmin, Cornwall

Contents

Figures

Tables

Contributors

Michael Arthur is Professor of Management at Suffolk University, Boston, USA. His work focuses on the relationships between careers, communities and employment arrangements in the knowledge-based economy. His previous books include *The Boundaryless Career*, *The New Careers*, *Career Frontiers* and *Career Creativity*. He has written extensively for academic and professional journals, and is a developer of the 'Intelligent Career Card Sort'® (ICCS®), which intends to help people manage their careers in contemporary times.

Marian Barnes is Professor of Social Policy at the School of Applied Social Science, University of Brighton, United Kingdom. She has undertaken national evaluations of significant partnership initiatives in England, namely, Health Action Zones and the Children's Fund, and has researched user involvement and public participation in a range of policy contexts.

Robert DeFillippi is Professor of Management and Director of the Centre for Innovation and Change Leadership, Suffolk University, Boston, USA. His scholarly writings focus on project-based organisations and careers as vehicles for knowledge creation and dissemination. His empirical research examines high technology and cultural industries. Additionally, he is Book Series Editor for Research in Management Education and Development and Associate Editor for the *International Journal of Management Reviews*.

Tobias Gössling is an Assistant Professor in Organisation Studies at Tilburg University, the Netherlands. He holds a PhD in Political Sciences from Witten/Herdecke University, Germany. His research focuses on institutions, inter-organisational relations and relations between organisations and society (Corporate Social Responsibility).

Barbara Gray is Professor of Organisational Behaviour and director of the Centre for Research in Conflict and Negotiation at the Smeal College of Business, USA. She is also a trained mediator and consults organisations about conflict and collaboration. Her research interests include inter-organisational relations, multiparty collaborative alliances, organisational and environmental conflict, team dynamics and sense-making. She is currently studying the impacts of the repair of relationship conflict on organisations and investigating leadership functions in multiparty alliances, which includes a project with the National Institutes of Health to study trans-disciplinary teams.

Paul Hibbert holds a PhD and an MBA from the University of Strathclyde Business School, United Kingdom, where he teaches in the MBA programme. His research on inter-organisational collaboration has been published in books and peer-reviewed journals such as *M@n@gement*, the *European Management Review* and the *International Journal of Public Administration*.

Chris Huxham is Professor of Management at the University of Strathclyde Graduate School of Business and Senior Fellow of the Advanced Institute of Management Research (AIM), United Kingdom. Her research concerns developing support for the management of inter-organisational collaboration, partnerships, alliances and networks. She received awards from the Academy of Management (Public and non-profit division) for this work in 1998 and 2001. She is on the Advisory board for *Public Management Review* and the Editorial Board of *Organization Studies*.

Rob Jansen is lecturer at the Department of Organisation Studies at Tilburg University, the Netherlands. He is currently writing his PhD thesis in the area of decision quality in organisational decision-making. His research interests lie in decision making, corporate social responsibility, and collaboration in inter-organisational settings.

Louise Knight is a Senior Research Fellow at the Centre for Research in Strategic Purchasing and Supply at the University of Bath School of Management, United Kingdom. She has led and contributed to a wide range of projects relating to supply management, public procurement, learning, and inter-organisational networks. Her work has been published in books and journals, including *Human Relations*, *Management Learning* and the *International Journal of Operations and Production Management*. She is the Associate Editor of the *Journal of Purchasing and Supply Management*.

Joris Knoben is a PhD student at the Department of Organisation Studies at Tilburg University, the Netherlands. He holds an MSc degree in economics from Tilburg University with a focus on regional economics. His main research interests lie on the tangential plane of regional economics and inter-organisational network theory.

Val Lindsay is Associate Professor of International Business and Head of the School of Marketing and International Business at Victoria University of Wellington, New Zealand. Her research work focuses on the international strategy of firms, the knowledge-based dynamics of networks and clusters in relation to international performance, and services internationalisation. She is a reviewer for a number of international business and management journals, and has consulted widely for businesses and government organisations on international strategy.

Elizabeth Matka is a Research Fellow at the Institute of Applied Social Studies, University of Birmingham, United Kingdom. She has undertaken research in Australia as well as the UK and was a core member of the Health Action Zones evaluation team.

Martine van Nuenen is currently involved in project management and works as a policy maker for the law department of a large Dutch insurance company. She holds an MSc degree in Organisation Studies from Tilburg University and a Bachelor degree in economics from the 's-Hertogenbosch Business School of Economics. Her main research interests lie in inter-organisational collaboration, group and network utilisation.

Leon Oerlemans is Professor in Organisational Dynamics in the Department of Organisation Studies at Tilburg University, the Netherlands, Extraordinary Professor in the Economics of Innovation in the Department of Engineering and Technology Management at the University of Pretoria, South Africa, and a research fellow of the Eindhoven Centre for Innovation Studies. His research focuses on the analysis of innovative behaviour of organisations in general and innovation and networks in particular. His work has been published in books and journals, including *Regional Studies, Research Policy, Organisation Studies, Technological Forecasting and Social Change, South African Journal of Science* and the *International Journal of Management Reviews*.

Derrick Purdue is Senior Research Fellow at the Cities Research Centre of the University of the West of England, Bristol, United Kingdom. He is author of *Anti-Genetix* (Ashgate, 2000), and editor of *Civil Societies and Social Movements* (Routledge, 2006). He has had articles published in several academic journals.

Annie Pye is Senior Lecturer in Management at the School of Management, University of Bath, United Kingdom. Her research question is about how small groups of people run large complex organisations. Publications include articles in *Journal of Management Studies*, *Organization Science*, *Corporate Governance*, *Management Learning* and the *Financial Times*. Her latest research project includes working with directors over time, developing skill and expertise in non-executive roles and board performance.

Helen Sullivan is Professor of Urban Governance at the Cities Research Centre, University of the West of England, United Kingdom. She specialises in the study of collaboration and partnerships and has researched these fields in a variety of governance settings. She is currently exploring the relationship between collaborative arrangements and democratic institutions.

Preface

The idea for this book was born at the 2004 MOPAN 'Collisions and Coalitions' conference which had been organised by the Department of Organisation Studies at Tilburg University in the Netherlands. One of the themes of the conference dealt with conflicts and failure in inter-organisational collaborations. The idea was to research and discuss the dysfunction of partnerships in order to better understand how they function. The convenors of the conference were asked to select the best papers of their respective research streams. While looking through these papers, we noticed that much of the research presented was based on an interaction perspective. This is intriguing as the majority of studies on inter-organisational relationships and networks focuses on the structural properties of networks. As we researched the relationship between interaction, on the one hand, and conflict and failure on the other, we noticed the importance and meaning of interactionist approaches for many questions related to network research. Many of the important network assets are interactionist assets. For example, control is a form of interaction; learning takes place in interaction; and trust is built in interaction. We then focused on the question as to what we can learn about networks from looking at interaction rather than structures. Coming from a social science background, we were intrigued by that perspective and the possibilities it provides.

Networks are all around us and we are all part of several networks: social networks, collegial networks, business networks, internet communities, clubs and cliques. Thus, we are 'inside networks'. Some of them are externally given; some constructed by ourselves; some are virtual, some temporary, and some heavily affect our action possibilities. Networks have become a default option in many contexts. Collaboration between public and private partners is stimulated; collaboration between businesses is seen as a precondition for success. The enormous growth of inter-organisational relationships and networks gave birth to the network approach, which comes in two different variations: the social network analytical perspective or the network governance perspective. Network analysis as an empirical tool can be considered a major innovation in social sciences, which further strengthened the dominance of the structural account of inter-organisational networks.

Although the structural account has produced many valuable insights on networks, it has an important drawback: it frequently treats network interaction and interactions in networks as a black box. That is, it only assumes interaction between actors to explain network phenomena. By opening the black box, going inside networks and studying processes such as controlling, learning, and resolving conflicts, our insights on the functioning of network can be deepened. Following this logic, we believe that there is a need for approaches that describe and explain network (inter)action and network behaviour, which can then complement insights derived from the structural account in network research.

Research on interaction aspects provides insight into network action. When we voiced this idea, many colleagues agreed with us and shared their thoughts on this topic with us. The resulting collection of concepts about network behaviour provides a richer understanding of their function than the focus on dysfunction alone could have brought forward. This volume answers questions about the nature, the functioning and the action of actors within networks. Additionally, it provides an overview of the field of interaction research on networks and highlights those questions that are in need of further exploration.

Acknowledgements

We are grateful to many academic colleagues who supported us in the process of creating this book. First, we would like to thank all members of MOPAN (Multi-Organisational Partnerships, Alliances and Networks) who allowed us to share our ideas about this challenging research theme and who were willing to discuss our ideas, both with us and with the other authors of this book. Second, we would like to thank the authors of the chapters for their contributions and thoughts. We enjoyed the constructive collaboration. Third, we thank our student assistants Mirjam van Buren and Anke de Bakker for their valuable support. Fourth, a special word of thanks goes to Nard Oerlemans for preparing the figures and to Jule Epp for proofreading.

Our biggest thanks go to those who provided the space, time and atmosphere for working on this volume: Natascha, Marion and Iris, Benjamin, Aurelia, Joris, Nard, Laura and Youri. Thank you for your patience! We thank the publishers, especially Francine O'Sullivan, Jo Betteridge and Emma Walker, for their kind support and the smooth collaboration.

Tilburg, the Netherlands
March 2007

Tobias Gössling
Leon Oerlemans
Rob Jansen

PART I

Monitoring and Control in Partnerships and
Networks

1. Inside Networks – A Process View on Inter-organisational Relationships and Networks

Leon Oerlemans, Tobias Gössling and Rob Jansen

INTRODUCTION

Inter-organisational networks and relationships are in fashion. Interest in organisational networks across a wide variety of fields has been rising very quickly for several years. Network studies have emerged in virtually every area of organisational research, including leadership, power, turnover, entrepreneurship, stakeholder relations, knowledge creation and utilisation, innovation, and inter-firm collaboration.

In a description of the state of the art of research on organisation networks, Borgatti and Foster (2003) conclude that most studies fall in one of four possible categories in a scheme consisting of two dimensions. The first dimension refers to the explanatory goal, which can be either performance or homogeneity. Some studies focus on explaining variation in success (e.g. performance or reward) as a function of inter-organisational relationships. Other studies concentrate on the explanation of homogeneity in actor attitudes, beliefs and practices, also as a function of inter-organisational relationships. The second dimension refers to the explanatory mechanisms in use, which can be either structuralist or connectionist. Studies differ in how they treat ties and their functions. In the structuralist approach, the focus is on the structure or configuration of ties in the (ego) network. It is a structural, topological approach that tends to neglect the content of ties and focuses on the patterns of interconnection. In the connectionist approach, the connectionist or relational stream, the focus is on the content and quality of such ties. Inter-organisational relationships and networks are seen as conduits through which information and aid flow.

A combination of the two dimensions results in four types of network studies. The first group is labelled 'structural capital' (structuralist and performance variation) and comprises of studies that concentrate on the benefits to actors of either occupying central positions in the network (e.g. Powell, Koput and Smoth-Doerr, 1996) or having an ego-network with a certain structure (e.g. Burt, 1992). The second group of studies (structuralist and homogeneity) seeks to explain common attitudes and practices in terms of similar network environments, usually indicated by centrality or structural equivalence (e.g. Galaskiewicz and Burt, 1991). In the group of studies combining performance variation and the connectionist approach, an organisation's success is a function of the quality and quantity of resources controlled by the organisation's alters (e.g. Stuart, 2000). This category comprises of research in the stakeholder and resource dependency traditions. The fourth and last group of studies is a combination of the connectionist approach and social homogeneity and seeks to explain attitudes, culture, and practices through interaction (e.g. Krackhardt and Kilduff, 2002). The spread of an idea, practice or material object is modelled as a function of interpersonal or inter-organisational interaction via friendship or other durable channels. Ties are conceived of as conduits along which information and influence flow. Actors are mutually influencing each other in a process that creates increasing structural inter-dependencies within structural subgroups. Structuralist accounts dominate the debate (Borgatti and Foster, 2003). Quantitative and conceptual research on entire networks allow for an understanding of the meaning of network structures, as well as positions and structural embeddedness in networks. Centrality and density are the two dominant independent variables used in network theory. However, criticism on this kind of research states that the focus on structural embeddedness does not lead to an understanding on relational embeddedness. Furthermore, it does not pay sufficient attention to dynamic network processes, because the description of networks is based upon stable social entities. Research addressing the qualitative aspects of relations in organisation networks is however significantly lacking.

This book contributes primarily to the fourth group of organisation network studies described above. The chapters of this book can all be placed in the connectionist tradition in network research. They all focus on the content of inter-organisational relationships and take patterns of interaction between actors as their starting point. Moreover, they seek to describe, explain or evaluate attitudes, beliefs and practices as a function of durable ties between actors. More specifically, the chapters deal with various processes (controlling, monitoring, learning, conflicts, managing conflicts) that take place in these interactions. Hence, this book contributes to the understanding of processes in multi-organisational partnerships, alliances and networks. As such, it provides insight into network processes. By taking a processual and interactionist approach on collaboration, this book clearly deals with criticism on dominant network research and fills an existing gap in the literature.

STRUCTURE OF THE BOOK

The book is organised into three parts. Each part begins with a chapter that provides a state-of-the-art literature review on aspects connected to the overall theme discussed in that specific part of the book. Each review chapter is followed by a number of chapters that provide empirical examples intended to further elaborate on or deepen insights. These empirical chapters make use of a variety of different research designs, such as case studies, surveys, inductive and deductive approaches.

Part I: Monitoring and Control in Partnerships and Networks

The first part of this book focuses on issues related to behaviour-guiding processes in multi-organisational partnerships, alliances, and networks. A key difference between inter-organisational networks and relationships, as compared to 'normal' or 'classical' organisations, is the absence of hierarchy. This confronts actors in networks with concerns about how to guide the behaviours of their collaborative partners. More generally speaking, it poses the question as to how the behaviours of actors in multi-organisations can be influenced. Some questions that surface are: how can appropriation concerns in inter-organisational networks be managed, or how can tasks in networks be coordinated in the absence of pure hierarchy? The literature proposes an array of formal and informal control mechanisms and processes ranging from outcome control (e.g. joint goal setting, performance monitoring and rewarding), behavioural control (e.g. planning, procedures, rules, norms and regulations) to social control (e.g. partner selection, trust building) and institutions. The contributions of the first part of the book deal with some of these mechanisms and processes.

In his chapter 'Inside Relationships', Tobias Gössling uses neo-institutional theory in order to analyse processes in inter-organisational relations. Institutions matter, also in inter-organisational relations. In other words, rules and regulations play a central role in networks. However, how do institutions influence the behaviour of members of such relations? Institutions develop, modify, persist and vanish in interaction; network actors use network structures in order to perform sanctioning on their interaction partners; and institutions alter the outcome of interaction processes. The literature review in this chapter outlines the contributions of research on this question. It pays special attention to the meaning of formal institutions for inter-organisational relations, the meaning of informal institutions and, finally, the development of normative and incentive structures within relations.

The chapter by Martine van Nuenen – 'Beyond Boundaries: A Cognitive Perspective on Boundary Setting' – deals with a form of social control, more specifically with partner selection (inclusion and exclusion) and, therefore, concentrates on boundary setting processes within networks. It argues that, in organisational theories, different assumptions have been made regarding how actors make choices. Contrary to rational choice models, the chapter proposes that groups of actors act, in part, upon the basis of shared frameworks of mental models that provide an interpretation of the environment as well as a prescription as to how that environment should be structured. The chapter departs from the relationship between aggregated cognition and embeddedness of social systems (e.g. network). It proposes that, underneath the formal rules and resources, entrenched cognitive processes appear to be in effect. These processes make up a cognitive substructure that is distinct from the network structure. The cognitive substructure as a set of relational ties is crucial for inclusion and exclusion processes.

Helen Sullivan, Marian Barnes and Elizabeth Matka, in their chapter on 'Building Collaborative Capacity for Collaborative Control: Health Action Zones in England', focus on partnership control. The empirical data for this study stem from projects in Health Action Zones (HAZs), which make up part of Area Based Initiatives (ABIs). ABIs are partnership initiatives of the United Kingdom's New Labour Government, which aim at change in the public sector. These initiatives were all based upon the application of partnership working between stakeholders from different sectors to achieve their goals. However, despite considerable evaluation efforts, relatively little attention has been paid to the ways in which ABIs have sought to generate or harness the necessary resources or capacity to work collectively and successfully. This chapter examines the ways in which actors in one of the HAZs set about channelling the necessary collaborative capacity to achieve their objectives. Moreover, the chapter illustrates that there has been a shift in attention from the more tangible, formal aspects of collaboration (e.g. the operation of contractual relationships) to the more intangible, informal aspects, such as the development of personal relationships, and the importance of collaborative organisational cultures.

Derrick Purdue, in his chapter 'A Learning Network Approach to Community Empowerment', reports extensively on an evaluation project. He applies an action learning methodology to enhance access to networks, decision-making power, and knowledge of what works. In this sense, the chapter deals with monitoring behaviour and outcomes in a network setting. The chapter draws on fieldwork at national networking events, regional workshops and individual projects. It presents an outline of the evaluation methodology and the findings. In an evaluation, the programme outcome is compared to the aims to improve the knowledge, networks and access to power holders of the participating community organisations. The evaluation is not simply a technical effort to monitor the progress of the project. It contributes to the process of empowerment through building more effective partnerships and networks.

The chapter by Purdue is in some ways connected to the chapters by Van Nuenen and Sullivan, Barnes and Matka as it basically addresses the question as to how networks know how they are doing. Furthermore, it refers to psychological processes underlying the behaviour of network actors. It also builds a bridge between Part I and Part II of this book, as it introduces the learning issue into the discussion on inter-organisational collaboration.

Part II: Learning in Partnerships and Networks

The second part of the book deals with 'learning in collaborative settings'. A significant and growing body of literature addressing the topic of organisational learning has evolved over the past years. Foundational work focused on learning as either a cognitive process or a function of behavioural change occurring through modification of an organisation's programmes, goals, decision rules, or routines. More recently, scholars have developed theories of how organisational learning occurs and how it impacts organisational performance. Learning is often claimed to be an explicit aim of, or potential benefit from, collaboration, and learning through collaboration is at the heart of many government policies. Therefore, learning processes and their outcomes are currently one of the most important aspects of collaborative efforts. The three chapters in Part II deal with these collaborative learning issues.

Paul Hibbert and Chris Huxham, in their chapter on 'Collaboration, Knowledge and Learning: Integrating Perspectives', investigate whether taking a broad view of the literature in the area of learning can lead synergistically to new and useful insights about the nature, role and impact of learning as it relates to inter-organisational collaborations. To investigate this area, Hibbert and Huxham survey a broad range of journals and books. This review was conducted in order to develop an emergent picture of the field of inter-organisational learning. Hibbert and Huxham's literature survey revealed that linkages and tensions were seen to be related, on the one hand, to learning outcomes, and, on the other hand, to learning processes and explanatory factors. As far as learning outcomes are concerned, the chapter discusses collaborative learning as a precondition for successful partnership outcomes; competitive versus collaborative learning; as well as other (un)intentional learning outcomes. Process and explanatory factors include: cultural influences on collaborative learning; the relevance of collaborative types, inter-organisational forms and partner characteristics for inter-organisational learning; and approaches for supporting learning. This chapter explores both of these two strands.

The chapter 'Brokerage, Closure and Community Dynamics: Implications for Virtual Knowledge Work Collaborations' by Robert DeFillippi, Michael Arthur and Valery Lindsay, provides the analytic framework for examining how knowledge work embodies both intra-community and inter-community dynamics in virtual collaborations. Brokerage involves the development of a community's ties with outsiders, through which knowledge can be usefully gained or traded. Closure refers to the ties that exist among a community's members and occurs through the members' mutual commitment to one another. The chapter proposes a systematic theoretical approach for examining these complementary phenomena, drawing particularly on ideas about social networks, social embeddedness and social capital. The chapter examines a number of contrasting examples, where the collaborating parties do not always have the opportunity for face-to-face interactions, but must rely, at least in part, on virtual channels of communication. Finally, the chapter describes the state of the art in the virtual intra-community and inter-community dynamics underlying knowledge work.

Louise Knight and Annie Pye describe 'The Search for Network Learning: Some Practical and Theoretical Challenges in Process Research'. This chapter draws on conceptual, empirical and methodological literature on networks and an empirical study of network learning – learning by a group of organisations as a group. The first part of this chapter describes a search process to find a theoretical concept for learning processes. This concept describes a learning context, learning content and learning process as key elements for analysis. The second part focuses on the implications for research processes. The appreciation of embeddedness as a social and relational phenomenon allows for a better understanding of the network process of 'learning'.

Part III: Conflicts and Failures in Partnerships and Networks

The third part of the book focuses on conflicts and conflict management in collaborative settings. Whenever organisations choose a collaborative setting, they have certain a priori positive expectations about the outcome of their collaborations. Given assumptions about instrumental rationality, actors will not choose to collaborate with other actors if they do not think it is beneficial for them to do so. These benefits of collaboration can be pecuniary and non-pecuniary: financial, market access, interaction, sympathy, legitimacy, etc. With respect to one or several of these dimensions, actors should have positive expectations in order to have an incentive to start and maintain an inter-organisational relationship. However, success in collaboration seems to be the exception rather than the rule (Park and Russo, 1996). Several studies show failure rates in collaborations ranging from 35 to 70 per cent (Reuer and Zollo, 2005; Park and Ungson, 1997; Kogut, 1989, Harrigan, 1988). Very inefficient collaborative settings, as well as failures of joint efforts, can be observed. Such failure, of course, is detrimental for the collaborating organisations, and, especially, for the joint goal. In order to learn from past experiences for the benefit of future collaboration, and to learn from the failure of others, it can be extremely helpful to analyse failure, to look for reasons for failure and to develop approaches to avoid collisions. Part III of the book focuses on the factors causing conflicts and on issues related to the management, development and solution of conflicts in collaborative settings.

The chapter 'Tie Failure: A Literature Review' by Leon Oerlemans, Tobias Gössling and Rob Jansen is a literature review on the ultimate form of inter-organisational conflict, namely tie dissolution, or, more precisely, factors influencing tie failure. It asks the question concerning why collaboration partners collide and why collaborations eventually fail. Three types of reasons for failures of collaboration, namely cognitive, motivational and behavioural reasons, can be analysed. Learning from the failures in and of collaborative settings means understanding the reasons for failure and analysing the existence of such reasons in actual interactions. In this review, three main factors for failures of coalitions emerge: environmental, organisational and relational. It appears that relational aspects dominate the factors causing coalition failure. It is proposed to come to a more detailed analysis of relational factors between partners in coalitions.

In a chapter on 'Frame-based Interventions for Promoting Understanding in Multi-party Conflicts', Barbara Gray proposes framing as a method for understanding and possibly solving conflicts in collaboration. The chapter discusses the necessity for parties and mediators in collaboration to adopt common frames for their efforts. Framing, in general, refers to the process of constructing and representing interpretations of a situation. Frames serve as lenses that enable parties to sort, synthesise and condense large amounts of information into manageable nuggets. Parties who are trying to negotiate joint agreements all use frames to identify, interpret and present salient elements of their experience of the issues and of each other. While the construction of joint frames may be desirable, shifting parties from contradictory frames to frames they can mutually embrace poses considerable challenges. The presence or absence of certain kinds of frames greatly contributes to intransigence in and escalation of many conflicts, particularly value-based or ideological conflicts. In this chapter, several frame-based interventions that have demonstrated some potential for opening a dialogue among the stakeholders in intractable conflicts are examined. In sum, this chapter proposes that frame-based interventions can be helpful for the management of conflicts.

In their chapter 'From Inter-organisational Conflict to Collaboration: The Case of the Music Recording Industry', Rob Jansen and Joris Knoben examine the origins and development of conflicts in an inter-organisational domain by focusing on the developments in the music recording industry. This chapter analyses the development that took place after the introduction of a new technology in this industry, which had a large impact on the composition of the industry as well as on its (internal) dynamics. After the entrance and subsequent spreading of the innovation, the industry was characterised by conflicts between organisations. Over time, however, collaboration between organisations emerged. By answering their research question concerning which factors play a part in the origins of inter-organisational conflict and in its development towards inter-organisational collaboration, they show that a longitudinal case study can give valuable insights into the interaction processes at work in an industry.

Part IV: Conclusions

The last chapter of this book 'Conclusions: Questions for Future Research' by Leon Oerlemans, Tobias Gössling and Rob Jansen provides an overview of the lessons learned from this volume. The last chapter categorises the results and conclusions from the different chapters in this volume and answers questions concerning the relational processes within networks. It offers an overview of the relevant research questions in the context of relational approaches towards networks and network theory.

REFERENCES

Burt, R.S. (1992), *Structural Holes: The Social Structure of Competition*, Cambridge, MA: Harvard University Press.
Borgatti, S.P. and P.C. Foster (2003), 'The network paradigm in organizational research: A review and typology', *Journal of Management*, **29** (6), 991-1013.
Galaskiewicz, J. and R.S. Burt (1991), 'Interorganization contagion in corporate philanthropy', *Administrative Science Quarterly*, **36** (1), 88-105.

Harrigan, K.R. (1988), 'Strategic Alliances and Partner Asymmetries', in F. Contractor and P. Lorange (eds), *Cooperative Strategies in International Business*, Lexington, MA: Lexington Books, pp. 205-226.

Kogut, B. (1989), 'The stability of joint ventures: Reciprocity and competitive rivalry', *Journal of Industrial Economics*, **38** (2), 183-198.

Krackhardt, D. and M. Kilduff (2002), 'Structure, culture and Simmelian ties in entrepreneurial firms', *Social Networks*, **24** (3), 279-290.

Park, S.H. and M.V. Russo (1996), 'When competition eclipses cooperation: An event history analysis of joint venture failure', *Management Science*, **42** (6), 875-890.

Park, S.H. and G.R. Ungson (1997), 'The effect of national culture, organizational complementarity, and economic motivation on joint venture dissolution', *Academy of Management Journal*, **40** (2), 279-307.

Powell, W.W., W.K. Koput and L. Smith-Doerr (1996), 'Interorganizational collaboration and the locus of innovation: Networks of learning in biotechnology', *Administrative Science Quarterly*, **41** (1), 116-145.

Reuer, J.J. and M. Zollo (2005), 'Termination outcomes of research alliances', *Research Policy*, **34** (1), 101-115.

Stuart, T.E. (2000), 'Interorganizational alliances and the performance of firms: A study of growth and innovation rates in a high-technology industry', *Strategic Management Journal*, **21** (8), 791-812.

2. Inside Relationships: A Review of Institutional Approaches towards Multi-organisational Partnerships, Alliances and Networks

Tobias Gössling

INTRODUCTION

Multi-organisational partnerships and networks are increasingly important phenomena in organisation studies as well as in the global economy, as production and services are increasingly often structured into such organisational forms (cf. Grugulis, Vincent and Hebson, 2003; Gössling, Jansen and Oerlemans, 2005). These organisational forms are particularly common in project management, product development and the provision of services, e.g. care (c.f. Sydow, Lindkvist and DeFillippi, 2004; Burgess, Carey and Young, 2005; Van Baalen, Bloemhof-Ruwaard and Heck, 2005). Organisational research approaches refer to the concept of inter-organisational relationships (or IORs), which are understood to be a specific form of economic interaction that is different from the atomized exchange on the markets, on the one hand, and different from the hierarchical relations in firms, on the other (c.f. Williamson, 1973; Williamson, 1975; Powell, 1990; Oliver, 1994). IORs provide shared access to resources, are more flexible than large organisations of mass production, can more easily meet the demand for specialised products and services, and are a mechanism that facilitates innovation (Powell and Smith-Doerr, 1994).

IORs are fashionable, although not new, research objects. In the last decennia, research on networks, and especially on IORs, has brought forward a wealth of knowledge. More specifically, it has answered questions about the nature of networks and of network members as actors. It has added to our knowledge about network development (c.f. Callander and Plott, 2005), network effectiveness (c.f. Chan, Kensinger, Keown and Martin, 1997; Provan and Milward, 2001), network management and coordination (c.f.

Jones, Hesterly and Borgatti, 1997; Vangen and Huxham, 2003), knowledge sharing and development within networks (c.f. Sydow et al., 2004 and other papers in that issue; Nielsen, 2005), as well as knowledge about partner selection (c.f. Rese, 2006). Structural accounts and classical network analysis provide us with research methods for visualising, quantifying and evaluating network relationships and structures (Cross, Borgatti and Parker, 2002; Provan, Veazie, Staten and Teufel-Shone, 2005). In the research literature, structural network characteristics have been studied and found to be related to benefits and opportunities of the respective network members (c.f. Burt, 1992). However, the relational aspects of IORs have to date received too little attention (Borgatti and Foster, 2003; Gössling and Jansen, 2006). Relational approaches in IOR research focus on the flows of resources between partners, e.g., information, valuation, thoughts or perceptions (Borgatti and Foster, 2003; Borgatti and Cross, 2003). Powell and Smith-Doerr (1994) mentioned this topic as one of the most relevant questions in qualitative network analysis.

Institutional approaches towards economic and organisational issues are prominent in current research as a consequence of the explanatory power of institutional theory (c.f. Kondra and Hinings, 1998; Hasselbladh and Kallinikos, 2000; Whitley, 2003; Redek and Susjan, 2005). Some scholars argue that institutions form the basic unit of analysis of economic interaction and are to be considered the fundamental building blocks of economic activity (c.f. Barnett, 2005). The discussions concerning institutions mainly focus on two aspects of institutions, namely the nature and causes of institutions, on the one hand, and the consequences of institutions, especially for economic and organisational behaviour and performance, on the other (c.f. North, 1990; Nelson and Sampat, 2001; Acemoglu and Johnson, 2005; De Cavalcanti and Novo, 2005). However, there is disagreement amongst scholars about the nature and definition of institutions. This disagreement not only highlights important differences between old institutional approaches and neo-institutional approaches (c.f. Nelson and Sampat, 2001) and differences between sociologists and economists (Scott, 2003) but also highlights the number of different ideas that can be found within these groups themselves. None of this lends itself well to the bringing of clarity into our understanding of institutions and their consequences. For example, Den Butter and Mosch (2003: 362), refer to 'government, unions, employer organisations, central banks, and advisory bodies' when they describe institutions, which is somewhat in contradiction with North's (1990: 3) definition of institutions as 'the humanly devised constraints that shape human interaction'. In order to understand the consequences of institutions for interaction in IORs, it is helpful to clearly define institutions and to understand the mechanisms that relate institutions with IOR action and behaviour.

Recently, scholars have approached IORs issues with institutional theory. Many of these research projects focus on the consequences of institutions for partnerships, and, more specifically, on the consequences of institutions and the level of institutional similarity between organisations for outcomes of partnerships (see Uzzi, 1997; Zaheer, McEvily and Perrone, 1998 for early approaches, and for more recent approaches see Barnett, 2005; Gössling et al., 2005; Matutinovic, 2005).

Since institutionalism essentially deals with interaction, it is presumably helpful for understanding and explaining relational aspects in IORs. In other words, institutions form conditions for interaction, and as such have consequences for actors. A common example of institutional consequences for relational aspects in interaction is the development of trust in IORs, which is a consequence of shared institutions (c.f. Gössling, 2004).

This chapter answers the following question: what are the consequences of institutions for interaction in IORs as discussed in the scientific literature? In order to answer this question, this chapter presents a literature review. In the first part, it presents an applicable definition of institutions as conditions for interaction. As such, it presents institutional theory as a theory of interaction. The second part discusses the relevance of interactional approaches in IOR research. Subsequently, the chapter reviews literature that addresses the consequences of institutions for IORs. In an overview, the chapter also presents the main contributions of institutional approaches to IORs research. In order to review the literature, a string of keywords that resulted from an iterative process was used. This string contained, for example, the concepts 'institutions, rules, collaboration, networks, partnerships, relations, IORs' and was applied on two different literature databases (ABI/Inform and ISI Web of Knowledge). The search resulted in a total of 345 articles. The abstracts of these articles were reviewed. Those articles that not only apply a definition of institutions that is compatible with our working definition, but also relate to IORs, were then included in the literature review discussed in this chapter. The inclusion criteria resulted in a total of 29 relevant articles (Tables 2.2 to 2.4). The conclusions answer the research question and discuss questions for further research in this tradition.

INSTITUTIONS

Three questions are relevant for understanding institutions: first, what are they? Second, how do they develop and change? Third, what are their consequences?

Research on institutions has undergone significant changes in the last decades. We can distinguish between an old and a new form of institutionalism. The old school of institutionalism defines institutions as typical patterns of interaction in social relationships. Institutions set the context for living and acting in societies (Ricoeur and Blamey, 1992; Bezes, Lallement and Lorrain, 2005). This definition of institutions can also be described metaphorically as the way in which the game of society is played (Nelson and Sampat, 2001). Hodgson (2004) stays in line with these old institutionalist approaches when he defines institutions as habits of thought and activity. This definition also encompasses organisations such as the state, churches, families and schools (Dubet, 2002).

Granovetter (1985) describes the old concepts of institutionalism as 'over-socialised'. These old concepts see institutions as predetermining individual behaviour. Actors are seen as rather slavishly following institutions without making use of individual reasoning and decision-making. From this understanding of institutions and their consequences for actors' behaviour, we can conclude that Granovetter is referring to old institutionalism in the following:

> Actors' behaviour results from their named role positions and role sets; thus we
> have arguments on how workers and supervisors, husbands and wives, or criminal
> and law enforcers will interact with one another, but these relations are not
> assumed to have individualised content beyond that given by the named roles.
> (ibid.: 486).

Old institutionalism has often been used to explain the phenomenon of group behaviour. However, old institutionalism is somewhat problematic for understanding, explaining and predicting individual behaviour. Following the logic of old institutionalism, two actors with similar institutional backgrounds would behave similarly under comparable conditions. However, actors do in fact show different behaviours when facing similar or same conditions (Oliver, 1991). Furthermore, old institutionalism does not relate institutions to theoretical models about decision-making. More specifically, it does not adequately deal with individual preferences and their consequences for decisions and actions.

Neo-institutionalism, on the other hand, relates institutions to preferences and decision-making. In neo-institutionalism, a metaphor used to describe institutions is 'the rules of the game' (North, 1990; Nelson and Sampat, 2001). In other words, institutions are 'durable systems of social rules that structure social interactions' (Barnett, 2005: 809). However, the existence of rules does not explain rule-following behaviour or deviations from rules. Rules may prescribe actions, but actors are not bound by these rules.

Institutions are seen as enabling constraints (Yack, 1988). Institutions normatively constrain or restrict the range of possible actions, but they also enable actions since they work out as decision-making aids that help reduce uncertainty.

The emphasis on constraints leads to a more elaborated definition: institutions are combinations of rules and sanctions (Gössling, 2003). As such, institutions contain three elements: the description of a situation; a normative statement or prescription about expectations; and a description about the possible consequences of rule-following behaviour and deviation. The formal structure of institutions contains these central elements: *in situation S always perform action A! Otherwise, you possibly will possibly have to face the consequence C.*

The first part of this definition thus refers to situations but also provides an inclusion/exclusion element as the description of situations can also encompass descriptions of a distinct social or juridical setting. The second part implies negative or positive normative statements, thus providing prohibitions or orders. The third part refers to consequences imposed by institutions that can be either positive or negative, consisting thus of rewards/incentives or punishments/sanctions.

This definition of institutions as combinations of rules and sanctions allows for a detailed analysis of institutions and their consequences. It is much more tangible than the definition used in old institutionalism, as it provides criteria for an analysis of the different elements of institutions. Furthermore, current research on organisations applies to a large extent to neo-institutionalism rather than to old institutionalism. Consequently, this present research focuses on neo-institutional research.

Formal and Informal Institutions

Institutionalism makes a distinction between formal and informal institutions. Some authors (c.f. North, 1990) describe the distinction between formal and informal institutions with respect to their formal appearance. Based on this understanding, formal institutions are written down, whereas the informal ones are traded orally or transported in shared mental models (Denzau and North, 1994). If we focus on the interaction between actors rather than on the formal textual conditions, we can pinpoint the distinction between formal and informal institutions to the sanctioning authority (c.f. Gössling, 2003). Formal institutions are enforced by a lawful authority, e.g. the government or a contractually defined third party, a lawyer, ombudsperson. Informal institutions, on the other hand, are enforced by actors who make up part of the social surrounding. The issue of sanctioning also highlights significant differences between formal and informal institutions. Sanctions in formal institutions are to a large extent defined within the institutions and consist of fines and penalties. Informal institutions and their related sanctions, on the contrary, are not clearly defined (Schlicht, 1998). The normative content of informal institutions allows for different types of action, and actors can be sanctioned in different forms, e.g. by inclusion/exclusion or reputation mechanisms (Gössling, 2003; 2004). In extreme forms, violence can serve as a sanction. In addition to this, formal institutions are planned and determined in a formalised process whereas informal institutions develop and change in interaction processes, which can involve either evolutionary or revolutionary processes.

Formal institutions are designed for distinct purposes. Constitutions, for example, are valid for an entire nation state; contracts bind the partners of a contractual relationship. Informal institutions are also specific to the respective institutional environment; however, there might be contingent overlap. An institutional environment is defined as a limited environment (e.g. a region) with a distinct set of institutions that are valid for every actor who acts within the respective environment (c.f. Hitt, Ahlstrom, Dacin, Levitas and Svobodina, 2004). Institutional environments can correspond with other institutional environments on the same, a higher or a subordinate level. For example, members of two different regions in the same state share to a certain extent typical informal national institutions, however, with respect to specific regional institutions; there might be differences, e.g. differences in formality.

Table 2.1 summarises this discussion about institutions by highlighting their appearance, form and sanctions.

Table 2.1   Form, occurrence and consequences of institutions

| | **Institutions** | |
	Formal	**Informal**
Appearance	Contracts, Law	Culture
Development	Codification	Evolution/Revolution
Sanctioned by	Legal Authority	Social Surrounding
Sanction	Fine	Inclusion/Exclusion, Reputation

Ways of looking at the consequences of institutions can differ between economic approaches on the one hand and sociological and behavioural approaches on the other. From an economic point of view, the main function of institutions is to influence transaction costs. Efficient institutions are designed in such a way that they reduce transaction costs (North, 1990;

Williamson, 1998; Howitt and Clower, 2000). Inefficient institutions, on the other hand, increase transaction costs. Sociological and behavioural approaches are helpful in understanding the mechanisms that relate institutions with, first, individual actions and, second, with the interaction between actors. Such approaches focus on the consequences of institutions for actors. Keeping in mind Granovetter's (1985) critique of over-socialised approaches, institutions do nevertheless influence the behaviour of those who take part in an institutional environment. However, the former does not completely determine the latter. In this context, three mechanisms are important. First, institutions form a normative framework that informs actors about the right, appropriate or desired behaviour in a given situation. Second, institutions provide security, as the normative framework is valid for every member of a specific community. Therefore, actors know how others are likely to behave. Third, institutions make it possible to calculate and evaluate consequences of behaviour, as they provide information about the possible reactions to compliance or non-compliance with the respective institutions. Actors will receive information concerning the possible consequences of compliance and non-compliance, as the sanctioning heavily depends on informational conditions (i.e., do other actors actually know about the actor's behaviour?), on the one hand, and the willingness of the respective actors to sanction the behaviour of their interaction partners on the other. The lack of sanctioning of non-compliance is positively related to non-compliance in the future (Oliver, 1991). In addition to this, institutions are not stable. They can change, and actors have an influence on these changes (c.f. North, 1990; Lawrence, Hardy and Philips, 2002). Consequently, actors are not just objects governed by institutions.

The term institutional setting is helpful for understanding the consequences of institutions on IORs and for appreciating the importance of the social surrounding for the sanctioning and rewarding of institution-oriented behaviour (c.f. Snyder, 1975; Boyes and McDowell, 1989). An institutional setting describes the sum of all formal and informal institutions that influence actors' behaviour. Different institutional settings are present and valid in different groups. Here, again, the distinction between formal and informal institutions is of relevance. Different organisations can have different formal institutions. However, even in cases where there is a significant similarity in the formal institutions of two organisations (e.g in the case of two organisational units or two organisations in one concern), the informal institutions can be very different. That is to say, even in the case of full formal institutional similarity, institutional settings in different organisations might differ from each other.

Informal institutions are often connected to culture (c.f. Nelson and Sampat, 2001). The rules and regularities of societies constitute their cultures. In this sense, informal institutional settings of organisations are part of their organisational cultures. Subcultures provide identity for those who take part in a specific subgroup (Kiesler, 1994). However, it excludes outsiders or at least creates a distance between insiders and outsiders. Organisational culture is an important and relevant research topic, yet it is a field with a wide variety of competing approaches (c.f. Riad, 2005). With respect to the term organisational culture, an institutional analysis allows for a clear analysis of elements of cultures. Examining the rules and sanctions allows us to study organisational culture, and also provides us with descriptors for organisational culture. Furthermore, members of a specific culture are part of an informal institutional setting.

Following this logic, every organisation forms an institutional setting for its members with its specific rules and possibilities for rewarding and punishing members for their behaviour. Individuals that are part of an organisation and thus members of the organisational culture are secondarily socialised within that specific institutional setting. Therefore, members of organisations are likely to know about the normative structures of the respective organisation. Second, they have certain – explicit and implicit – expectations about colleagues' behaviour. Third, they know about the incentive/disincentive structures, reward and punishment, enforcement and reinforcement mechanisms that are relevant for institution-related behaviour.

Figure 2.1   Institutions, institutional setting and environment

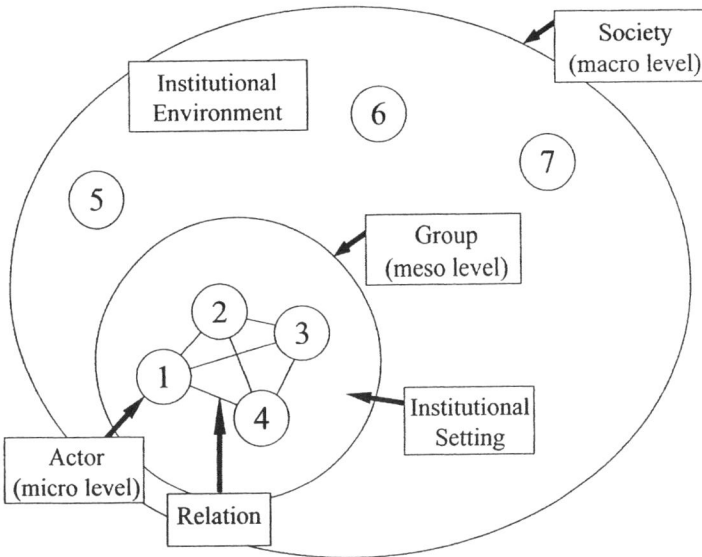

Figure 2.1 shows the different levels of institutions and their possible influence on actors. Institutions influence the behavioural options of an individual on the micro level. On the meso level, an actor has an (in)direct relation with one or several interaction partners of a group. The institutions that are specific for this group are referred to as 'institutional setting'. On the macro level, institutions exist and are relevant for the members of a society. The institutions that are specific to the society are referred to as 'institutional environment'.

NETWORKS AND INTER-ORGANISATIONAL RELATIONSHIPS

A simple definition of networks is 'a set of actors connected by a set of ties' (Borgatti and Foster, 2003: 992) with actors being 'persons, teams, organisations, concepts, etc' (ibid.). There are two network discussions that are only partly connected. One discussion involves theories of social networks and describes the multiple social relations of actors (c.f. Granovetter, 1973; Burt, 1992; Wasserman and Faust, 1994). The other discussion focuses on network theories in organisation studies and examines organisational networks (c.f. Powell, Koput and Smith-Doerr, 1996; Uzzi, 1997; Oliver and Ebers, 1998).

In organisational networks, the actors or 'nodes' in the above definition are organisations. A link between the two discussions consists in the fact that organisational networks partly contain multiple social networks that, for example, facilitate interaction (Uzzi, 1997). Furthermore, organisational networks can be embedded in social networks (c.f. Van Nuenen in Chapter 3 of this volume).

Organisational networks consist of organisations (nodes) and the present and absent relations between these organizations (IORs). IORs are relatively stable connections between organisations, consisting in 'transactions, flows, and linkages' (Oliver, 1990: 241). From a transaction cost perspective, IORs are specific governance structures that are used in order to coordinate economic interaction between partners (c.f. Kay, 1997; Williamson, 1970; Powell, 1990; Powell and Smith-Doerr, 1994). Such relations involve several hierarchically independent actors that make the decision to interact in order to achieve a certain goal or perform a certain task.

With respect to the explanatory mechanism of network theory, we can distinguish between structuralist approaches on the one hand, and connectionist or relational approaches, on the other (Borgatti and Foster, 2003; Roweley, Behrens and Krackhardt, 2000; Moran, 2005). Structuralist approaches focus on the consequences of network structures, namely, the ties, nodes, patterns or structural holes. Connectionist approaches, on the other hand, focus on the consequences of the content of ties and allow for a relational analysis. A similar distinction can be found in the two different aspects of the concept of embeddedness (Roweley, Behrens and Krackhardt, 2000). Structural embeddedness is a quantitative variable that refers to the structural position of an actor in an (ego-)network (Wasserman and Faust, 1994). Relational embeddedness, on the other hand, also provides qualitative criteria of (social) relations (Moran, 2005). A difference between these two approaches thus concerns the unit of analysis. Connectionist approaches are relational in nature and focus more extensively on the relationship between organisations than on entire networks. Dyads are the smallest structural unit of networks. They also contain the smallest possible IORs, as there are only two partners involved. In more complex relationships, several partners are involved, who, in turn, are linked via different contractual ties made up of both formal and informal contracts. Relational approaches focus on the content and quality of relationships between organisations, whereas structuralist approaches systematically focus on the entire network level.

Figure 2.2   Network, dyads and structural holes

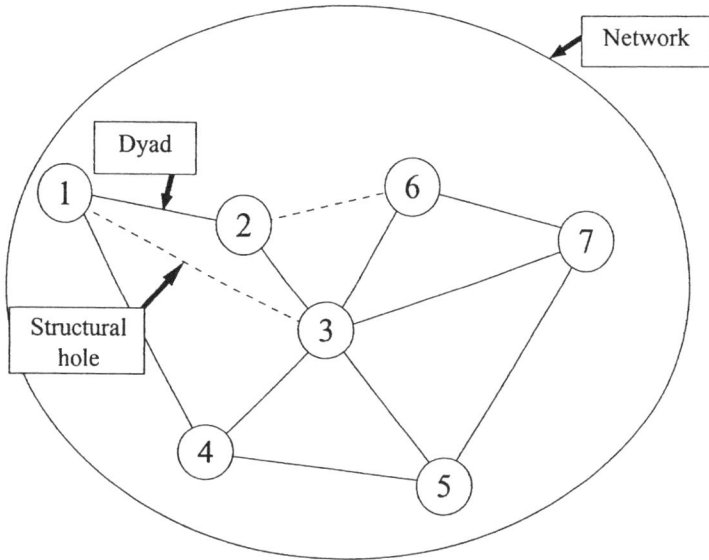

Source: Adapted from Burt (1992).

Consequently, the analysis of relational aspects focuses on IORs, and thus on the relationship between organisations.

However, a central aspect of the structural approaches has significance for the relational aspects of collaborations. Burt's (1992) theory of structural holes describes an important structural feature of networks. Within networks, actors can be related without having a direct relationship. In other words, a missing direct tie between two actors can be partially substituted by the existence of indirect ties. Figure 2.2 displays network relations, dyadic relations and structural holes. All actors 1...7 are members of a common network. The relationship between actor 1 and actor 2 is a dyad; the relationship between actor 1 and 3 is only indirect (structural hole). The circle around the network does not represent a network border, but symbolises the restriction of the researcher's focus (Brass, Galaskiewicz, Greve and Tsai, 2004).

Summarising the above discussion on networks and IORs, organisational networks consist of organisations and the multiple relationships between organisations, including structural holes. IORs are relatively stable relationships between organisations. Ties between nodes represent relationships. Organisational networks are multiply embedded in social networks and vice versa. Structural holes are indirect relationships between network actors.

INSTITUTIONS AND IORS

In order to clarify the consequences of institutions for IORs, it is helpful to make a distinction between the different possible levels of analysis. On the micro level, the focus is on individuals. Individuals are members of social or professional groups, e.g. organisations (meso level I). These groups imply institutional settings on a group level. Organisations can have relationships with other organisations (IORs, meso level II). Such relationships between groups imply that groups with their specific institutional settings interact. Organisations in relationships are exposed to institutions that are not part of their specific institutional setting. However, partners of IORs form groups and can develop institutions that are specific to their respective relationship. Hence, IORs imply institutional settings on an IOR level.

Furthermore, organisations as well as the relations between them can be part of organisational networks (meso level III). Finally, individuals, organisations, IORs and networks are part of societies (macro level). The multiple relations between members of societies are not specific. Societies form institutional environments.

With respect to institutions and IORs, the following general questions concerning institutions will be discussed in the subsequent section. What are institutions in the context of IORs? Where do they stem from and how do they change? What are their consequences? The question concerning the consequences of institutions is central to institutional theory and also essential for understanding IORs. In the following, I will discuss the different aspects of formal and informal institutions and their relationship to IORs. The subsequent section discusses the consequences of formal institutions for IORs, thus taking formal institutions as independent variables and focusing on the different possible and relevant dependent variables. The next section takes informal institutions as the independent variable and analyses their possible consequences. These two sections are very much in line with institutional theory, which focuses on the consequences of institutions and takes institutions as independent variables. The last section focuses on institutional change and isomorphism. Institutions in organisations have consequences for institutions in the partner organisations as well as in the entire IOR.

Consequences of Formal Institutions for IORs

IORs are influenced by a larger formal institutional environment, i.e. the legal conditions of the respective national or international environment. That is to say, the formal rules and sanctions of the respective national or international formal institutional environment have an impact on the action possibilities of IORs and their respective members. These institutions are external to IORs. Five of the ten papers concerning the consequences of formal institutions for IORs focus on external institutional conditions for IORs, meaning institutions at work at the macro level.

Ebrahim (2004) stresses the importance of reliable formal institutions for IOR formation. However, he does point out that a certain degree of fuzziness or vagueness in institutions can have a positive influence for IORs. In the case of a lack of formal institutions, interaction partners are more likely to engage in informal networks than in formal networks (Murphy, 2002). This would be consistent with Kalil's (1999) argument that suggests that partners use their IORs in order to substitute or evade formal institutions. De Mesquita and Stephenson (2006) suggest that the optimal size of networks decreases with the existence and effectiveness of government enforcement of actors' behaviour. Hence, the characteristics of formal institutions have an influence on network size. Hitt et al. (2004) argue that the existence of a stable institutional environment is crucial for collaboration between partners. In a less stable institutional environment, organisations are less likely to engage in long-term relations.

There is some empirical evidence concerning the consequences of formal institutions for IORs – however, it is limited. It suggests that the stability of formal institutions is important for the stability of IORs. This would be consistent with the description of the key features of institutions in institutional theory. Institutions reduce uncertainty and provide predictability. A lack of stability decreases predictability. Furthermore, the rigidity of formal institutions has a rather negative influence on IORs. Rigid institutions only allow for a limited number of responses. This finding is consistent with Gössling's (2003) idea about the importance of the openness of institutions, Schlicht's (1998) view on the significance of fuzziness – i.e. a lack of rigidity – and Oliver's (1991) findings concerning diverse strategic responses on institutional pressure.

Formal IORs are contractual relationships between partners. This statement does not deny the possibility of informal collaboration. However, informal collaboration is not based upon formal contracts. Partnerships consist at least in part of explicit contractual relationships that represent formal institutional settings. In many cases, the contractual structure is the constituent of organisational, as opposed to social networks. Formal organisational networks are defined as structured sets of organisations and their respective contractual relations (c.f. Jones et al., 1997). It is important to note that this view only partly covers IORs, as many IORs exist without formal collaboration contracts. However, if formal contracts exist, they constitute the internal formal institutional settings of IORs. Six of the eleven papers on consequences of formal institutions for IORs in this review take a meso approach and focus on these IOR settings.

Gaggio (2006) states that formal institutions are likely to promote trust between IOR members. He refers to business associations and consortia, which represent the framework for formal institutions. Although the empirical evidence for his findings is somewhat thin, the argument concerning the social consequences (trust) of formal institutional settings is convincing and consistent with institutional theory. At the same time, however, there is also evidence about the crowding out effects of trust: too many formal institutions, especially in combination with the threat of sanctions and too much control, diminish trust levels. The question remains as to the extent to which, and the ways in which, formal institutions have an influence on trust in IORs.

Contractual relationships can be designed and implemented into IORs. They are more juridical than social phenomena. Organisations can make explicit choices about how to shape their contractual relations (Gulati and Singh, 1998), and it is therefore relatively easy to provide a definition and a description of their occurrence. It has often been argued that actors are embedded in network relations that 'provide opportunities for and constraints on behaviour' (Brass et al., 2004: 795). However, this description of relations is somewhat imprecise: it is not a relationship as such that creates opportunities but rather its content and quality. Rules, being part of contracts, provide security. The relationship as such does not provide restrictions in and of itself. Rather, it is the implications of the content of the contracts which does so. In terms of institutional theory, the possible sanctions form the incentives for behaviour.

Williams (2005) proposes that cooperative advantages stem from high density between network members, a medium level of intensity (in terms of investment) in the relationship between the members, a low level of centrality, and the provision of stability and predictability. With this list of advantages, Williams can be seen to be referring to the effects of institutions, particularly with respect to the last two points.

Gulati and Singh (1998) suggest that the appropriateness of a contractual collaborative setting depends on the anticipated transaction costs. Gulati and Singh (ibid.: 811) explicitly refer to institutions by pointing to organisational forms that '[...] also provide an organisational context that determines the rules of the game [...]'. Their research proposes that organisations can choose between three contractual forms, namely, 'joint ventures, minority investment, and contractual alliances' (ibid.: 792). The choice of the contractual form influences the costs of the eventual collaboration. In other words, outcomes depend on the chosen institutions.

However, the distinction between the three contractual forms is rather crude. A more fine-tuned analysis is one that refers to the degree of formalisation of IORs. Following Williams (2005), a high degree of formalisation has a negative influence on the performance of IORs. This finding is congruent with Park's (1996) assumption that formalisation is needed only to a certain degree: too much formalisation undermines the efficiency of collaboration. Luo and Chung (2005) suggest that kinship relations like family relations can improve the performance of IORs. Kinship relations are less dependent on formalisation than business relations between otherwise unrelated partners. These findings are consistent with the previous comments concerning rigidity versus openness or the fuzziness of institutions on the macro level, as kinship relations are closed with respect to membership but more open with respect to content than clear-cut formal contractual relationships.

Summarising, the papers that concern themselves with the consequences of formal institutions for IORs, be it on a micro or a macro level, suggest that formal institutions are likely to provide action possibilities and stability for IORs. A high degree of formalisation, on the other hand, is described as being too rigid for allowing IORs to flourish. Apparently, there is a certain break-even point, after which formal institutions are more constraining than enabling. However, little is known about when too much is too much. Furthermore, there is little knowledge about the content of specific institutions and their respective consequences. In other words: what kind of formal institutions provide incentives or stability for IORs?

Table 2.2   Formal institutions in networks

Macro perspective (formal part of the institutional environment)		
Institutions in Networks	Consequences	Author/year Approach
Rules and regulations	A certain vagueness of property rights can be beneficial for collaboration. Formal incentive structures enhance collaboration	Ebrahim (2004) Historical
Contracts	Business networks are substitutes for formal institutions	Kalil (1999) Theoretical
Institutions as formal and informal norms in networks	Existence of 3rd party contract enforcement (formal inst.) decreases the optimal size of informal trade networks. Legal enforcement has little effect on networks until law becomes sufficiently inexpensive	De Mesquita and Stephenson (2006) Theoretical
Ties, relations, laws	In the case a lack of formal institutions, entrepreneurs are more likely to rely on their informal networks than to engage in formal business networks	Murphy (2002) Empirical (N= 41)
Institutions are shared collective understandings, norms and rules	A stable institutional environment helps 'firms take a longer-term view of alliance partner selection, focusing more on the potential partner's intangible assets along with technological and managerial capabilities'	Hitt et al. (2004) Empirical (N= 121)
Meso II perspective (formal part of the institutional setting on the IOR level)		
Agreements, density	'ION structures are more likely to promote and sustain cooperation if: (3) the intensity of the ION is great enough for them to be concerned about and (5) they provide stability and predictability in network relationships'	Williams (2005) Theoretical/ Literature
Contracts, licensing, franchises, joint ventures,	Rigidity (= formalization) is needed, too much rigidity is counter-productive for collaboration	Park (1996) Theoretical
Formal institutions exist within governance structures	Hierarchical control in IOR is influenced by the anticipated coordination costs	Gulati and Singh (1998) Empirical (N= 1570)
Family relations and prior social ties	These ties improve group performance in transition processes	Luo and Chung (2005) Empirical (N= 100)
Socially constructed, embedded in networks and used for binding actors	Existence of institutions increases trust in networks Examples: local bank, business associations and consortia	Gaggio (2006) Empirical (N= 2)

Table 2.2 provides an overview of the selected research literature describing the influence of formal institutions in IORs.

Consequences of Informal Institutions for IORs

Nelson and Sampat (2001: 38) stress the importance of informal institutions for understanding multi-party partnerships: 'As a special effect of the above [i.e., the discussion about the consequences of informal institutions, T.G.], but a central one for this discussion, for activities requiring effective interaction among different parties, mutual knowledge about and use of the standard appropriate meshed routines may be essential for coordination to be achieved.' Thus, in order to understand interaction between IOR partners, it is essential to comprehend the consequences of informal institutions for actors' behaviour.

IORs form interaction conditions that are different from single-organisational working and behavioural conditions. First of all, IORs are embedded in multiple institutional settings. The settings of the partners can be very different or quite similar. Partners with similar institutional settings show a high degree of institutional proximity. Institutional proximity is defined as the degree of sameness of the institutional setting, or, in other words, their similarity with respect to their incentives and constraints (Torre and Gilly, 2000).

At first sight, this may also be true for formal institutions. However, once formal institutions are set up for IORs, these institutions are valid and uniform for both parties involved. In other words, in the case of a formal IOR, there is only one formal institutional setting. Nevertheless, possibly divergent informal institutional settings continue to exist in the different organisations of an IOR. They influence the behaviour of the members of the respective organisations and they might be different from the settings of the respective partners.

Organisations collaborate for different purposes and reasons (Oliver, 1990). Certainly, many of these reasons are related to the fact that the partner is different in the sense of being able to provide something that the other organisation cannot or does not provide. In other words, the partner is always the other and not the self. Therefore, partnerships between different partners potentially consist of several different institutional settings. That is to say, as long as the institutional settings of the respective organisations differ, a multi party collaboration has to deal with differing institutional settings. Furthermore, in the case of the collaboration of n institutionally diverse parties, the collaboration faces *(n+1)* institutional settings. The additional institutional setting results from the collaboration that is specifically taking place between the respective collaborative partners themselves (Gössling,

2005). Hence, in a dyadic relationship, three institutional settings are possibly present and valid: the institutional settings of the two partners and the institutional setting of the IOR.

It does not necessarily follow from this that the conflicts that arise in the collaboration between organisations are always a result of institutional differences (c.f. Riad, 2005, with reference to Larsson and Lubatkin, 2001; Vaara, 2003). In fact, a certain level of diversity of collaboration partners can be productive and have an additional value (Milliken and Martins, 1996). However, it can possibly result in misunderstanding that is due to the behavioural consequences of institutions. Organisational differences, and, more specifically, differences in organisational cultures, are often associated with clashes, problems, miscommunication, failure and so on (c.f. Riad, 2005; Bruce and Forbes, 2004; Kiesler, 1994; Oerlemans, Gössling and Jansen, Chapter 9 in this volume). The institutional setting of an organisation provides a normative framework, which influences the behaviour and expectations about behaviour of the respective organisation. Moreover, it provides incentive/disincentive structures. In the case of institutional differences between two collaboration partners, members of one organisation are likely to behave differently than members of the other organisation. Furthermore, members of one organisation can decide to sanction members of the other organisation if the other's behaviour does not match one's own normative expectations. This sanctioning, however, is only understandable given the background of the specific institutional setting. Hence, institutional diversity possibly can be a source of misunderstanding between individual members of IORs.

In addition to this, IORs provide the possibility for interaction that is based upon informal institutions. Actors can, for example, exert institutional pressure. They can impose normative expectations on others concerning their actions and behaviour. Pressure comes into play on the basis of relational power. Relational power in multi-organisational relationships can be either direct or indirect. In the case of direct relational power, actors can exert pressure on their direct interaction partners by providing a sanctioning potential for their normative statements. Such a potential can take different forms. An extreme and very efficient form is the threat of discontinuing an inter-organisational relationship (Gössling, 2004). Indirect relational power can exist in structural holes (Burt, 1992). In indirect relationships, actors can exert their normative claims by threatening reputation effects or second-order sanctioning. In the case of reputation effects, the first actor activates the sanctioning potential of a third actor in order to sustain her normative claims towards a second actor. This can be done by providing information about the behaviour of the second actor that does not match the normative expectations of the third actor (Gluckler and Armbruster, 2003; Gössling, 2004). In the case of second-order sanctioning or second-order punishment, the first actor uses her sanctioning potential towards a third actor in order to make the third actor sanction the second actor (Fehr and Fischbacher, 2004). In both cases, institutions form the basis for actors' behaviour.

Sanctions are threats that are only relevant in case of non-compliance or the perception thereof. With respect to rule-following behaviour, actors have several options. In the simplest models, scholars describe the possibility either for rule-following behaviour or for deviation (Meyer and Rowan, 1977; Powell and DiMaggio, 1983; c.f. Oliver, 1991). Oliver, however, combines resource dependence theory and institutional theory and describes different options for actors to react to institutional pressure. These possible reactions can range from acquiescence via compromise, to avoidance and defiance, and can go as far as manipulation. The important point is that institutions are not rigid per se but do allow for different reactions.

Empirical studies and literature studies concerning the consequences of institutions in networks uphold the assumption that informal institutions matter for the different aspects of collaborative outcomes. Five of the eleven articles in this part of the review emphasise the importance of trust. Uzzi (1996), in his seminal research concerning the meaning of direct personal relations as opposed to arm's length ties, indicates that the former is more likely to produce collaborative advantages than the latter. Trust as a consequence of personal relations allows for efficient exchange and collaboration. Parkhe (1998) suggests that informal institutions allow for the building of trust and that trust is a necessary condition for collaborative action and performance. Lyon (2000) supports this idea. Williams (2005) concludes that the reliance on informal agreements and trust between partners positively affects the productivity of IORs. Farrell and Knight (2003) explain the existence of trust on the basis of shared social institutional structures: Members who stem from a similar social background possess shared informal institutions and are therefore likely to develop a high level of trust. Farrell and Knight's work thus refers to two aspects that are central to research about institutional consequences for IORs, namely trust and culture. Culture is a well-researched phenomenon in the field of institutionalism and IOR research. Four of the eleven papers in this review make reference to culture.

Luo, Shenkar and Nyaw (2001) focus on control and its effectiveness in IORs. Their findings suggest that cultural and institutional distance in the sense of differences in informal institutions in IORs decrease the effectiveness of control. Pothukuchi, Damanpour, Choi, Chen and Park (2002) support these findings. Organisational culture differences decrease IOR performance even more than national culture differences.

Table 2.3   Informal institutions in networks

Central Variable	Institutions in Networks (definition/ examples)	Consequences	Author/year Approach
	Embeddedness, network proximity	Proximity (as opposed to arm's-length ties) produces collaborative advantage	Uzzi (1996) Empirical (N= 23)
Trust	Informal agreements	Mutual trust and informal agreement provide stability for IORs	Williams (2005) Theoretical/ literature
	Rules and incentives in interaction	Institutions allow for trust, trust is crucial for the success of collaboration.	Parkhe (1998) Theoretical/ literature
	Norms of interaction, related to trust	Shared norms allow for social capital, trust is a basis for inter-organisational collaboration success	Lyon (2000) Empirical N=4
Trust and culture	Rules and punishment (incentives)	The existence of institutions in common social settings enhances trustworthiness and the willingness to engage in collaboration Institutional change affects trustworthiness	Farrell and Knight (2003) Theoretical/ empirical 1 region
	Organization culture	Non-conflicting cultures and trust allow for control	Dekker (2004) Theoretical/ empirical. N=1
Culture (informal part of the institutional setting)	Culture (national/regional culture)	Cultural distance decreases the positive influence of control on performance in collaboration	Luo, Shenkar and Nyaw (2001) Empirical N=295
	Culture, organizational culture, social embeddedness	Organisational culture differences produce conflicts and negative performance in joint ventures	Pothukuchi et al. (2002) Empirical, N=127
Culture, informal part of the inst. environment	regulative and normative resources	Regional differences in institutional thickness explain differences in the growth and viability of project networks	Sydow and Staber (2002) Empirical N=2
Proximity	Social structure, embeddedness	Social structure shape prices: embeddedness decrease prices	Uzzi & Lancaster (2004) Empirical, N=250
	Undefined in the paper	Institutional isomorphism and social proximity enhance collaborative learning	Greve (2005) Theoretical/literature

Sydow and Staber (2002) relate performance differences to informal institutional differences in different regions. A difference in institutional thickness, which is defined as the presence and relevance of informal regional institutions, is attributed particular importance when looking at positive influences on network performance. Dekker (2004) suggests that the possibility of controlling IORs is highly dependent on non-conflicting cultures.

A third concept in this context that is referred to by four of the eleven papers is institutional similarity. Next to trust and culture, a high level of institutional similarity produces different positive effects for IORs: Uzzi and Lancaster (2004) refer to social structures and a high level of social embeddedness that is likely to decrease transaction costs in collaboration. Greve (2005) refers to learning as an IOR outcome. Learning is more likely to occur once partners show a high level of institutional isomorphism and social proximity.

Institutional Change and Isomorphism in IORs

Institutional change is defined as changes in normative and incentive structures (North, 1990). A central statement coming from institutional theory is that institutional isomorphism produces legitimacy (Deephouse, 1996; Powell and DiMaggio, 1983). Organisations receive legitimacy by following the institutions of their respective institutional environments and settings. When it comes to interaction partners, isomorphism creates institutional proximity between the IOR partners. In other words, the institutional settings of IOR partners tend to become more similar to each other. Furthermore, this process leads to institutional changes at least in one of the partners. The underlying mechanism that generates legitimacy is explained as follows: partners possess similar normative expectations about behaviour. There is a shared understanding about appropriate and normal behaviour, making institution-oriented behaviour similar or at least understandable. Consequently, IOR partners are not likely to punish each other for their normal or regular behaviour.

Powell and DiMaggio (1983) suggest in their seminal paper that institutional pressure leads to isomorphism: Over time, partners tend to look like each other in many respects. Their paper provoked an intense academic debate about the phenomenon of isomorphism between partners and their central theses received empirical support in many research projects. Mizruchi and Fein (1999) support this idea of isomorphism in IORs. Davis, Desai and Francis (2000) described network embeddedness as a moderating variable that increases the impact of institutional pressure on isomorphism. Lu (2002) came to similar results, indicating that common experience and a shared socio-cultural background are likely to foster isomorphism. Lee and Pennings (ibid.: 156) also support the consequences of IOR embeddeness for institutional similarity.

Table 2.4   Development and change of institutions in networks

Central Variable	Institutions in Networks (definition/ examples)	Consequences	Author/year Approach
Isomorphism	Institutional pressure	Institutional pressure leads to institutional isomorphism: Organisations in networks tend to look like each other	Powell and DiMaggio (1983) Theoretical Mizruchi and Fein (1999) Theoretical/ literature Davis et al. (2000) Empirical, N=129 Lu (2002) Empirical, N=1.194
	Structures, systems and practices established in the past		
	Implicit, reference to Scott: normative structures	Social networks, size and sector similarity and spatial proximity are likely to produce institutional isomorphism	Lee and Pennings (2002) Empirical, N=301
Institutional entrepreneurship	Sets of cultural rules	Institutions and collaboration are inter-dependent: institutions provide rules and resources, collaboration provides the context	Phillips et al. (2000) Theoretical
Proto-institutions	Widely diffused practices, standards, rules and norms	Collaboration as a source of institutional change: proto-institutions	Lawrence et al. (2002) Empirical N=1
Institutional change	The rules of the game in society	Networks can supplement or replace formal institutions when they are weak	Ahlstrom and Bruton (2006) Theoretical/ empirical, N=65
Institutional diversity	Normative patterns	Seemingly contradictory institutions can coexist in networks	Smith-Doerr (2005) Empirical, N=41

Phillips, Lawrence and Hardy (2000) suggest that institutional settings and collaborations are interdependent. Institutional settings provide the structures and norms for collaboration partners to live by, on the one hand. Interaction within the collaboration, on the other hand, provides the resources for the development and change of institutions. On an organisational and IOR level, this suggestion is consistent with the initial assumptions made by research on institutional change, namely that institutions and institutional development and changes underlie evolutionary processes that change and sustain institutions. In an empirical study, Lawrence et al. (2002) are able to support their assumptions and show that IORs are able and likely to foster a certain path towards institutional change.

That is to say that collaboration partners are able to develop 'proto-institutions' that are different from the specific institutions of the respective partners and that are specific and valid for the IOR. Smith-Doerr (2005) describes the non-conflicting co-existence of different, contradictory institutional settings within collaborations. He relates this to the ability of individuals to handle contradictory normative information. Ahlstrom and Bruton (2006) describe the importance of network institutions. In the case of the absence or weakness of the formal institutions of a society, networks can provide institutional stability for the IOR partners.

In line with the discussion above, this literature review shows that institutional processes, especially the process of institutionalisation, matter greatly for IORs. The strongest emphasis in this stream of literature is on isomorphism (five out of nine papers). Institutional change is an evolutionary process (North, 1990). This process is influenced, fostered and triggered by collaboration as collaboration partners tend to develop institutional similarity. In this way, IORs tend to develop institutions that are typical and specific for the respective IORs and their members. Table 2.4 provides an overview of the research literature (selection) on institutional changes in IORs.

CONCLUSION

Institutions matter, as institutional theory suggests, for inter-organisational collaboration as well. Collaboration takes place within multiple institutional environments and settings. Formal institutions matter, as they form the contractual basis and conditions for collaboration. Contracts define the tasks of interaction partners and the behavioural rules of collaboration. The juridical institutional setting determines whether or not the contracts can be closed and whether and at which costs they can be enforced. In other words, formal institutions are relevant for the external and internal legality of the collaboration. Formal institutions represent the framework for behaviour within relationships.

This chapter discussed what institutions are and the different forms and contexts in which they exist and matter for IORs. It explained the occurrence of institutions in IORs, and it described the possible, theoretically probable, and empirically observed consequences of institutions for IORs. Table 2.5 below summarises this discussion by focusing on appearance, form and consequences of institutions in IORs.

The appropriate question concerning the institutionalists' claim that 'institutions matter' is the question concerning which specific institutions matter (Bardhan, 2005) and how they matter.

To begin with, an overall analysis of the literature shows that the importance of institutional theory, in the form of neo-institutional theory, is widely accepted within IOR research. Institutions are analysed in most cases as being normative structures. Furthermore, institutions are described as part of specific settings. The normative function of institutions can be ascribed to those who take part in an institutional setting.

Second, the above discussion concerning formal institutions suggests that the legal institutions of a society are important for the possibility of collaborating at all. Although not explicitly mentioned in the literature, an example of this would be the presence of clearly defined and ascribed property rights that allow for collaboration. The functioning of a legal enforcement system is a further precondition for collaborative success.

Table 2.5   Form, occurrence and consequences of institutions in IORs

	Institutions Formal	Informal
Appearance		
Institutional environment	Law	Regional culture, Institutional thickness
Institutional setting	Contracts	Org. culture, IOR culture
Development		
Institutional environment	Not discussed in the literature	
Institutional setting	Contracting	Adaptation
Consequences		
Institutional environment	Possible stimulation of IOR occurrence and performance, importance of the institutional design	Possible stimulation, importance of the institutional fit
Institutional setting	Influence on collaboration, importance of the appropriate contracts	Influence on collaboration and behaviour, importance of the institutional fit, institutional similarity (isomorphism)

Third, formal institutions within IORs matter. In the organisation science literature, however, there is surprisingly little discussion concerning the appropriate formal institutions and the particular elements of collaboration contracts.

A fourth conclusion refers to the efficiency of institutions in organisations and organisational networks. Institutions possibly evolve to minimise transaction costs (Lyon, 2000). Informal institutions are crucial throughout the entire lifecycle of an IOR. Lyon (2000) mentions the lack of empirical evidence concerning normative settings despite their economic consequences. We know that institutional similarity or institutional proximity fosters the development of trust and increases the likelihood of collaborative success. Institutional conflicts, on the other hand, are rather dysfunctional for collaboration. However, a detailed analysis of institutions that advance collaboration versus those that are more counter-productive is missing in the literature.

A fifth conclusion is that organisations in IORs are able to influence the institutional settings of their partners. They can either develop 'proto-institutions' or cope with institutional diversity. However, given the limited empirical evidence on this subject, we know relatively little about the conditions that foster the development of proto-institutions, on the one hand, and the conditions that allow for the non-conflicting co-existing of contradicting institutions, on the other. It seems important, however, with respect to legitimacy, that either one or the other occurs.

There is a wealth of literature on institutions. The literature on institutions in IORs is, however, limited. In particular, empirical research on the consequences of institutions in IORs is relatively scarce, given the enormous importance that is given in institutional theory. This is certainly due to the nature of both institutions and networks. Both phenomena pose serious challenges for researchers. The biggest challenge for studying institutions in networks certainly is the fact that it is virtually impossible to research institutions independently under *ceteris paribus* conditions. Given the great variety of institutions and their appearance, they are intangible, complex and difficult to observe. However, this statement does not support North's (1990) remark that institutions are impossible to see, feel and touch. Repeated interaction and normative statements about behaviour are indicators of the existence of institutions (Gössling, 2003). More in-depth research on the meaning of institutions in IORs could provide insight into their consequences.

This chapter focuses foremost on institutions as being relational aspects of IORs. However, in the following presentation of ideas and paths for future research, this chapter integrates structural and relational approaches. With respect to the three fields of discussion presented in this chapter, the following questions for future research are proposed:

- Which legal settings, constitutions, and laws could enable collaboration and allow for collaborative prosperity and success?

- Which IOR contracts could enhance collaboration and allow for collaborative prosperity and success?
- To what extent and in which ways can we analyse and identify specific informal institutions that foster collaborative prosperity and success?
- To what extent does the network position (density and centrality) of an actor matter with respect to successfully relying on informal rather than formal institutional mechanisms (e.g. trust versus contracts)?
- To what extent does the network position (centrality) of an actor matter for the emergence of proto-institutions?
- Which underlying institutions (e.g. openness, tolerance) can be related to institutional diversity versus coercion or isomorphism within IORs?

ACKNOWLEDGEMENT

I am grateful to Bram Kaashoek for his work as research assistant on this chapter.

REFERENCES

Acemoglu, D. and S. Johnson (2005), 'Unbundling institutions', *Journal of Political Economy*, **113** (5), 949-995.
Ahlstrom, D. and G.D. Bruton (2006), 'Venture capital in emerging economies: Networks and institutional change', *Entrepreneurship Theory and Practice*, **30** (2), 299-320.
Baalen, P. van, J. Bloemhof-Ruwaard and E. van Heck (2005), 'Knowledge sharing in an emerging network of practice: The role of a knowledge portal', *European Management Journal*, **23** (3), 300-314.
Bardhan, P. (2005), 'Institutions matter, but which ones?', *Economics of Transition,* **13** (3), 499-532.
Barnett, V. (2005), 'Institutions, network relations, and economic systems: A counter to Oleinik's reply', *Journal of Economic Issues*, **39** (3), 808-812.
Bezes, P., M. Lallement and D. Lorrain (2005), 'Les nouveaux formats de l'institution', *Sociologie du Travail*, **47** (3), 293-300.
Borgatti, S.P. and R. Cross (2003), 'A relational view of information seeking and learning in social networks', *Management Science*, **45** (4), 432-445.

Borgatti, S.P. and P.C. Foster (2003), 'The network paradigm in organizational research: A review and typology', *Journal of Management*, **29** (6), 991-1013.

Boyes, W.J and J.M. McDowell (1989), 'The selection of public utility commissioners: A re-examination of the importance of institutional setting', *Public Choice*, **61** (1), 1-13.

Brass, D.J., J. Galaskiewicz, H.R. Greve and W. Tsai (2004), 'Special research forum on building effective networks – Taking stock of networks and organizations: A multilevel perspective', *Academy of Management Journal*, **47** (6), 795-818.

Bruce, A. and T. Forbes (2004), 'Community care in Scotland: Can joint management bridge the gap?', Sixth International Conference of Strategic Issues in Health Care Management, University of St Andrews.

Burgess, J.F., K. Carey and G.J. Young (2005), 'The effect of network arrangements on hospital pricing behaviors', *Journal of Health Economics*, **24** (2), 391-405.

Burt, R.S. (1992), *Structural Holes: The Social Structure of Competition*, Cambridge, MA: Harvard University Press.

Butter, F.A.G. den, and R.H.J. Mosch (2003), 'The Dutch miracle: Institutions, networks, and trust', *Journal of Institutional and Theoretical Economics*, **159** (2), 362-391.

Callander, S. and C.R. Plott (2005), 'Principles of network development and evolution: an experimental study', *Journal of Public Economics*, **89** (8), 1469-1495.

Cavalcanti, T.V. de and B.A. Novo (2005), 'Institutions and economic development: How strong is the relation?', *Empirical Economics*, **30** (2), 263-276.

Chan, S.H., J.W. Kensinger, A. Keown and J. Martin (1997), 'Do strategic alliances create value?', *Journal of Financial Economics*, **46** (2), 199-221.

Cross, R., S.P. Borgatti and A. Parker (2002), 'Making invisible work visible: Using social network analysis to support strategic collaboration', *California Management Review*, **44** (2), 25-46.

Davis, P.S., A.B. Desai and J.D. Francis (2000), 'Mode of international entry: An isomorphism perspective', *Journal of International Business Studies*, **31** (2), 239-258.

Deephouse, D.L. (1996), 'Does isomorphism legitimate?', *Academy of Management Journal*, **39** (4), 1024-1039.

Dekker, H.C. (2004), 'Control of inter-organisational relationships: Evidence on appropriation concerns and coordination requirements', *Accounting, Organisations and Society*, **29** (1), 27-49.

Denzau, A.T. and D.C. North (1994), 'Shared mental models: Ideologies and institutions', *Kyklos*, **47** (1), 3-31.

Dubet, F. (2002), *Le Déclin de L'Institution*, Paris: Seuil.

Ebrahim, A. (2004), 'Institutional preconditions to collaboration: Indian forest and irrigation policy in historical perspective', *Administration & Society*, **36** (2), 208-242.

Farrell, H. and J. Knight (2003), 'Trust, institutions, and institutional change: Industrial districts and the social capital hypothesis', *Politics and Society*, **31** (4), 537-566.

Fehr, E. and U. Fischbacher (2004), 'Third-party punishment and social norms', *Evolution and Human Behaviors*, **25** (2), 63-87.

Gaggio, D. (2006), 'Pyramids of trust: Social embeddedness and political culture in two Italian Gold jewellery districts', *Enterprise and Society*, **7** (1), 19-58.

Gluckler, J. and T. Armbruster (2003), 'Bridging uncertainty in management consulting: The mechanisms of trust and networked reputation', *Organization Studies*, **24** (2), 269-297.

Gössling, T. (2003), 'The price of morality. An analysis of personality, moral behaviour, and social rules in economic terms', *Journal of Business Ethics*, **45** (1-2), 121-131.

Gössling, T. (2004), 'Proximity, trust and morality in networks', *European Planning Studies*, **12** (5), 675-689.

Gössling, T. (2005), 'What is in a Relationship?', in T. Gössling, R.J.G. Jansen and L.A.G. Oerlemans (eds), *Coalitions and Collisions*, Nijmegen: Wolf Publishers, pp. 143-152.

Gössling, T. and R.J.G. Jansen (2006), '*Network Social Responsibility*', in N. Gould (ed.), Proceedings of the 12th International Conference on Multi-Organisational Partnerships, Alliances & Networks, 'Engagement', Exeter: Small Run Press.

Gössling, T., R.J.G. Jansen and L.A.G. Oerlemans (2005), 'Coalitions and Collisions: The Benefits and Problems in the Context of Collaboration', in T. Gössling, R.J.G. Jansen and L.A.G. Oerlemans (eds), *Coalitions and Collisions*, Nijmegen: Wolf Publishers, pp. 385-398.

Granovetter, M.S. (1973), 'The strength of weak ties', *American Journal of Sociology*, **78** (6), 1360-1380.

Granovetter, M.S (1985), 'Economic action and social structure: The problem of embeddedness', *American Journal of Sociology*, **91** (3), 481-510.

Greve, H.R. (2005), 'Interorganizational learning and heterogeneous social structure', *Organization Studies*, **26** (7), 1025-1047.

Grugulis, I., S. Vincent and G. Hebson (2003), 'The rise of the "network organisation" and the decline of discretion', *Human Resource Management Journal*, **13** (2), 45-59.

Gulati, R. and H. Singh (1998), 'The architecture of cooperation: Managing coordination costs and appropriation concerns in strategic alliances', *Administrative Science Quarterly*, **43** (4), 781-814.

Hasselbladh, H. and J. Kallinikos (2000), 'The project of rationalization: A critique and reappraisal of neo-institutionalism in organization studies', *Organization Studies*, **21** (4), 697-720.

Hitt, M.A., D. Ahlstrom, M.T. Dacin, E. Levitas and L. Svobodina (2004), 'The institutional effects on strategic alliance partner selection in transition economies: China versus Russia', *Organization Science*, **15** (2), 173-185.

Hodgson, D.E. (2004), 'Project work: The legacy of bureaucratic control in the post-bureaucratic organization', *Organization*, **11** (1), 81-100.

Howitt, P. and R. Clower (2000), 'The emergence of economic organization', *Journal of Economic Behavior & Organization*, **41** (1), 55-84.

Jones, C., W.S. Hesterly and S.P. Borgatti (1997), 'A general theory of network governance: Exchange conditions and social mechanisms', *Academy of Management Review*, **22** (4), 911-945.

Kalil, R. (1999), 'Endogenous business networks', *Journal of Law, Economics and Organization*, **15** (3), 615-636.

Kay, N.M. (1997), *Pattern in Corporate Evolution,* Oxford: Oxford University Press.

Kiesler, S. (1994), 'Working together apart', *Cause/Effect*, **17** (3), 8-12.

Kondra, A.Z. and C. R. Hinings (1998), 'Organizational diversity and change in institutional theory', *Organization Studies*, **19** (5), 743-767.

Larsson, R. and M. Lubatkin (2001), 'Achieving acculturation in mergers and acquisitions: An international case survey', *Human Relations*, **54** (12), 1573-1607.

Lawrence, T.B., C. Hardy and N. Phillips (2002), 'Institutional effects of interorganizational collaboration: The emergence of proto-institutions', *Academy of Management Journal*, **45** (1), 281-290.

Lee, K. and J. Pennings (2002), 'Mimicry and the market: Adoption of a new organizational form', *Academy of Management Journal*, **45** (1), 144-162.

Lu, J.W. (2002), 'Intra- and inter-organizational imitative behaviors: Institutional influences on Japanese firms' entry mode choice', *Journal of International Business Studies*, **33** (1), 19-37.

Luo, X. and C.N. Chung (2005), 'Keeping it all in the family: The role of particularistic relationships in business group performance during institutional transition', *Administrative Science Quarterly*, **50** (3), 404-439.

Luo, Y., O. Shenkar and M.-K. Nyaw (2001), 'A dual parent perspective on control and performance in international joint ventures: Lessons from a developing economy', *Journal of International Business Studies*, **32** (1), 41-58.

Lyon, F. (2000), 'Trust, networks and norms: The creation of social capital in agricultural economies in Ghana', *World Development*, **28** (4), 663-681.

Matutinovic, I. (2005), 'The microeconomic foundations of business cycles: From institutions to autocatalytic networks', *Journal of Economic Issues*, **39** (4), 867-898.

Mesquita, E.B. de and M. Stephenson (2006), 'Legal institutions and informal networks', *Journal of Theoretical Politics*, **18** (1), 40-67.

Meyer, J.W. and B. Rowan (1977), 'Institutionalized organizations: Formal structure as myth and ceremony', *American Journal of Sociology*, **83** (2), 340-363.

Milliken, F.J. and L.L. Martins (1996), 'Searching for common threads: Understanding the multiple effects of diversity in organizational groups', *Academy of Management Review*, **21** (2), 402-433.

Mizruchi, M.S. and L.C. Fein (1999), 'The social construction of organizational knowledge: A study of the uses of coercive, mimetic, and normative isomorphism', *Administrative Science Quarterly*, **44** (4), 653-683.

Moran, P. (2005), 'Structural versus relational embeddedness: Social capital and managerial performance', *Strategic Management Journal*, **26** (12), 1129-1151.

Murphy, J.T. (2002), 'Networks, trust, and innovation in Tanzania's manufacturing sector', *World Development*, **30** (4), 591-619.

Nelson, R.R. and B.N. Sampat (2001), 'Making sense of institutions as a factor shaping economic performance', *Journal of Economic Behavior & Organization*, **44** (1), 31-54.

Nielsen, B.B. (2005), 'The role of knowledge embeddedness in the creation of synergies in strategic alliances', *Journal of Business Research*, **58** (9), 1194-1204.

North, D.C. (1990), *Institutions, Institutional Change and Economic Performance*, Cambridge: Cambridge University Press.

Oliver, A.L. (1994), 'In between markets and hierarchies – Networking through the life cycle of new biotechnology firms', Institute for Social Science Research – ISSR Working Papers (6), 1-38.

Oliver, A.L. and M. Ebers (1998), 'Networking network studies: An analysis of conceptual configurations in the study of inter-organizational relationships', *Organization Studies*, **19** (4), 549-583.

Oliver, C. (1990), 'Determinants of interorganizational relationships – Integration and future directions', *Academy of Management Review*, **15** (2), 241-265.

Oliver, C. (1991), 'Strategic responses to institutional processes', *Academy of Management Review*, **16** (1), 145-179.

Park, S.H. (1996), 'A framework of the institutional mechanism for network control', *Organization Studies*, **17** (5), 795-824.

Parkhe, A. (1998), 'Understanding trust in international alliances', *Journal of World Business*, **33** (3), 219-240.

Phillips, N, T.B. Lawrence and C. Hardy (2000), 'Interorganisational collaboration and the dynamics of institutional fields', *Journal of Management Studies*, **37** (1), 23-43.

Pothukuchi, V., F. Damanpour, J. Choi, C.C. Chen and S.H. Park (2002), 'National and organizational culture differences and international joint venture performance', *Journal of International Business Studies*, **33** (2), 243-265.

Powell, W.W. (1990), 'Neither Market nor Hierarchy – Network Forms of Organization', in B. Store and L.L. Cumming (eds), *Research in Organizational Behaviors*, Greenwich: JAI Press, pp. 295-336.

Powell, W.W. and P.J. DiMaggio (1983), 'The iron cage revisited: Institutional isomorphism and collective rationality in organizational fields', *American Sociological Review*, **48** (2), 147-160.

Powell, W.W. and L. Smith-Doerr (1994), 'Networks and Economic Life', in R. Swedberg and N. Smelser (eds), *The Handbook of Economic Sociology*, New Jersey: Princeton University Press, pp. 368-402.

Powell, W.W., K.W. Koput and L. Smith-Doerr (1996), 'Interorganizational collaboration and the locus of innovation: Networks of learning in biotechnology', *Administrative Science Quarterly*, **41** (1), 116-145.

Provan, K. and H.B. Milward (2001), 'Do networks really work? A framework for evaluating public-sector organizational networks', *Public Administration Review*, **61** (4), 414-423.

Provan, K.G., M.A. Veazie, L.K. Staten and N.I. Teufel-Shone (2005), 'The use of network analysis to strengthen community partnerships', *Public Administration Review*, **65** (5), 603-613.

Redek, T. and A. Susjan (2005), 'The impact of institutions on economic growth: The case of transition economies', *Journal of Economic Issues*, **39** (4), 995-1027.

Rese, M. (2006), 'Successful and sustainable business partnerships: How to select the right partners', *Industrial Marketing Management*, **35** (1), 72-82.

Riad, S. (2005), 'The power of "organizational culture" as a discursive formation in merger integration', *Organization Studies*, **26** (10), 1529-1554.

Ricoeur, P. and K. Blamey (1992), *Oneself as Another*, Chicago: University of Chicago Press.

Roweley, T., D. Behrens and D. Krackhardt (2000), 'Redundant governance structures: An analysis of structural and relational embeddedness in the steel and semiconductor industries', *Strategic Management Journal*, **21** (3), 369-386.

Schlicht (1998), *On Custom in the Economy*, Oxford: Clarendon Press.

Scott, J. (2003), 'The new economic sociology', *Sociological Review*, **51** (4), 562-564.

Smith-Doerr, L. (2005), 'Institutionalizing the network form: How life scientists legitimate work in the biotechnology industry', *Sociological Forum*, **20** (2), 271-299.

Snyder, D. (1975), 'Institutional setting and industrial conflict: Comparative analyses of France, Italy and the United States', *American Sociological Review*, **40** (3), 259-278.

Sydow, J. and U. Staber (2002), 'The institutional embeddedness of project networks: The case of content production in German television', *Regional Studies*, **36** (9), 215-227.

Sydow, J., L. Lindkvist and R.J. DeFillippi (2004), 'Project-based organizations, embeddedness and repositories of knowledge: Editorial', *Organization Studies*, **25** (9), 1475-1489.

Torre, A. and J.-P. Gilly (2000), 'On the analytical dimension of proximity dynamics', *Regional Studies*, **34** (2), 169-180.

Uzzi, B. (1996), 'The sources and consequences of embeddedness for the economic performance of organizations: The network effect', *American Sociological Review*, **61** (4), 674-698.

Uzzi, B. (1997), 'Social structure and competition in interfirm networks: The paradox of embeddedness', *Administrative Science Quarterly*, **42** (1), 35-67.

Uzzi, B. and R. Lancaster (2004), 'Embeddedness and price formation in the corporate law market', *American Sociological Review*, **69** (3), 319-344.

Vaara, E. (2003), 'Post-acquisition integration as sensemaking: Glimpses of ambiguity, confusion, hypocrisy, and politicization', *The Journal of Management Studies*, **40** (4), 859-894.

Vangen, S. and C. Huxham (2003), 'Nurturing collaborative relations: Building trust in interorganizational collaboration', *Journal of Applied Behavioral Science*, **39** (1), 5-31.

Wasserman, S. and K. Faust (1994), *Social Network Analysis: Methods and Applications*, Cambridge: Cambridge University Press.

Whitley, R. (2003), 'The institutional structuring of organizational capabilities: The role of authority sharing and organizational careers', *Organization Studies*, **24** (5), 667-695.

Williams, T. (2005), 'Cooperation by design: Structure and cooperation in interorganizational networks', *Journal of Business Research*, **58** (2), 223-231.

Williamson, O.E. (1970), *Corporate Control and Business Behaviors*, Englewood Cliffs: Prentice-Hall.

Williamson, O.E. (1973), 'Markets and hierarchies: Some elementary considerations', *The American Economic Review*, **63** (2), 316-325.

Williamson, O.E. (1975), *Markets and Hierarchies: Analysis and Antitrust Implications*, New York: The Free Press.

Williamson, O.E. (1998), 'Transaction cost economics: How it works; Where it is headed', *The Economist*, **146** (1), 23-58.

Yack, B. (1988), 'Toward a free marketplace of social institutions: Roberto Unger's "super liberal" theory of emancipation', *Harvard Law Review*, **101** (8), 1961-1977.

Zaheer, A., B. McEvily and V. Perrone (1998), 'Does trust matter? Exploring the effects of interorganizational and interpersonal trust on performance', *Organization Science*, **9** (2), 141-159.

3. Beyond Boundaries: A Cognitive Perspective on Boundary Setting

Martine van Nuenen

Our choices are constrained by the contexts within which we act, but these constraints do not enslave us. Far from it: contexts themselves provide opportunities for action and therefore make liberation possible.
Somerville, 2000

INTRODUCTION

The main question addressed in this chapter is: how are boundaries set within a network context? The aim is to investigate the processes of inclusion and exclusion that underlie boundary setting in networks rather than determining the aim or exact location of network boundaries themselves.

Processes result from the individual, yet intricately interlocked behaviours exhibited by two or more people. The behaviours of the one person are contingent on the behaviours of the other person. Weick (1979: 89) has termed these contingencies 'interacts' and illustrates how sets of interacts are assembled into processes and how these processes then constitute the organisation. According to him, a preliminary convergence of interest occurs when an individual anticipates that the other can provide a benefit and when each has a similar notion as to how this can be accomplished. This reasoning emphasises the fact that individuals choose to come together because each wants to perform some act and needs the other person in order to make that performance possible. So having first converged on shared ideas concerning how a structure can form, the persons then activate a repetitive series of interlocked behaviours. Such interlocked behaviours form the basis of a collective structure (ibid.: 90). The preceding description emphasises the fact that action appears to be a prerequisite for the formation of a collective structure and that, in the stage prior to this, choice is involved in the activation of a repetitive series of interlocked behaviours. Hence, it is argued

45

that in order to be able to adequately describe the dynamic process of the development of any collective structure, a focus on the interplay between choice, action and structure is opportune.

The scientific discourse concerning organisational forms in general and inter-organisational networks in particular has been dominated for a considerable period of time by static analyses. The lack of dynamic theories is one reason why much network research to date remains of little relevance to the practice of network management (Sydow, 2004: 202). Most (empirical) investigations tend to rely exclusively on measures of structure (e.g. in terms of density and centrality) and *ex post* evaluations of strategy (e.g. Ahuja, 2000; Provan and Milward, 1995; Williams, 2005), thereby neglecting considerations concerning perception and intent in determining the process of network development. Sydow (2004) discusses two prominent theoretical perspectives in which the dynamics of inter-organisational networks are an almost natural object of study: evolutionary and co-evolutionary approaches, on the one hand, and interventionist approaches subscribing to the idea of trans-organisational development, on the other hand. He argues, though, that both approaches fall short of an adequate conceptualisation of the interplay of action and structure. Whereas evolutionary theory lacks an explicit concept of agency, interventionist approaches overemphasise the possibilities of agency while neglecting structures (ibid.: 203). According to him, advanced network theories should offer a more thorough understanding of the complex interplay between (network) action and (network) structure.

In the following sections, a dynamic approach towards boundary setting within a network context will be introduced by elaborating on the interplay between the theoretical concepts that underlie the main question of this chapter: choice, action and structure. Subsequently, a case study from the field of facility management will be presented as an application of this approach. On the basis of this case study, the concept of inclusion and exclusion and its contribution to the development of a collective structure will be analysed. The chapter will conclude with some final observations.

AGENCY AND SOCIAL STRUCTURE: A DYNAMIC APPROACH

In a sociology of social structure, social actors are pictured as being very much at the receiving end of the social structure. In total opposition to this, a sociology of social agency conceptualises the social structure as the derivative of social action and interaction. In seeking to come to grips with problems of action and structure, structuration theory offers a conceptual scheme that enhances our understanding of how actors are both the creators of social systems while, at the same time, being created by them (Giddens, 1991).

According to Giddens (1979), social systems involve regularised relations of interdependence between individuals or groups, that can typically be best analysed as recurrent social practices. Social systems are systems of social interaction. Systems have structures, or more accurately, have structural properties; they are not structures in themselves. He defines structures as rules and resources, organised as properties of social systems. To study the structuration of a social system is to study the ways in which that system, via the application of generative rules and resources, and in the context of unintended outcomes, is produced and reproduced in interaction. He emphasises the duality of structure, in which the structural properties of social systems are both medium and outcome of the practices they recursively organise. With this view, he is referring to the way in which social activities regularly reconstitute the circumstances that generated them in the first place.

Some critics argue that structuration theory still provides too little space for free action, or alternatively, that it underestimates the influence of structural constraint. Archer (1990) points out that action is, of course, ceaseless and essential both to the continuation and further elaboration of the system, but subsequent interaction will be different from earlier action due to the conditioning of the structural consequences of a prior action. According to her, Giddens' theory of structuration does not denote a point reached in development, as does the concept of morphogenesis. Morphogenesis, like structuration, is also a process referring to the complex interchanges that produce change in a system's given form, structure or state. However, morphogenesis has an end product, structural elaboration, which, according to Archer is quite different from Giddens' social system, understood merely as a visible pattern. Hence, according to her, the morphogenetic perspective is not only dualistic but also sequential, dealing in endless cycles of structural conditioning, social interaction and structural elaboration, thereby unravelling the dialectical interplay between structure and action. Although interesting, it would be beyond the scope of the present chapter to extensively elaborate on both structuration and morphogenetic approaches. Both approaches concur that action and structure presuppose one another: structural patterning is inextricably grounded in practical interaction (Archer, 1990: 74). However, since structuration theory does not denote fixity, it is always a process and never a product. Hence, the structuration approach seems apt for conceptualising the dynamic interplay between action and structure.

BOUNDARY SETTING

A Social Construction of Organisational Choice

Sydow (2004: 202) argues that many organisations may have the choice of entering different networks. One way to define choice is as 'the logics that determine social action' (Scott, 1995). Different assumptions have been made in organisational theories regarding how actors make choices (e.g. Elster, 1985; Jones, 2002; Scott 1995; Abell, 1991; Zey, 1992). Rational choice models assume that actors behave expediently to pursue their preferences within a situation (Abell, 1991; Zey, 1992), although analysts in this camp vary considerably in terms of how restricted the assumptions concerning rationality are made. Other theorists refer to choice as being oriented towards a moral dimension that takes into account one's relations and obligations to others in the situation (Scott, 1995; Elster, 1985), while yet others see choice as a result of the meanings we attribute to objects and activities, the latter being referred to as cognitive choice theories (Huff and Schwenk, 1990; Scott, 1995; Jones, 2002). According to these theories, preferences are not taken as given: the identities of actors and their interests are viewed as the product of social interaction.

Some contributions that devote significant attention to the dynamic processes between (groups of) actors are Berger and Luckmann's (1967) classic book *The Social Construction of Reality* and Weick's four-stage model of group development (1979). Berger and Luckmann (1967) focus on the processes by which any body of 'knowledge' comes to be socially accepted as 'reality'. According to them, the world of everyday life is not simply taken for granted as reality by the members of society within the subjectively meaningful conduct of their lives. It is a world that, in fact, originates in their thoughts and actions, and is maintained as real by these. Moreover, they argue that the process consists of three dialectical moments: externalisation, objectivation and internalisation. Scott (1995) also refers to the cognitive dimensions of human existence. He indicates (ibid.: 43) that 'the social construction of actors is not limited to persons: collective actors are similarly constituted and come in a wide variety of forms'. The implication that theories concerning the social construction of reality are also applicable to the organisational level is an important one within the context of this chapter. Weick (1979) examines how meanings convert in the formation of a collective structure. He describes a four-stage model of group development in which individuals agree to exchange means and to facilitate the accomplishment of one another's designs. Hence, organisations in interaction may come to share a framework of mental models that provide both an interpretation of the environment and a prescription as to how that environment should be structured. According to cognitive theories, choice is informed and constrained by the ways in which the environment is perceived (Scott, 1995). If interacting organisations come to share similar interpretations of their environment, and interpretations of the environment influence organisational choice, it seems valid to propose the following:

Proposition 1:
Shared beliefs between mutually interacting organisations regarding the perceived environment, contribute to the development of similar organisational choices.

According to Giddens (1979), the total social field is a field of forces acting on group members and shaping their actions and experiences. Any collective structure is therefore comprised of groups of organisations that share similar mental models. Porac, Thomas and Baden-Fuller (1989) refer to such groups as cognitive communities. Denzau and North (1994: 4) define mental models as 'the internal representations that individual cognitive systems create to interpret the environment'. Drawing from the above definition, it seems possible to assume a relationship between the mental representation of social relationships and the development of a collective structure: the latter being based on the former.

According to Somerville (2000), the creation of rights, which includes actors in membership, by the same token excludes others from that membership. In strictly rational terms, cooperation should arise only where there is 'balanced reciprocity': that is, where the action of one actor that is benefiting another is 'balanced' by a reciprocal action from the other actor. He indicates, however, that group boundaries are drawn in a way that cannot fully be explained on the basis of rational choice. A sense of identity with or commitment to a group cannot be explained entirely in terms of the benefits that membership in the group brings. It is exactly this observation that contains the essence of the next proposition:

Proposition 2:
The aggregation of organisational choice within a network setting will expose a consistent pattern of included and excluded groups of relational ties.

Institutionalisation

Berger and Luckmann (1967) identified institutionalisation as a core process in the creation and perpetuation of enduring social groups. Tolbert and

Zucker (1996) use the theoretical analyses put forward by Berger and Luckmann (1967) as a point of departure in their study and go on to suggest that there are three sequential processes involved in the initial formation of institutions and in their spread. Their analysis was focused on the occurrence of institutionalisation processes among individual actors. Tolbert and Zucker (1996) extended the analysis to organisations.

Researchers have examined the role played by managers' conceptions of field boundaries by asking, for example, what business they are in or who their primary competitors are (e.g. Porac et al., 1989). Such studies illustrate the role that micro-processes, such as perception and cognition, play in creating macro-level phenomena, such as organisation and industry boundaries (Tolbert and Zucker, 1996; Abrahamson and Fombrun, 1994). Abrahamson and Fombrun (1994) acknowledge a possible transition from micro- to macro-culture and define inter-organisational macro-cultures as 'the relatively idiosyncratic, organisation-related beliefs that are shared among top managers across organisations.'

When going back to the propositions that have been made in the previous section, a cognitive categorisation into included and excluded groups of relational ties could restrict managers' attention to a fixed set of symbionts or competitors and to fixed ways of cooperating and competing, thereby reinforcing these cognitively established structures of cooperation and competition (ibid.). This tendency persistently exposes them to a similar set of attributes that they must interpret, which, according to Abrahamson and Fombrun (ibid.) is one of the reasons why greater macro-cultural homogeneity tends to emerge between the organisations involved. Based on this reasoning, it seems valid to propose that:

Proposition 3:
Managerial beliefs about network outcomes will vary between in- and excluded groups of relational ties within a network.

THEORETICAL COMPATIBILITY

When comparing the reasoning presented so far with the dialectical processes of externalisation, objectivation and internalisation as outlined by Berger and Luckmann (1967), there seems to be congruence. The process of externalisation appears to correspond with the first proposition and the observations that have been made. Organisations in interaction actively construct a shared framework of reference that provides both an interpretation of the environment and a prescription as to how that environment should be structured. These organisations are then projecting their own meanings into reality. They refer to this process as externalisation. Proposition 2 suggests that the aggregation of organisational choice within a network setting will expose a consistent pattern of included and excluded groups of relational ties. This pattern then seems to be cognitively imposed upon the organisations involved. This suggestion seems to match Berger and Luckmann's (1967) process of objectivation. The final proposition refers to processes of institutionalisation and the existence of different macro-cultures between groups of organisations. They argue that whenever actors engage in internalisation, they are conforming to the expectations of existing social institutions, and they are also recreating that social institution. Jepperson (1991: 149) claims that, while some analysts equate contextual or environmental effects with institutional ones, they are analytically quite distinct. All institutional effects have contextual qualities, but not all contextual effects are institutional ones. That is, contextual effects often refer to effects of the proportional distribution of individuals across groups within a collective, or to rates of interaction between individuals in different social locations. Many contextual effects are aggregative in character rather than institutional. This remark is an important one within the context of this chapter: shared beliefs may lead to similar organisational choices (proposition 1), but this is merely an aggregated contextual effect. It is not until the social relations involved internalise the result of their choices that this effect becomes an institutional one.

THE PROCESS OF BOUNDARY SETTING: A CASE STUDY

Relevance

The empirical part of this study will be carried out in the field of facility management. Regterschot (1988: 19) defines facility management as: 'The integral management (planning, allocation and control) of housing, services and resources in order to support the organisation's primary process with an effective, efficient, flexible and creative realisation of objectives within a changing environment.' The turbulent environment of facility management and the increasing necessity of a market-oriented approach forces facility service companies in the field under study to expand their boundaries. The integration of various supporting services in facility service companies creates the opportunity for management to concentrate on their core activities. Complexity, flexibility and the necessity of having, have a market-oriented focus that is an important incentive for the development of facility management. Facility service companies have to make conscious choices about contracting out or collaborating on parts of the primary process. This implies that within the specific context of facility management, a proactive creation and maintenance of relational ties seems particularly important. The practical relevance of this study is to increase the awareness of a relational approach within the field of facility management and potentially within other fields, as well. It is expected that an increased focus on a relational context could bring about new possibilities for organisational change and innovation. This increased focus could illuminate possible limitations in the considerations entertained by decision-makers when they attempt to employ innovative partnering and transacting as a means of improving organisational performance. By means of this study, the discussion concerning structural patterning and practical interaction within a network context that was raised by earlier studies and in this chapter is once again addressed. By combining a structuration approach with an understanding of the cognitive processes that underlie boundary setting, this study intends to transcend the limitations of earlier investigations.

Research Methods

The field under study is a field of facility management that orients towards a focal organisation: the facility services department of St Elisabeth Hospital located in Tilburg, the Netherlands. This focal organisation served as a point of entry into the field, as they provided us with provided a file of with names and addresses of those that are (a) key suppliers and (b) suppliers that sell more than 10,000 euros a year to the focal organisation. The list contained 107 suppliers. From this list, a random sample was taken. The study was carried out as a web survey among 50 suppliers. The website was made up of four pages and included the survey questions.

The objective of the first web page was to find empirical evidence for research propositions 1 and 2 by mapping the mental models of the research respondents. In addition, the web page provided the respondent with a list of the names for all 50 research respondents. The respondent was first asked to indicate which organisations he or she knew, and subsequently, whether the relational tie was considered to be relevant for the realisation of his or her own company's strategy. As will become apparent in the next subsection, the aggregation of the output of this first page exposes a consistent pattern of those groups that are included and those that are excluded in the network of relational ties.

The aim of the second page was to find empirical evidence for research proposition 3: namely, to measure managerial beliefs about network outcomes and compare these with respect to the in- and excluded groups identified by the respondents. For this purpose, the respondent was first exposed to a series of questions and then to a series of statements. Answers to both questions and statements were given on a five-point Likert Scale, ranging from 'very negative' to 'very positive' for the questions or 'highly disagree' to 'highly agree' for the statements. The questions were based on a study by Lant and Baum (1993). They examined the ways in which hotel managers categorise other firms as being within or outside of their competitive set. In addition to examining this using objective indicators, such as price or location, softer dimensions, such as performance attributions, perceived environmental predictability and perceived managerial roles, were also considered important and were consequently included in the investigation. The attitudes and perceptions of managers from various hotels were examined, as well. They intended to make these dimensions operational by using the indicators mentioned in Table 3.1.

Table 3.1   Measurement of managerial beliefs

Dimensions	Indicators
Performance attributions	Market position
	Strategic decisions
	Actions by others in the field
	Internal operations
Perceived environmental predictability	Strategic decision outcomes
	Impact of environmental change
Perceived managerial roles	Monitoring environmental trends
	Staffing
	Setting organisational policy

Source: Lant and Baum (1993).

Five of the indicators were considered to be relevant within the context of the present study: market position, strategic decisions, internal operations, impact of environmental change and monitoring environmental trends. Lant and Baum (1993) defined these indicators as follows:

- Market position: managers' assessments of the impact that their organisation's market position has on their organisation's performance.
- Strategic decisions: managers' assessments of the impact of the organisation's strategic decisions on the organisation's performance;
- Internal operations: managers' assessments of the impact that internal operations have on the organisation's performance.

- Impact of environmental change: managers' assessments of how accurately they are able to predict the impact that environmental changes will have on their organisation.
- Monitoring environmental trends: the extent to which the manager is involved in this activity.

The statements used in this study are based on a study conducted by Ali and Al-Shakhis (1989). They examine and compare managerial beliefs in two different cultures. Their definition of managerial beliefs is based on Rokeach (1968) and is as follows: 'assumptions about the world in which a person lives, the validity of which he or she does not question'. Ali and Al-Shakhis used *The Beliefs about Work Questionnaire* to measure managerial beliefs, which was designed by Buchholz (1977), who, in turn, had based his ideas on Rokeach (1968). The questionnaire was used several times in the United States and can be regarded as a reliable and valid tool to analyse and describe managerial beliefs.

To be able to put the research responses into perspective, the respondent was asked to answer some general questions on the third web page concerning size, for example, number of years employed and product range. Finally, on the fourth page of the web site, the respondent was given the possibility to indicate whether he or she was interested in the outcome of the study.

Methodology

The respondent's selection of relational ties on the first page of the web survey was considered to be the raw data from which to map a network of linkages. A categorisation of one organisation as tied to another has been referred to as a linkage. A linkage was defined as present when one respondent identified another organisation. The interest of this study lies in the identification of groups of relational ties, or 'cliques', within the network of linkages among the research respondents. According to Scott (2000: 114), a clique can be defined as 'a sub-set of points in which every possible pair of points is directly connected by a line and the clique is not contained in any other clique'. He does admit that this concept is rather restrictive for real social networks as such tightly knit groups are very uncommon. Therefore, he proposes the concept of the n-clique. In this concept, n is the maximum path length at which members of the clique will be regarded as connected. The present study will focus on the identification of cliques with a value of n equal to one. According to Scott (2000), there will be a considerable amount of overlap among the various cliques in any but the smallest graphs. A relatively dense network will tend to comprise of a large number of overlapping cliques, with many points being members of numerous different cliques. Alba (1982) suggests that overlapping cliques could be aggregated into circles if they have more than a certain proportion of their members in common. This can be done in two steps. The criterion for identifying circles in the first step is that cliques are merged into a circle if two-thirds of their members are identical. The result of this first step then might be one or more circles, together with a number of separate cliques and isolated points. In the second step, the remaining cliques can be merged with those circles with which there is a lower level of overlap. Alba (1982) suggests that a one-third overlap in membership might be appropriate in this second step. The result of this aggregation will be a large circle or a set of smaller circles surrounded by a periphery of less well-connected cliques and points. When applying the above arguments to the objective of the web survey's cognitive mapping exercise, the criteria for the inclusion and exclusion of groups of relational ties within the context of the present study can be summarised in Table 3.2.

Table 3.2   Criteria for in- and exclusion

Circles	Included relational ties
Less well-connected cliques & Isolated points	Excluded relational ties

In order to be able to identify these circles, as well as the less-well connected cliques and the isolated points, a network analysis was carried out using software of UCINET and Visone. UCINET is a comprehensive package for the analysis of social network data, as well as other 1-mode and 2-mode data. Visone is a program for visualising both 1-mode and 2-mode social network data. UCINET can run an enormous number of statistical analyses. The present study focused however on the identification of cliques, circles and isolated points. After entering the required size of the cliques into the program, UCINET runs the clique analysis. The output from the clique analysis then reports the number of cliques found, followed by a listing of the nodes that belong to each clique. After the listing of cliques, an actor-by-actor clique co-membership matrix indicates the number of cliques each pair of actors has in common. The final bit of output contains a clique-by-clique co-membership matrix. Hierarchical clustering of this data gives an overview of the number of nodes that the different cliques have in common. Based on this output, circles can be identified: those cliques that have a specified level of nodes in common are merged into a circle. These cliques can then be referred to as included groups in the network of relational ties. In the present study, cliques were merged at 'level two': those cliques that had at least two nodes in common were merged into a circle. The remaining cliques were considered to be less well-connected. Those nodes that had not been assigned to a clique were considered to be isolated points. After importing the UCINET output into the Visone package, the network could be drawn and the in-and excluded groups of relational ties could be visualised.

Since the answers to all questions and propositions of the second part of the survey were indicated on a five-point Likert-scale, SPSS appeared to be the appropriate statistical package to analyse the results. A one-way analysis of variance was applied as the technique of causal analysis.

Results

Out of the 50 respondents, 20 filled out the first part of the web survey, resulting in a response rate of 40 per cent. The aggregation of the output exposes a consistent pattern of included and excluded groups of relational ties (Figure 3.1). The analysis first focused on the identification of cliques with a value of n is one. This resulted in the identification of 24 cliques ranging from a size of three to maximally four nodes per clique. These results are presented in Figure 3.1. Based on a hierarchical clustering of overlap between the cliques, 23 of the 24 cliques could be merged into one circle. This circle included clique numbers one to 22 and clique number 24. Hence, clique number 23 was the only clique excluded from the circle (white clique in Figure 3.1).

When applying these results to the level of the individual nodes, it appears that 22 relational ties were identified as being included in the circle (black nodes in Figure 3.2). The remaining 28 relational ties belonged to the less-well connected clique or were (completely) isolated and were therefore identified as being excluded relational ties (white nodes in Figure 3.2).

Figure 3.2 indicates that those respondents that were identified as excluded nodes can actually be classified into three sub-groupings. Nodes 22, 26 and 33 represent clique number 23, the only clique that was excluded from the circle. Clique number 23 is considered to be a less well-connected clique. Nodes 5, 6, 18, 21, 23, 29, 32, 42, 44 and 47 appear to be completely isolated from the network. None of the respondents identified one of these nodes as being relevant for the realisation of their own company strategy. Nor did the isolated nodes identify any other relational tie as being a relevant one. These nodes will be considered true isolates and it is assumed that their influence on the nodes within the network is minimal. The remaining fifteen nodes were not assigned to any clique, but they were also not considered to be true isolates. The reason for this is that the nodes in question did not identify any other relational tie as being relevant for the realisation of the own company strategy, but the remaining nodes within the network did identify them as being relevant relational ties.

Figure 3.1   Identification of cliques

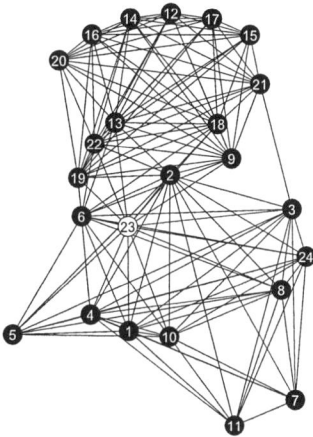

The data for research proposition 3 was collected by performing a one-way analysis of variance on the output that resulted from the second part of the web survey. Seventeen of the fifty respondents filled out the second part of the web survey, resulting in a response rate of thirty-four percent. The respondents were first identified as either being included or excluded (Figures 3.1 and 3.2) in order to be able to compare the deviation of scores between the groups. Table 3.3 presents an overview of the measured effects per question (or statement) for the in- and excluded groups of relational ties. A description of each question and statement can be found in the appendix of this chapter.

There seemed to be a general tendency towards scores that lie between a 'neutral' and 'positive' attitude. The outcomes appeared to be internally consistent. Most differences between in- and excluded groups were based on: variations in attitudes towards the organisations' market positions and the influence of this on organisational performance; the influence of direct relational ties on strategic decision-making; the influence of relational ties on environmental predictability; inter-organisational dependency; outsourcing in relation to innovative power; and discriminating power in relation to an organisation's market performance.

The overall measured effect appeared to be rather small, although there were some exceptions. The deviation of scores between in- and excluded groups with respect to questions concerning the organisations' market positions and the influence of this on organisational performance was considerable.

Figure 3.2   Identification of in- and excluded relational ties

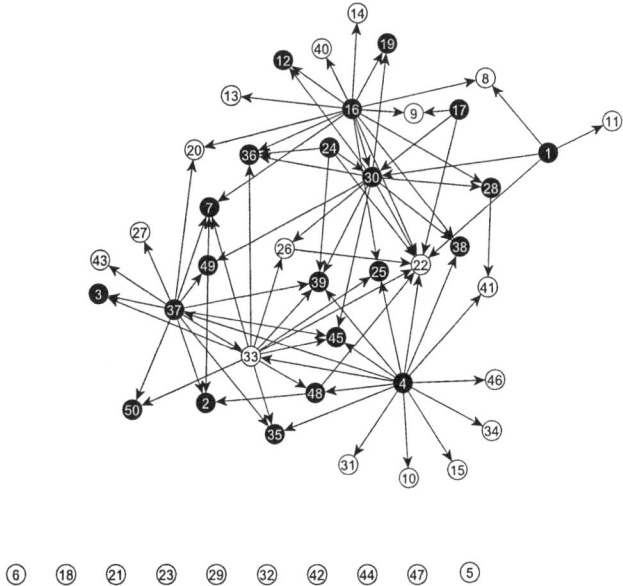

The excluded nodes demonstrated a more favourable attitude in answering both of these questions. Furthermore, the excluded nodes judged the influence of their direct relational ties on their strategic decisions and on the environmental predictability more positively. This can be considered noteworthy, as one would expect included nodes to have a more positive attitude concerning these issues. The following reasoning could possibly underlie these results. Excluded groups of relational ties may be less aware of the influence that direct relational ties could actually exert on them and could therefore demonstrate a more favourable attitude towards the respective questions. This would be different in the included groups of relational ties, where members are likely to be more aware of the network of relational ties they are situated in and may therefore more explicitly perceive both the positive and negative influences that this might have on them.

One of the statements in the second part of the web survey claimed that inter-organisational dependency should be avoided at all times. Exclusive groups in the network of relational ties were considerably more in favour of this statement than the included groups. This score appears to correspond with the expectations of the study. The score of the included nodes on this statement, when compared to all other scores, was also the lowest score on the questionnaire, meaning that the included nodes highly disagreed with the statement. Another statement claimed a clear preference for network collaboration over individual operations. The included nodes demonstrated an overall positive attitude towards this statement, while the excluded nodes were less in favour of the statement. Again, this score corresponds with the expectations of the study.

Table 3.3   Measured effects between in- and excluded groups of ties

Question/ statement	Overall mean	Effect of included ties in relation to overall mean	Effect of excluded ties in relation to overall mean	Effect between in- and excluded ties
1	4.00	−0.08	+0.20	−0.28
2	3.59	−0.17	+0.41	−0.58
3	3.82	−0.15	+0.38	−0.53
4	3.94	−0.02	+0.06	−0.08
5	3.65	−0.07	+0.15	−0.22
6	3.53	−0.11	+0.27	−0.38
7	3.76	−0.01	+0.04	−0.05
8	3.88	+0.04	−0.08	+0.12
9	3.59	−0.01	+0.01	−0.02
10	3.82	−0.07	+0.18	−0.25
11	3.76	−0.01	+0.04	−0.05
12	3.53	−0.11	+0.27	−0.38
13	2.94	−0.11	+0.26	−0.37
14	3.82	+0.10	−0.22	+0.32
15	3.59	+0.08	−0.19	+0.27
16	3.12	−0.04	+0.08	−0.12
17	4.12	+0.05	−0.12	+0.17
18	3.59	−0.09	+0.21	−0.09
19	3.29	−0.21	+0.51	−0.72
20	4.06	+0.11	−0.26	+0.37
21	3.94	−0.02	+0.06	−0.08

The largest measured effect was found for a statement concerning how contracting out knowledge and capacity will reduce an organisation's innovative power. The deviation in scores on this statement between in- and excluded groups was considerable. The excluded nodes clearly had a more positive attitude towards the statement. Finally, the last statement of the study claimed that an organisation's discriminating power determines the organisation's market performance. The included nodes demonstrated a more favourable attitude towards the statement, meaning they agreed more highly with it than the excluded nodes.

Analysis

The objective of the first part of the web survey was to map the mental models of the research respondents and to find empirical evidence for the existence of noticeable groups of in- and excluded nodes. The results offered insufficient evidence for the acceptance of the first proposition of the chapter, even though the theoretical reasons that underlie this proposition did give a clear indication that shared organisation-related beliefs can contribute to the development of similar organisational choices between mutually interacting organisations. It is expected that face-to-face dialogues with the research respondents would better support this argument. Proposition 2 is however accepted, as the cognitive output appears to demonstrate a perceptible classification into in- and excluded groups within a network of relational ties (Figures 3.1 and 3.2).

Based on the average effect, it seems that in- and excluded groups do maintain differing managerial beliefs about network outcomes. In order to clarify whether the overall measured effect is important enough in the field under study, the Squared Variance (R^2) was calculated by dividing the between-group variance (Sum of Squares Between) by the total amount of variance (Sum of Squares Total). A high Squared Variance would imply that a high percentage of variance between the groups can be ascribed to actual differences between the groups and not to random error (Hinkle, Wiersma and Jurs, 1998). The average Squared Variance of the data from the present web survey is 4.26 per cent, indicating that about 4 per cent of the variance between the in- and excluded groups can be attributed to actual differences between the groups. Based on the above and the level of significance (0.05) of the results of the second part of the web survey, the third proposition in this study cannot be accepted. A higher response rate might possibly have resulted in a different effect, but more empirical evidence is required in order to be able to make some valid observations concerning the movement of the level of significance in relation to an improved response rate. However, the results of the analysis do acknowledge a variance in attitudes between in- and excluded groups concerning some important organisational issues, such as organisational decision-making, environmental predictability, inter-organisational dependency, knowledge-sharing and innovative power (on some organisational issues the average Squared Variance even exceeded 10 per cent). With respect to the chapter's practical relevance, one of the objectives of this study was to demonstrate that the homogeneity of beliefs within groups can inhibit organisational members from adapting to changing environments. Based on the results of the empirical part of the analysis and the preceding discussion, there seems to be at least sufficient empirical support to claim a perceptible amount of heterogeneity between in- and excluded groups and homogeneity within the respective groups. Hence, it seems worthwhile to call attention to the relational context within the field under study.

CONCLUSION

The focus of the present chapter was been on the interrelation between 'choice', 'action' and 'structure'. The chapter intended to outline how an understanding of the underlying cognitive processes can be used to progress organisational collaboration within a network context. The main contribution of the study can be found not so much in the exploration of the individual variables, but more in the focus on how these variables relate. After a thorough theoretical exploration, the interplay between the variables 'choice', 'action' and 'structure' seemed to show congruency with the three phases of externalisation, objectivation and internalisation, as described by Berger and Luckmann (1967). An understanding of how this ongoing dialectical process could relate to cognitive processes of inclusion and exclusion within a network context seems to be very valuable in order to determine what organisational behaviour is merely contextual and what behaviour has indeed been institutionalised (Jepperson, 1991). As claimed above, shared beliefs between interacting organisations may indeed lead to similar organisational choices, but this is merely an aggregated contextual effect. It is not until the nodes involved internalise the results result of their choices that this effect becomes an institutional one. As Weick (1979) already claimed, organisations should be more self-conscious about and spend more time reflecting on the actual things they do. An organisation needs to find ways to separate out the effects of its own interventions from the effects that would have happened anyway. An understanding of how organisations actually behave within a network context and how coalitions they enter into go through several stages could contribute to more efficient group and network utilisation.

Further research on the constructs in the field, as well as tests for the accepted propositions in other contexts, would be valuable contributions to the present study. An interesting question for future exploration concerns the effectiveness of weak ties versus the effectiveness of strong ones. It would be lucrative to further explore the argument that weak ties cumulatively produce more knowledge than strong ties. This argument seems to correspond with the reasoning of the present study concerning how homogenisation originates within groups of strong ties and how this blocks innovative power when compared to groups of more weakly linked ties. It is expected that building on this argument by examining whether this reasoning can be applied to in-

and excluded groups in a network of relational ties would be a valuable and possibly very interesting extension of the present case study.

Another interesting discussion that could be raised concerns the limitations of social network analysis. This especially concerns the risks involved when trying to frame a multi-organisational collaborative attempt. A question that could be raised here is: would boundaries not become less flexible, and the organisations involved consequently less creative, when organisations can visualise the structure they are situated in? If we apply this argument to the present study, Figures 3.1 and 3.2 could possibly direct the attention of the 50 research respondents to those nodes that had been assigned to the same clique or circle, thereby possibly increasing increase homogeneity within the group and leading to a decrease in creativity and innovative power. It would be interesting to empirically examine this assumption, for example, by means of a time-series design.

Although the aforementioned arguments could result in interesting discussions, it is be beyond the scope of the present study to expand on them. However, these final comments emphasise the importance of further research in this area.

REFERENCES

Abell, P. (1991), 'The New Institutionalism and Rational Choice Theory', in W.R. Scott and S. Christensen (eds), *The Institutional Construction of Organizations: International and Longitudinal Studies*, California: Sage Publications, pp. 3-14.

Abrahamson, E. and C.J. Fombrun (1994), 'Macrocultures: Determinants and consequences', *Academy of Management Review*, **19** (4), 728-755.

Ahuja, G. (2000), 'Collaboration networks, structural holes and innovation: A longitudinal study', *Administrative Science Quarterly*, **45** (3), 425-455.

Alba, R.D. (1982), 'Taking stock of network analysis: A decade's results', *Research in the Sociology of Organizations*, **1**, 39-74.

Ali, A. and M. Al-Shakhis (1989), 'Managerial beliefs about work in two Arab states', *Organization Studies*, **10** (2), 169-186.

Archer, M. (1990), 'Human Agency and Social Structure: A Critique of Giddens', in J. Clark, C. Modgil and S. Modgil (eds), *Anthony Giddens: Consensus and Controversy*, Wiltshire: Redwood Press Limited, pp. 73-84.

Berger, P.L. and T. Luckmann (1967), *The Social Construction of Reality: A Treatise in the Sociology of Knowledge*, London: Allen Lane Penguin Press.

Buchholz, R. (1977), 'The belief structures of managers relative to work concepts measured by a factor analytic model', *Personnel Psychology*, **30** (4), 567-587.

Denzau, A.T. and D.C. North (1994), 'Shared mental models: Ideologies and institutions', *Kyklos*, **47** (1), 3-31.

Elster, J. (1985), 'Rationality, morality and collective action', *Ethics*, **96** (1), 136-155.

Giddens, A. (1979), *Central Problems in Social Theory: Action, Structure and Contradiction in Social Analysis*, London: MacMillan Press.

Giddens, A. (1991), 'Structuration Theory: Past, Present and Future', in C.G.A. Bryant and D. Jary (eds), *Giddens' Theory of Structuration: A Critical Appreciation*, London: Routledge, pp. 201-221.

Hinkle, D.E., W. Wiersma and S.G. Jurs (1998), *Applied Statistics for the Behavioural Sciences*, Boston: Houghton Mifflin.

Huff, A.S. and C.R. Schwenk (1990), 'Bias and Sensemaking in Good Times and Bad', in A.S. Huff (ed.), *Mapping Strategic Thought*, Somerset: John Wiley, pp. 89-108.

Jepperson, R.L. (1991), 'Institutions, Institutional Effects and Institutionalization', in W.W. Powell and P.J. Dimaggio (eds), *The New Institutionalism in Organizational Analysis*, Chicago: University of Chicago Press, pp. 143-163.

Jones, B.D. (2002), 'Bounded rationality and public theory: Herbert. A. Simon and the decisional foundation of collective choice', *Policy Sciences*, **35** (3), 269-284.

Lant, K.L. and J.A.C. Baum (1993), 'Cognitive Sources of Socially Constructed Competitive Groups: Examples from the Manhattan Hotel Industry', in W.R. Scott and S. Christensen (eds), *The Institutional Construction of Organizations: International and Longitudinal Studies*, California: Sage Publications, pp. 15-38.

Porac, J.H., H. Thomas and C. Badden-Fuller (1989), 'Competitive groups as cognitive communities: The case of the Scottish knitwear manufacturers', *Journal of Management Studies*, **26** (4), 397-415.

Provan, K.G. and H.B. Milward (1995), 'A preliminary theory of interorganizational network effectiveness: A comparative study of four community mental health systems', *Administrative Science Quarterly*, **40** (1), 1-33.

Regterschot, L.J. (1988), *Facility Management: Het Professioneel Besturen van de Kantoorhuisvesting,* Deventer: Kluwer Bedrijfswetenschappen.

Rokeach, M. (1968), *Beliefs, Attitudes and Values*, San Francisco: Jossey-Bass.

Scott, J. (2000), *Social Network Analysis: A Handbook*, London: Sage Publications, Second edition.

Scott, W.R. (1995), *Institutions and Organizations*, California: Sage Publications.

Somerville, P. (2000), *Social Relations and Social Exclusion: Rethinking Political Economy*, London: Routledge.

Sydow, J. (2004), 'Network development by means of network evaluation? Explorative insights from a case in the financial services industry', *Human Relations,* **27** (2), 201-220.

Tolbert, P.S. and L.G. Zucker (1996), 'The Institutionalization of Institutional Theory', in S. Clegg, C. Hardy and W. Nord (eds), *Handbook of Organization Studies*, London: Sage Publications, pp. 169-183.

Weick, K.E. (1979), *The Social Psychology of Organizing*, Massachusetts: Addison-Wesley Publishing Company, Second edition.

Williams, T. (2005), 'Cooperation by design: Structure and cooperation in interorganizational Networks', *Journal of Business Research*, **58** (2), 223-231.

Zey, M. (1992), 'Criticisms of Rational Choice Models', in M. Zey (ed.), *Decision Making: Alternatives to Rational Choice Models*, California: Sage Publications, pp. 9-31.

Table 3A.1 Measurements

#	Questions
Market position	
1	How would you rate your organisation's market position?
2	How would you rate the influence of your direct relational ties on the organisation's market position?
3	How would you rate the influence of your organisation's market position on the organisation's performance?
Strategic decision-making	
4	How would you rate your organisation's ability regarding strategic decision-making?
5	How would you rate your ability to accurately assess the outcomes of your strategic decisions?
6	How would you rate the influence of your direct relational ties on strategic decision-making within your organisation?
7	How would you rate the influence of strategic decision-making on the organisation's performance?
Internal operations	
8	How would you rate the internal operations (planning, allocation and control) within your organisation?
9	How would you rate the influence of your direct relational ties on your organisation's internal operations?
10	How would you rate the influence of internal operations on the organisation's performance?
Environmental predictability	
11	How would you rate the influence of environmental change on your organisation's performance?
12	How would you rate the influence of your direct relational ties on the environmental predictability?
Statements	
13	Inter-organisational dependency should be avoided at all times.
14	Being part of a relational network is more fruitful than operating individually.
15	Decisions made within the context of a relational network are better than individual decisions.
16	Organisational conformity increases an organisation's chance of survival.
17	An organisation should maintain its own identity at all times.
18	An organisation's innovative power depends on the available technical know-how within the organisation.
19	Contracting out knowledge and capacity will reduce an organisation's innovative power.
20	An organisation's discriminating power determines the organisation's market performance.
21	Organisational ability determines an organisation's competitiveness.

4. Building Collaborative Capacity for Collaborative Control: Health Action Zones in England

Helen Sullivan, Marian Barnes and Elizabeth Matka

INTRODUCTION

Public policy discourse acknowledges that the role of the nation state has changed in the last decades of the 20th century. A combination of challenges, such as the emergence of multi-level governance, the fragmentation and increasing social differentiation of society, and the complexity of core policy concerns including social exclusion, health inequalities and environmental sustainability, has undermined traditional approaches to governing through hierarchy and made necessary the development of alternative forms of governing and a new role for the nation state (Pierre and Peters, 2000; Rhodes, 1997; Skelcher, 2000).

For Kooiman meeting these challenges necessitates 'a mix of all kinds of governing efforts by all manner of social-political actors, public as well as private; occurring between them at different levels, in different governance modes and orders' (2003: 3). Collaboration (working together across organisations) is one way of realising this, particularly at the community or local level where public, private, voluntary and community sectors come together. Such collaborations may also attempt to engage with the 'non-organised' public, but there is often ambiguity about this (Barnes, Bauld, Benzeval, Judge, Mackenzie and Sullivan, 2005). Kooiman sees these collaborative endeavours as 'microcosms' of the wider environment, illuminating key issues inherent in attempting to govern together rather than alone, such as, power relationships, the 'pull' of context and history, the dynamics of membership (individual and organisational) and the overlapping nature of tasks and roles. Collaborations therefore exemplify the challenges associated with moving away from governing through hierarchy, towards what some authors consider to be a network mode of governing (Klijn and Koppenjan, 2000). They highlight the potential redundancy of longstanding traditions, rules and norms that govern activity within and between organisations and point to the need for the development of new forms of control.

This chapter has as its focus the ways in which collaborations seek to establish a range of 'controls' that are fit for purpose, that is, they are able to support the achievement of desired outcomes while at the same time adhering to the values and ethos of collaboration. It argues that in order to secure appropriate measures of control, collaborations need to be able to draw on a reservoir of collaborative capacity. However, it also argues that other factors outside the immediate collaboration (such as those suggested by Kooiman, above), can impact, positively and negatively, on the exercise of collaborative capacity and hence on the operation of collaborative control.

In the UK, collaboration has become a significant instrument in the delivery of public policy objectives since the late 20th century (Sullivan and Skelcher, 2002). Most often operationalised through partnerships, collaborative effort has been evident in a number of spheres but is manifest most clearly in New Labour's use of Area Based Initiatives (ABIs) as vehicles for change. These ABIs bring together a range of actors from the public, private, voluntary and community sectors, for the purposes of neighbourhood regeneration (New Deal for Communities), improved life chances for children (Sure Start), and health improvement/reduced health inequalities (Health Action Zones). Consequently the UK provides fertile ground for the study of collaborative control in the context of a unitary state.

This chapter examines the kinds of collaborative capacity needed to support the necessary collaborative control drawing on the experience of a particular partnership initiative, Health Action Zone (HAZ), in England. It will explore the incidence of formal and informal controls, arguing that both are needed in sustainable collaborations, but that the relative significance of either will depend on a variety of factors. The case study of HAZ will also highlight the particular role of central government in informing the possibilities and limitations of collaborative capacity and collaborative control.

EXERCISING CONTROL IN COLLABORATIONS

There are three primary reasons why control is important in collaborations. First, it helps to maintain a clear focus on the purpose of the collaboration, ensuring that the outcomes sought by the collaboration are identified, clarified and shape the plans and activities of the actors in the collaboration. There are a number of ways in which this kind of control can be achieved: through joint goal setting or visioning, through the development of a performance management framework that is linked to the achievement of shared goals/outcomes, and through the operation of incentives to support activity in the direction of key collaborative outcomes. Second, control also helps to regulate the conduct of actors in the collaboration, supporting ways of working that fit with the wider values of society and penalising 'bad' behaviour. This kind of control is activated through the application of rules and regulations, norms and ways of behaving in relationships with others that are considered to be appropriate to the effective working of the collaboration and to the workings of a democratic society. Third, control is important in securing the optimal performance of the collaboration. This needs to be undertaken at a number of levels and in a number of ways and involves ensuring that the 'right' people are involved in collaborative action, such as those with the appropriate skills and capacities, that the structures, processes and activities of the collaboration are 'fit for purpose', that is they function in support of the achievement of the primary purpose of the collaboration, and that collaborative activities are effectively managed and coordinated.

In essence control in collaboration is important for the same reasons that it is important in hierarchical relationships (the achievement of outcomes, regulation of conduct and optimal operational performance). However, in collaborations, exercising that control is considerably more difficult because many of the levers present in hierarchical relationships are unavailable, for example, established chains of command, and universal rules and norms of appropriate behaviour. Consequently control needs to be negotiated rather than mandated (Moore, 1995). Reaching the point of control in any collaboration reflects the achievement of a delicate balance between actors in the collaboration that will need to be constantly reviewed and renegotiated.

One way of understanding the nature of control in collaboration is to view it through the lens of complexity theory. The term 'complexity theory' is often used in the social sciences to describe a range of theoretical approaches developed in the natural sciences, including systems theory, chaos theory and theories of complex adaptive systems. According to Howard (2006) the 'application of complexity theory to social phenomena is a way of providing a conceptual framework to understand the interconnectivity and interplay of elements within a complex social system and between this system and its environment'. For Howard the connectivity displayed in complex systems is of great importance in understanding human organisation as it allows for actors to be influenced by their histories and cultures but to be able to transcend these to create something 'emergent'. This understanding of actors as informed but not imprisoned by their professional experiences and able to generate new ideas, opportunities and ways of doing things through interaction with others, is a good description of the possibilities of collaborations, that are normatively assigned to them.

In the evaluation of Health Action Zones (which forms the empirical basis for this chapter) we drew on complexity theory in a way that 'emphasizes the significance of open systems in which different elements interact dynamically to exchange information, self-organize and create many different feedback loops, where relationships between cause and effects are non-linear, and where the system as a whole has emergent properties that cannot be understood by reference to the component parts' (Barnes, Matka and Sullivan, 2003). In open systems the boundaries between context and the collaboration are at best blurred allowing for the 'intersection and interaction' of different parts of the system in ways which are non-hierarchical and frequently unpredictable, and which result in change both to the 'context' as well as to the collaboration (Byrne, 2001). Cilliers (2000) concurs with this emphasis on unpredictability, arguing that it is due to the 'rich interaction' and 'abundance' of feedback generated within such systems. We found this a helpful way of appreciating the interaction between the collaboration (the HAZ) and central government (purportedly 'external' to the HAZ but influential over it, and in practice influenced by it).

Complex systems pose considerable problems for control. In the first place the non-linearity of the interactions in complex systems makes them inappropriate for the application of top-down control strategies or problem solving (Stacey, Griffen and Shaw, 2000). Second, the dynamic nature of complex systems and their propensity to 'self-organise at points of criticality ... for ... survival' means that they 'cannot survive when there is too much control, ... control should be distributed throughout the system' (Medd, 2001). Gilchrist (2000) describes this in the context of community development as networks operating on a continuum between rigidity and randomness, where the ability to adapt to changes is regulated by the system itself.

This is not to say that in practice actors outside the collaboration cannot have a benign influence on the workings of the collaboration, but that any intervention will need to be carefully considered for its intended and unintended consequences. In the context of the HAZ and the role of central government, one option is for it to provide what Mayntz calls 'contextual control', the setting of framing rules and norms that can enable local actors to maximise their capacity to act effectively through 'self-regulation and horizontal co-ordination' (1993: 15).

COLLABORATIVE CAPACITY FOR COLLABORATIVE CONTROL

For collaborations to perform as self-regulating systems requires a reservoir of system capacity that enables the various elements of the system to operate to facilitate survival (as a minimum) but also to encourage creative emergence. In collaborations this kind of capacity is known as collaborative capacity (Sullivan and Skelcher, 2002).

Hudson, Hardy, Henwood and Wistow provide a useful definition of collaborative capacity, suggesting that it 'refers to the level of activity or degree of change a collaborative relationship is able to sustain without any partner losing a sense of security in the relationship. This sense of security encompasses not only the tangible resources which are central to collaborative endeavour, but less obvious matters such as perceived loss of autonomy and perceived change in relative strength' (1999: 245-246). This definition and the work of others including Huxham and Vangen (2000) emphasise the dynamic and fluid nature of collaborative capacity and the need for it to be regularly remade.

Collaborative capacity facilitates joint decision-taking and action and enables the management of power differentials between stakeholders in the collaboration (Stewart, 2003). This in turn supports the achievement of collaborative advantage, which, according to Huxham and Vangen (2000: 3) is the achievement of outcomes unavailable to any of the organisations acting alone. In these ways collaborative capacity enables the exercise of collaborative control in the key areas of activity identified above.

In practice the history of UK public policy is littered with examples of 'failed collaborations'. Reported causes of failure regularly include those factors that introduce insecurity into collaborative capacity thereby reducing the efficacy of the operation of collaborative control, such as the failure to include all relevant stakeholders, power imbalances amongst partners and inadequate means of facilitating action. Where collaborations have been considered successful, the attributes of key individuals and the quality of inter-personal relationships have often been cited as being more important than management processes or technical capacity in generating success (Stewart, Goss, Gillanders and Grimshaw, 2002).

Therefore any examination of the key components of collaborative capacity needs to explore the contribution of individuals and organisations and that of the collaboration itself (Huxham and Vangen, 2000). Sullivan and Skelcher (2002) provide a framework for examining collaborative capacity that is multi-dimensional and draws on a range of research to identify key components of collaborative capacity. In brief they argue that the generation of collaborative capacity amongst individuals requires the demonstration of particular leadership and boundary spanning skills to catalyse and sustain collaborative action. It also relies upon the existence of strong trust relationships between individuals. Finally the development and demonstration of the skills and attributes of individual collaborative capacity needs to be considered worthwhile by individuals, i.e. there has to be some kind of 'fit' between the investment in collaborative capacity and the prevailing environment or context (Hudson et al., 1999). Within organisations collaborative capacity also needs to be demonstrated through organisational leadership and inter-organisational trust. However, to achieve this requires other attributes to be in place, specifically a collaborative organisational culture and an orientation towards learning (Newman, 1996).

A considerable amount of attention has been focused on the contribution of individuals and/or organisations in 'making collaborations work' (e.g. Hardy, Hudson and Waddington, 2000; Osborne, 2000). However, what remains relatively unexplored is how the capacity generated or harnessed amongst individuals and organisations is then utilised within the collaboration, for example, for the purposes of control. Sullivan and Skelcher's (2002) framework suggests that this capacity needs to be expressed in a variety of ways.

Strategic Capacity
Agents in collaboration will have their own particular mission and purposes. Achieving collaborative advantage necessitates the identification of a distinct collaborative mission that aligns agents' agendas, specifies collaborative interventions and their means of delivery. Strategic capacity is necessary to enable partners to act collectively to determine their mission and framework for collaborative action coupled with the necessary infrastructure support. This capacity focuses on 'outcome control' and highlights the importance of 'catalytic leaders' in generating this kind of capacity and control.

Governance Capacity
This concerns the development of mechanisms to secure the 'good governance' of collaborative action. ABIs aim to deliver public purpose by combining a range of resources. To do this necessitates the establishment of an appropriate constitutional form that can manage the resource flows. It also requires the development of appropriate accountability mechanisms, so that the activities of the collaboration are transparent and open to scrutiny by relevant stakeholders. This capacity is concerned with control for the regulation of conduct in and of the collaboration. The differing cultures of the organisations that sponsor actors to be part of the collaboration will influence the nature of the governance form and accountability mechanisms that will be necessary to exercise this kind of control.

Operational Capacity

This refers to the ways in which partners make use of the variety of mechanisms at their disposal, such as pooled budgets, joint appointments and/or lead commissioning, to maximise the collaboration effort in order to deliver new types of services or projects. This capacity focuses on control of operational performance. The kinds of structures, processes and mechanisms adopted will be contingent upon the culture of the organisations that contribute to the collaboration, with particular reference to the promotion of learning as a means of facilitating creative emergence in the collaboration. Central here too is the role of network managers, those individuals whose job it is to establish an appropriately enabling collaborative infrastructure.

Practice Capacity

This focuses on the skills and abilities of professionals and others, ensuring that these, whose interventions will be essential to the achievement of collaborative advantage, are equipped with the necessary skills and support. This capacity focuses on control both in terms of regulating conduct and in supporting operational performance. Important in influencing each of these is the nature of trust relationships between practitioners in the collaboration and the presence of 'reticulists' in the collaboration. These are individuals with appropriate 'boundary spanning' skills who can accelerate the rate of collaborative performance and intensify its quality.

Community Capacity

Involving 'the public' as services users or community members is a core element of many government initiatives. Consequently collaborations need to be attuned to the needs of the public in their engagement, supporting the involvement of communities and citizens in opportunities opened up by the collaboration. This capacity requires consideration of all three aspects of control: connecting community capacity contributes to outcomes; fostering an ethos in the collaboration that supports community involvement, and establishing ways of working and specific initiatives that can help ensure that community involvement in the collaboration is productive.

The relationship between collaborative capacity and collaborative control is a dynamic one. Collaborations need sufficient capacity to enable them to exercise appropriate control, as without this collaborations risk the domination of powerful actors, the collapse of the collaboration into a state of inertia (Huxham and Vangen, 2000: 772), or the involvement of the collaboration in a range of irrelevant and/or ineffective activity.

Reflecting on the above discussion it is possible to identify two key and interlinked factors that can influence the operation of collaborative control.

The first is the level of collaborative capacity present in the collaboration; high levels of collaborative capacity enable self-regulation, while low levels inhibit collaborative performance. The second is the degree of control the collaboration has over itself compared to the control that is exercised (or attempted to be exercised) from outside the collaboration. Collaborations that exercise considerable control over their operations have high levels of internal authority. Conversely collaborations that are subject to control from external sources have low levels of internal authority. In the UK this translates into a discussion about the level of central government control (external) that is sought and achieved over the collaborative effort.

Figure 4.1   Dimensions of collaborative control

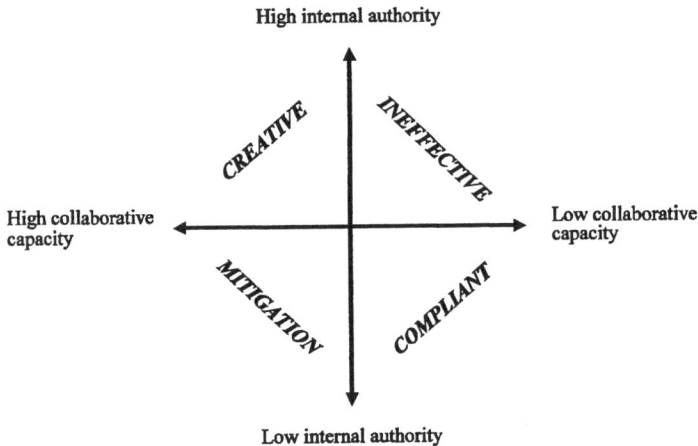

These factors can be mapped onto a simple matrix in order to produce a number of possible outcomes for collaborative control (see Figure 4.1). Collaborations with high collaborative capacity and high internal authority generate control which is creative in all dimensions. Collaborations with high collaborative capacity and low internal authority focus control on mitigating the unwelcome external influence in order to create space for the collaboration to operate. Collaborations with low collaborative capacity and high internal authority operate control in a way that complies with the demands of the external body. Collaborations with low collaborative capacity and low internal authority usually operate ineffective control systems. The remainder of this chapter focuses on the dimensions of collaborative control in Health Action Zones.

THE HEALTH ACTION ZONE INITIATIVE

Health Action Zones were one of the first policy initiatives of the New Labour Government elected in 1997. In total 26 HAZs were established following two rounds of bidding between 1997 and 1999. There was a high expectation that HAZs would act as 'trailblazers', developing 'bespoke approaches to local problems and challenges' (Department of Health, 1997a: section 3) and devising innovative ways of working which could act as a model for agents of central and local governance. They were set broad aims relating to a reduction in health inequalities, health improvement, modernising health services, and achieving better collaboration across the NHS, local government, voluntary and private sector organisations, as well as engaging with communities, service users and citizens in developing and delivering the change agenda.

In common with other policy initiatives introduced by New Labour, HAZ status was accompanied by an evaluation requirement commissioned by the Department of Health (DH). The overarching aim of the national evaluation was to 'identify and assess the conditions in which strategies to create a more substantial capacity for local collaboration result in the adoption of change mechanisms that lead to the modernisation of services and a reduction in health inequalities' (Bauld and Judge, 2002: 9). The 'building capacity for collaboration' component of the national evaluation, that this chapter draws on, worked with five HAZs. The evaluators followed the experiences of each of the five HAZs between 1999 and 2002, undertaking two rounds of interviews with key players, using postal questionnaires to obtain wider views on partnership working and community involvement in the HAZs, developing and employing a project reporting instrument to gain the views of sampled HAZ projects about partnership working and community involvement and attending and observing a variety of HAZ events and meetings (for details see Sullivan, Barnes and Matka, 2002; Barnes, Sullivan and Matka, 2004). Details of the five HAZs are contained below.

Bradford HAZ

Bradford HAZ comprised the area covered by both the Bradford Metropolitan District Council and the then Health Authority. It had a population of just under 500,000, a significant proportion from ethnic minority communities, the fastest growing of which were the Pakistani and Bangladeshi communities. The Bradford HAZ Implementation Plan (1998) cited parts of the South Asian community populations as being particularly vulnerable to ill health, specifically those resident in the inner city areas of

Bradford, although health inequalities and social exclusion were common concerns in a variety of geographical contexts, whether inner city, outer estates or in outlying towns such as Keighley. Inequalities in health within the district and between the district and other areas (the region and England as a whole) were recognised as particularly pronounced and this was reflected in health being identified as one of the key priorities contained in Bradford's Community Plan and latterly the district's 20/20 vision statement.

Bradford HAZ's strategy was outlined in the HAZ Implementation Plan published in October 1998. It was underpinned by three key features: that HAZ money and activity should be focused on supporting change to mainstream programmes and organisations; that HAZ status should enable the district to build upon its experience of collaboration in relation to health; and that community involvement in a number of different forms was essential to the HAZ objectives of meeting needs, addressing inequalities and promoting heath across the district.

A partnership board was appointed to have oversight of the HAZ programme. Comprised of key representatives and senior officers of partner organisations (including the Training and Enterprise Council (TEC), Chamber of Commerce, Community Health Councils (CHCs), Race Equality Council and the Trade Union Congress (TUC)) the HAZ partnership was one of a number of linked strategic partnerships in the district. The board was supported by a steering group – an officer body with responsibility for implementing HAZ priorities and monitoring performance. Key agents for implementation were the four Primary Care Groups (PCGs) and the Implementation Plan identified the need to set up local HAZ partnerships in each PCG area to bring local stakeholders together.

Lambeth, Southwark and Lewisham (LSL)

Lambeth, Southwark and Lewisham (LSL) HAZ was a 'complex' HAZ made up of a three inner London unitary local authorities and the LSL Health Authority and covering a population of 730,000. The population of the HAZ was extremely diverse and also extremely mobile, in part because of the areas' refugee and asylum seeker populations. This presented particular challenges for the appropriate identification of health needs and delivery of health and related services.

LSL HAZ articulated a strong focus on children and young people from the outset; the HAZ Implementation Plan being entitled 'Children First'. The HAZs' stated mission was to, 'use the opportunities presented by the HAZ to improve the future for children and young people in South East London by promoting health, improving services and building on strong local partnerships'. This was to be done through nine HAZ programmes, focusing on: building healthier environments and communities; improving parenting support and skills; improving opportunities for disabled children and young people with special needs; working with excluded children and young people to bring them back into the mainstream; reducing unwanted teenage pregnancies and improving sexual health; reducing youth crime; reducing substance misuse; increasing employment opportunities and health through work; and smoking cessation.

LSL HAZ appointed a partnership board, supported by an executive group to oversee the delivery of the HAZ programme. Members of the partnership board included representatives from the three local authorities and the health authority as well as the emerging PCGs and representatives from other key sectors. Close links were maintained between the HAZ partnership and other key bodies such as Education Action Zones and community/voluntary bodies.

Manchester, Salford and Trafford (MaST)

Manchester, Salford and Trafford (MaST) HAZ was another 'complex' HAZ covering an urban area of 880,000 people and involving multiple local and health authorities, specifically: Manchester City Council, Salford City Council, Trafford Metropolitan Borough Council, Manchester and Salford & Trafford Health Authority. Health inequalities between the HAZ and the rest of England were recognised as being particularly acute, particularly in relation to Manchester where life expectancy was significantly lower for both men and women than anywhere else in England. This factor was compounded by the fact that suicide rates for young people, particularly young men, were a cause for concern. Like Bradford and LSL, the MaST HAZ population was very diverse. It had a number of long established minority ethnic communities lately being joined by newer communities.

The main thrust of the initial HAZ implementation plan was to tackle the problems faced by children and young people, such as accident prevention, sexual health and substance abuse. Increased participation and promotion of health issues among older people in the community was also a priority, as was targeting those with mental illness.

A partnership board and executive group were appointed to oversee the workings of the HAZ. As with LSL, the MaST partnership needed to include amongst its membership representatives of each of the host local authorities and health authorities as well as key representatives from other sectors, in particular the voluntary sector.

Northumberland HAZ

Northumberland HAZ had a rather different profile to that of the other case study HAZs as it was a HAZ with a significant rural dimension and one which operated with a two-tier local government structure. The core partners to the HAZ were therefore: Northumberland County Council, Northumberland Health Authority, Alnwick District Council, Berwick upon Tweed Borough Council, Blyth Valley Borough Council, Castle Morpeth Borough Council, Tynedale District Council, Wansbeck District Council and the NHS Trusts in Northumberland. The HAZ covered a population of 310,000 spread over a large geographic area.

The Northumberland HAZ was borne out of pre-existing relationships between health and social services in the county and complemented by the development of the Northumberland Strategic Partnership (NSP) which brought together the key players in the county from a range of sectors. The HAZ partnership occupied the space in between these two layers of partnership activity – its focus on health distinguishing it from the NSP which considered regeneration in the widest sense and its focus on involving the public and the private/voluntary sectors distinguishing it from the service focused relationships of health and social services.

Northumberland HAZ was managed through the HAZ development group, chaired by the chief executive of the health authority and made up of all the eight HAZ programme board directors plus key additional representatives. The HAZ development group was linked to the NSP via a management board which comprised chief executives of the various key public bodies. A partnership reference group had been established under the umbrella of the NSP. This reference group comprised a range of stakeholder representatives with a specific interest in the workings and objectives of the HAZ.

Sandwell HAZ

Sandwell HAZ comprised a coterminous health and local authority, serving a population of 300,000, living mainly in the six local towns that made up the borough of Sandwell. The HAZ was predominantly urban with a diverse population, which like MaST was made up of well established minority ethnic communities (mainly South Asian) that had latterly been joined by newer communities. An area with deep seated deprivation, Sandwell had long been in receipt of targeted funding streams from Government initiatives for the purposes of regeneration. Consequently partnership working and community involvement were important foci for the borough well before the opportunity arose to become a Health Action Zone.

Another important dimension to the Sandwell context was the nature of the area as an administrative aggregate of six towns, each with its own identity and issues. This context contributed to certain ways of doing things within Sandwell – for example the establishment of Local Town Committees for each of the six localities – and the same approach flowed through into the HAZ, resulting in the setting up of six community fora to engage with the HAZ.

The main focus of the HAZ according to the Implementation Plan was to tackle the problems faced by children and young people, older people and socially excluded groups in the borough. This was to be achieved by working in a fairly wide-ranging way to establish the prerequisites for health, promote social inclusion and contribute to the economic regeneration of the area.

As with the other case study HAZs the Sandwell HAZ was overseen by a (large) partnership board comprising a cross-section of the key local partners with operational management overseen by a small executive group. Close links were developed with the emerging Sandwell civic partnership, the body that sought to provide coherence to all cross-cutting partnership activity in the borough.

These five case studies provide the empirical basis for the analysis of collaborative control in HAZs which is considered in the remainder of this chapter.

COLLABORATIVE CAPACITY AND CONTROL IN HAZ

Central Government and 'Contextual Control'

As indicated above HAZs were the one of the first initiatives of a Labour Government committed to make a significant impact on key public concerns about levels of social exclusion. The creation of HAZs reflected the new government's commitment to transforming the role of the state (and people's perceptions of it) into an instrument for creating the conditions in which citizens could achieve good health and well-being. The importance that was attached to the potential achievements of HAZs and the government's determination to tackle intractable issues such as health inequalities meant that it paid close attention to the design and delivery of HAZs in localities. This set the tone for what would come to be known as New Labour's 'centralising' and 'controlling' tendencies, and had important implications for the freedom to act later experienced by local HAZ partnerships (Stoker, 2004).

Central government's influence over HAZs was evident from the beginning of the initiative. HAZs were selected by the Department of Health following a competitive round of 'bidding' for HAZ status in which localities had to respond to a set of bidding criteria established by the department. In some cases localities were advised as to the configuration of local geography that would best 'fit' with central government's own priorities. This had particular implications for the shape of at least one of our case studies – Manchester, Salford and Trafford HAZ – which brought together a number of local and health authorities in what many respondents described as a 'shotgun marriage' for the purposes of achieving HAZ status.

On achieving HAZ status, central government continued to influence HAZs in relation to all aspects of control identified above. In relation to 'outcomes control', the Department of Health required all successful HAZs to produce and submit an 'Implementation Plan' to the department for consideration. This plan was to describe in some detail the key outcomes the HAZs were aiming to achieve, their strategies for achieving these outcomes, the infrastructural arrangements that would support implementation and their means of assessing their progress towards their goals. HAZs were also required to report regularly on their progress to central government. While initial HAZ guidance emphasised the importance of 'local' priority setting based on local circumstances, this was later compromised in two ways. First, DH officials keen to see 'results' from the investment in HAZ began to question the link between the wide range of local activities and improved outcomes. This led to the creation of a national 'performance management' system for HAZs which required localities to produce 'high level statements' of performance regularly for submission to the department. Individual HAZs were assessed on the basis of these submissions and a 'traffic light' system was used to denote whether they were performing well ('green light') or whether their performance gave significant cause for concern which needed to be addressed ('red light') (Barnes et al., 2005). Second, a change in the Secretary of State for Health presaged a change in priorities for the Department of Health. Coronary heart disease, cancer and mental health became core areas for attention and each HAZ was required to demonstrate how their activities were contributing towards improved outcomes in each of these areas. Among our case studies this change had particular consequences for Lambeth, Southwark and Lewisham whose Implementation Plan had been developed with a particular focus on children and young people, and which therefore did not sit easily with the new priorities.

In terms of 'regulating conduct', the DH published seven principles which were designed to underpin the philosophy of local HAZ working and to be reflected in their plans and activities. These were: achieving equity, engaging communities, working in partnership, engaging front-line staff, taking an evidence-based approach, developing a person-centred approach to service delivery, and taking a whole-systems approach (Department of Health, 1997b). One of these principles, 'working in partnership' was linked to a requirement that each HAZ should establish a strategic partnership mechanism (a 'board') to oversee and direct local action in relation to the following key objectives: achieving health improvements and reductions in health inequalities, the joint provision of improved services, systems of governance that are efficient and accountable, and more successful and embedded cross-agency and cross-sector working. As our case study descriptions illustrate, HAZs responded to the 'working in partnership' principle in similar but locally specific ways, informed by their own histories and experiences of partnership working as well as the practicalities of establishing partnership arrangements in very different local contexts.

Here, too, changes in central government priorities impacted on the development of these partnership arrangements. Prior to the general election in 2001, the government announced radical new proposals in its reform of the health and service and local government, as well as new proposals for partnership working at the local level (Barnes et al., 2005). Relevant here are the demise of health authorities (the lead bodies in HAZs) and the establishment of new primary care organisations (PCGs), and the establishment of Local Strategic Partnerships (LSPs), new institutions charged with the oversight of a new programme of local regeneration ('Neighbourhood Renewal') and with bringing together existing partnership arrangements (including HAZs) under a single coordinating partnership umbrella. Amongst our case studies, these changes had particular implications in Sandwell and Bradford HAZs.

In Sandwell the well-established relationships that existed between the Health Authority and the local authority, in particular the social services department, were the basis on which the HAZ was built. The shift of focus to new primary care organisations ('trusts') introduced new partners into the HAZ arena and challenged these established relationships. In contrast, in Bradford it was the demise of the Health Authority that caused the problems. The move from coterminous district health and local authorities to a configuration of primary care organisations, local government and a Strategic Health Authority had a major impact on those driving the health agenda on all sides (Barnes et al., 2004). The LSP agenda also had a profound effect on the way in which all HAZs planned for the future, reorienting HAZ perspectives on the contribution of health to local community strategies and influencing the way HAZs worked in relation to neighbourhood based initiatives such as neighbourhood renewal.

The DH also sought to facilitate the 'optimal performance' of HAZ operations via the provision of some very particular incentives. At an individual level it sought to foster the innovative and entrepreneurial spirit it believed to be central to the success of HAZ through the provision of a range of developmental and learning support offered from within the department and from both national and local evaluation processes. It funded HAZNet, a web-based system that offered specific interest led networks, alerted subscribers to national and local evaluation developments, and provided a route for dissemination between HAZs and their wider audience. The National Fellowship scheme was also established. This aimed to foster learning amongst front-line staff by providing individuals with small resources to undertake a research project in their area of practice. At HAZ level the DH also offered HAZs the opportunity to identify organisational or institutional barriers to innovation, with a view to granting specific 'freedoms and flexibilities' to HAZs who could demonstrate how the removal of a particular barrier could improve performance. In practice this offer achieved little, in part because some key 'freedoms' had been granted in the Health Act (1999), and also because HAZs found it difficult to identify barriers that the department was able or willing to remove – very often their removal would require changes in primary legislation, something that the central government was not prepared to commit to.

The above analysis illustrates the ways in which central government sought to exercise control over HAZs primarily through its instruments for 'outcomes control' and to a lesser extent through the guidance and support offered by the centre in relation to 'regulating conduct' and securing 'optimal operational performance'. Below we consider the extent to which localities were able to generate sufficient collaborative capacity to exercise control over the HAZ from within, drawing on the dimensions of collaborative capacity identified earlier in the chapter.

Collaborative Capacity in HAZ

Strategic collaborative capacity is necessary to establish the vision and key themes pertaining to its achievement within the HAZ. In support of this each HAZ initially developed strategic partnership bodies comprising a wide ranging steering group supported by a smaller executive body to act as the driver. None of these bodies sought to accommodate community representatives (outside of elected local authority councillors) directly, opting instead for other mechanisms to link with communities.

While the HAZ structures frequently looked similar, greater insight into the strategic capacity of the collaborations is gained by examining the approach to strategic planning adopted in each HAZ. For example in Bradford where there was considerable experience of partnership working and a strong network of health stakeholders, a central element of the HAZ vision was a reorientation of mainstream services towards effective community involvement. This was manifest in a strategic intent to influence the design of new primary care organisations so that community involvement was integral. It was also evident in the development of a shared strategy for community development that included but went beyond the health sector.

By contrast in MaST the HAZ was faced with a significant challenge of holding together powerful strategic interests with limited convictions about the benefits of working together. Here Bryson's (1988) 'think big, act small' approach – the development of ambitious goals to give the partners something meaningful to strive for, coupled with small steps to avoid alienating partners in practice, was adopted. The subsequent vision for MaST supported interventions across a range of community configurations – population groups, localities, individuals and interest groups – with HAZ wide strategic capacity built and utilised to support these interventions but not necessarily to be sustained beyond the life of the HAZ.

Regardless of the different strategies adopted by the HAZs, all of our case studies reflected the importance of leadership in facilitating the development and implementation of appropriate strategies. For Luke (1997) collaborations require the attention of 'catalytic leaders', individuals with certain core skills: the capacity to think and act strategically, the application of interpersonal skills to relate to and successfully motivate others, an ability to focus on results and the possession of personal integrity that is acknowledged by others.

This leadership capacity emerged in different ways and in different locations in HAZ. For some, the HAZ initiative represented an opportunity to use existing skills and capacities in the pursuit of shared goals. Here HAZ was a vehicle or conduit for pre-existing capacity. For others HAZ represented an opportunity for personal growth, to develop new skills or capacities through taking a leadership role in HAZ or to test out the utilities of existing skills and capacities in an entirely new partnership environment.

The style and emphasis of leaders and leadership varied between and within HAZs over time. In some cases this change of emphasis was managed within the existing leadership group, with individuals taking on different roles. However, in most cases the change of emphasis coincided with or was precipitated by the loss of a key leader to a role outside the HAZ. In Northumberland where the HAZ had devolved considerable power and responsibility to programmes, the loss of the key leader was seen as an opportunity to reshape the leadership of the initiative throughout the implementation phase. Whilst a change in the style and embodiment of leadership was sometimes valuable or necessary as HAZs evolved, in some cases it could have a destabilising effect.

Governance capacity refers to the capacity of partners to develop ways of securing the good governance of collaborative action within the HAZ. Sullivan and Skelcher (2002) identify two aspects to the governance of collaboration – the constitutional form taken and the accountability arrangements made. The case-study HAZs were constituted as 'unincorporated associations' meaning that they had no separate legal identity and could not control assets, requiring a key partner (usually the health authority) to act as the 'accountable body' for financial purposes. This is the most common form of partnership governance arrangement in England and one which, while subject to constraints, is attractive because of its flexibility in terms of the range of representation on the partnership group.

Accountability arrangements need to embrace accountability to the public, accountability for performance and accountability for finance. Health Authorities were directly accountable to the Department of Health for the financial management of HAZ resources and were required to report to the department regularly on HAZ performance towards outcomes using a standard pro forma. Where HAZs had greater flexibility was in the way in which they operationalised their accountability to the public. There was an awareness that the traditional methods of accountability were in tension with the objectives of new initiatives like HAZ. For example the need to meet functional performance indicators and targets set by different government departments often restricted partners in their capacity to contribute to shared local health outcomes. In Sandwell the HAZ tried to encourage partners into the habit of joint accountability, including developing shared measures whilst fulfilling obligations to government departments. This was accompanied by attempts to give an account of HAZ to local people by way of major stakeholder events, an approach further developed as part of Sandwell's LSP and neighbourhood renewal strategy.

Lack of trust is often cited as a limiting factor in collaborations (e.g. Huxham and Vangen, 2000). Cropper (1996) suggests that one way in which trust can be fostered in and between organisations is through what he terms 'principled conduct', modes of operating that provide the framework for 'a sense of inclusion, of predictability or dependability, and of unequivocality in relationships' (ibid.: 96). Cropper identifies two elements to principled conduct – 'fair dealings' in relation to how the potential benefits of collaboration will be distributed, and 'fairness in procedure', including the development of shared codes of conduct that organisations agree to abide by in their collaborative relationships.

In relation to 'fairness in procedure', case study HAZs found the formalisation of codes or 'ground rules' for collaboration helpful and important. Unsurprisingly formal codes of conduct were developed early on in artificial or complex HAZs where there had been little prior collaboration.

Formal agreements were said to help 'prevent misunderstandings' and to ensure that meetings did not 'get out of hand'. However formalised arrangements were also evident amongst partners who had worked together previously and considered themselves adept at collaboration; here they provided a reminder of the shared basis for action that guided the collaboration. In some HAZs the development of 'principled conduct' was referred to primarily at the strategic level. However in others 'ground rules' were considered vitally important in exchanges at all levels.

While these different approaches did succeed in building and sustaining trust between some partners, there remained scepticism – particularly amongst voluntary sector partners – about the extent to which all partners really played by the same rules and the consequences of this for 'fair dealings'. Examples were given of funding being allocated to 'big players' apparently outside the formal frameworks and justified on the basis of other rules and relationships that were external to HAZ and went beyond what could be captured in formal protocols.

Operational capacity refers to the ways in which partners make use of the variety of mechanisms at their disposal to maximise the collaboration effort in order to deliver new types of service arrangements. The case studies provided evidence of the use of a range of mechanisms to deliver HAZ programmes including contracts, secondment opportunities, joint appointments and processes for sharing information between partners. However, there was little evidence that these mechanisms were applied systematically or that the HAZ was understood to offer particular opportunities to try out new mechanisms.

It might have been expected that those HAZs that were most focused on working with the mainstream would be most likely to try out new arrangements and mechanisms and indeed there was evidence of 'joint' arrangements in both Bradford and Northumberland. However in both cases high profile work with the mainstream meant the development of new organisations rather than the application of mechanisms to link existing organisations, including the development of PCG and later primary care trusts (PCTs) in Bradford and the decision to pursue a Care Trust in Northumberland.

Elsewhere in HAZs with less focus on the mainstream it was often difficult to predict how the operational capacity built and applied in HAZ could impact more widely and deeply in partners' organisations. In LSL there was no attempt at a systematic approach. Instead operational mechanisms were used as appropriate to individual circumstances. As a result there was concern that what was described as the 'scattergun' approach to HAZ commissioning had resulted in too few local project partnerships being able to demonstrate operational capacity. This led to greater attention being paid to capacity building in the later phases of the HAZ and to developing new models of service provision such as developmental commissioning, which aimed to tackle discrimination in service commissioning and delivery by involving voluntary and community sector bodies more directly in developments.

Throughout the HAZ evaluation respondents emphasised the use of informal agreements and relationships to promote collaborative endeavour and some expressed considerable disquiet at the adverse consequences of formalising arrangements. Nonetheless particular project experiences also highlighted the extent to which the reliance on 'good working relationships' between individuals could jeopardise operational capacity. For example in Northumberland one project manager spoke of the difficulty he experienced in trying to manage a project worker who had been 'lent' to the organisation by a partner but without any clarity about hours of work, line management or role.

Ensuring the smooth running of the HAZ was usually the responsibility of a key individual – the HAZ manager or coordinator. The importance of the role played by these individuals in collaborations is highlighted by Klijn and Koppenjan (2000) who argue that securing cooperation between members of a network over a particular issue will not necessarily arise simply from the interaction of network members, but requires some form of 'steering' or network management. Klijn and Koppenjan identify two types of network management: process management, which is concerned with strategies to improve the quality of network interactions by 'seek[ing] to unite the various perceptions of actors and solve the organisational problem that various organisations, in having autonomously developed their own strategies, are not automatically in concert with one another' (ibid.: 140); and network constitution, which seeks to make changes to the network itself (bringing in new actors, changing the rules of operation or reframing the problem or issue the network is concerned with). The approaches are fundamentally different and neither is easy, in each case the role of the network manager(s) being that of a mediator or stimulator rather than director. For HAZ managers these difficulties were compounded by the fact that the HAZ 'networks' might (in theory at least) comprise actors from the 'non-organised' public as well as actors linked to organisations.

Practice capacity refers to the skills and abilities of workers and their capacity to embrace and further the collaborative agenda. The HAZ evaluation's focus on community involvement allowed us to explore the development of practice capacity in this important area for HAZs. In some HAZs the key challenge was to transfer capacity from community involvement specialists to those within the targeted organisations. So in Bradford the approach of attaching community involvement specialists to new primary care organisations as they developed appeared to be successful in building in a commitment to public engagement into these organisations and to support this via the resourcing of individuals to fulfil this function. However there remained wider concerns about the extent to which this commitment to community involvement had penetrated the middle management tier. In other HAZs there was greater emphasis on developing community involvement capacity in response to specific circumstances, for example, the Community Development Coordinators in LSL sought out opportunities for innovation within the very different contexts of the three boroughs.

Important in the development of practice capacity was the contribution of 'reticulists or boundary spanners' at all levels in the HAZ. Reticulists or boundary spanners are able to play a variety of roles in collaborations to facilitate action amongst others (Sullivan and Skelcher, 2002). The most commonly articulated capacities of reticulists cited in the case studies were networking, creativity, coordination, problem solving and communication. Those most obviously identified as reticulists were those whose job it was to 'add value' to action on the ground, usually with a specific community involvement/development focus. The Community Involvement workers in the primary health care organisations in Bradford, the Healthy Living Development Managers in Northumberland, and the Community Development Coordinators in LSL all fulfilled this role.

Also important in enhancing the degree of practice capacity in the collaboration was the existence of trust relationships between key individuals. Mayer, Davis and Schoorman (1995) emphasise that the development of trust between individuals is based upon a combination of personal and professional attributes, for example combining a technical ability to do the job with altruistic motivations and individual integrity. Maintaining trust relationships over time requires the demonstration of reliability and dependability in relation to these attributes (Rousseau, Sitkin, Burt and Camerer, 1998; Jones and George, 1998).

These aspects of trust were resonant with the case studies. For HAZ staff particularly, the ability to demonstrate their competence to other stakeholders was key to building trust, although it worked both ways, as in Bradford where the pre-existing area coordinators and the HAZ Community Involvement workers had many shared interests. For the area coordinators it was not only important that they were confident in the competence of the HAZ staff, it was also necessary to demonstrate their own competence to these staff. This was accomplished by offering to organise and co-facilitate a community event. The success of this helped to build trust between the relevant individuals and led to further, deeper collaboration. Stakeholders in Northumberland were also keen to highlight the power of trust, emphasising that trust relationships last beyond individual roles or jobs and that once trust is built collaborative action can be sustained through informal rather than formal mechanisms.

The demonstration of collaborative community capacity refers to the capacity of communities and citizens to engage with and take part in the opportunities opened up by HAZ. Here HAZs had some success in involving communities in a number of ways, particularly at project level. Much less success was had (or indeed sought) in relation to building community capacity to participate in the strategic decision-taking of the HAZ although the experience of HAZ informed the subsequent development of LSPs.

In Sandwell's the HAZ was used as a means of providing new opportunities for widening and deepening engagement with communities. This was achieved through the development of particular work streams, including work with older people, but was also attempted on a HAZ-wide basis, such as holding big events where community members could share experiences of the HAZ and also have the opportunity to influence future directions. In Northumberland the focus on making change to the mainstream generated a different approach, focusing on the development of community research to support the promotion of particular policy or service changes in the county.

Barnes and Prior (1998) discuss the significance of trust in renewing relationships between public services and their users. Fundamental to this is the notion of reciprocal trust – if citizens and service users are to have trust in public services, service providers must demonstrate trust in them. There are examples of this in HAZ, even if the purposes of action were not expressed in this way. Thus apparently 'risky' projects involving young men on the verge of criminal activity acting as mentors to others, giving teenagers more power to take control over their sexuality, or enabling mental health service users to find ways of dealing with their problems outside the medical model, can all be considered examples of ways of working which can build reciprocal trust. In a different way, enabling community members to take on significant leadership roles: chairing groups, deciding on the allocation of grants, and running community projects, are indicative of a greater preparedness on the part of 'officials' to trust 'the public' and to recognise their competence as collaborators. However, this aspect of the HAZ initiative did not develop or sustain the profile which some hoped it would have and, in practice, the emphasis on developing trusting relationships between organisations was greater than with communities.

CONCLUSION

This chapter has focused on the importance of control in collaborations. It has identified why control is important and for what purposes, and has highlighted the particular difficulties associated with exercising control in 'complex systems' such as collaborations. The chapter has highlighted two key dimensions to control in collaborations: the balance between internal and external authority and the availability of sufficient collaborative capacity. The examination of control in English Health Action Zones has revealed the critical importance of central government in providing 'contextual control' to the operation of HAZs. It has illustrated how the instruments of that contextual control are designed to, and in practice can, both constrain and facilitate the activities of local collaborations. However, the analysis of HAZs also revealed the extent to which local HAZs were able to operate within these contextual controls, to develop strategies, interventions and ways of working that were consistent with their local circumstances and not merely reflections of national design. The extent to which local HAZs were able to do this depended very much on the amount of collaborative capacity the HAZ could draw upon. The greater the reservoir of collaborative capacity within the locality, the more the HAZ was able to mitigate the constraining effects of central government's contextual controls, and develop instead a system of internal authority to guide the operations of the local HAZ (see Figure 4.1). The analysis of English HAZs suggests that, in England at least, central government influence over collaborative activity remains strong, particularly (and unsurprisingly) where collaborative initiatives have their origins in central government, but that local collaborative capacity is also present and is fed and facilitated by local circumstances (history and traditions).

REFERENCES

Barnes, M. and D. Prior (1998), 'Trust and the Competence of the Welfare Consumer', in A. Coulson (ed.), *Trust and Contracts. Relationships in Local Government, Health and Public Services*, Bristol: The Policy Press.

Barnes, M., H. Sullivan and E. Matka (2004), 'The Development of Collaborative Capacity in HAZs', Final Report of the national evaluation to the Department of Health, University of Birmingham and the University of the West of England.

Barnes, M., E. Matka and H. Sullivan (2003), 'Evaluation, understanding and complexity: Evaluation in non-linear systems', *Evaluation*, **9** (3), 265-284.

Barnes, M., L. Bauld, M. Benzeval, K. Judge, M. Mackenzie and H. Sullivan (2005), *Building Capacity for Health Equity*, London: Routledge.

Bauld, L. and K. Judge (2002), 'The Development of Health Action Zones', in L. Bauld and K. Judge (eds), *Learning from Health Action Zones*, Chichester: Aeneas, pp. 1-16.

Bryson, J. (1988), 'Strategic planning – Big wins and small wins', *Public Money and Management*, Autumn, 11-15.

Byrne, D. (2001), 'Complexity science and transformations in social policy', *Social Issues*, **1** (2), www.whb.co.uk/socialissues/index.htm, (2 August 2002).

Cilliers, P. (2000), 'Knowledge, complexity and understanding', *Emergence*, **2** (4), 7-13.

Cropper, S. (1996), 'Collaborative Working and the Issue of Sustainability', in C. Huxham (ed.), *Creating Collaborative Advantage*, London: Sage, pp. 80-100.

Department of Health (1997a), 'Health Action Zones – Invitation to Bid', Executive Letter, No. 65, London: Department of Health.

Department of Health (1997b), 'Health Action Zones', Circular EL (97)145, Leeds: NHSE.

Department of Health (1999), *The Health Act 1999*, London: Department of Health.

Gilchrist, A. (2000), 'The well-connected community: Networking to the "edge of chaos"', *Community Development Journal*, **35** (3), 264-275.

Hardy, B., B. Hudson and E. Waddington (2000), 'What Makes a Good Partnership?', Leeds: Institute for Health/NHS Executive Trent.

Howard, J. (2006), 'Local governance: the local, the "sub-local", and public participation – managing complexity?', Paper to the 10th annual International Research Symposium on Public Management, Glasgow: Caledonian University, April 10-12.

Hudson, B., B. Hardy, M. Henwood and G. Wistow (1999), 'In pursuit of inter-agency collaboration in the public sector', *Public Management*, **1** (2), 235-260.

Huxham, C., and S. Vangen (2000), 'Ambiguity, complexity and dynamics in collaboration', *Human Relations*, **53** (6), 771-806.

Jones, G.R. and G.M. George (1998), 'The experience and evolution of trust: implications for co-operation and teamwork', *Academy of Management Review*, **23** (3), 531-46.

Klijn, E.-H. and J.F.M. Koppenjan (2000), 'Public management and policy networks', *Public Management*, **2** (2), 135-158.

Kooiman, J. (2003), *Governing as Governance*, London: Sage.

Luke, J.S. (1997), *Catalytic Leadership: Strategies for an Interconnected World*, New York: Jossey-Bass.

Mayer, R.C., J.H. Davis and F.D. Schoorman (1995), 'An integrative model of organizational trust', *Academy of Management Review*, **20** (3), 709-734.

Mayntz, R. (1993), 'Governing Failures and the Problems of Governability: Some Comments on a Theoretical Paradigm', in J. Kooiman (ed.), *Modern Governance: New Government-Society Interactions*, London: Sage, pp. 9-20.

Medd, W. (2001), 'Making (dis)connections: Complexity and the policy process?', *Social Issues*, **1** (2), www.whb.co.uk/socialissues/index.htm (2 August 2002).

Moore, M.H. (1995), *Creating Public Value: Strategic Management in Government*, Cambridge, MA: Harvard University Press.

Newman, J. (1996), 'Beyond the vision: Cultural change in the public sector', *Public Money and Management*, April/June, 59-64.

Osborne, S.P. (ed.) (2000), *Public-Private partnerships: Theory and Practice in International Perspective*, London: Routledge.

Pierre, J. and B.G. Peters (2000), *Governance, Politics and the State*, London: Macmillan.

Rhodes, R.A.W. (1997), *Understanding Governance*, Buckingham: Open University Press.

Rousseau, D.M., S.B. Sitkin, R.S. Burt and C. Camerer (1998), 'Not so different after all: A cross-discipline view of trust', *Academy of Management Review*, **23** (3), 339-404.

Skelcher, C. (2000), 'Changing images of the state: Overloaded, hollowed out, congested', *Public Policy and Administration*, **15** (3), 3-19.

Stacey, R.D., D. Griffen and P. Shaw (2002), *Complexity and Management*, London: Routledge.

Stewart, M. (2003), 'Towards Collaborative Capacity' in M. Boddy (ed), *Urban Transformation and Urban Governance – Shaping the Competitive City of the Future*, Bristol: Policy Press, pp. 79-90.

Stewart, M., S. Goss, G. Gillanders, and L. Grimshaw (2002), *Collaboration and Co-ordination in Area Based Regeneration Initiatives*, London: DETR.

Stoker, G. (2004), *Transforming Local Governance*, Basingstoke: Palgrave.

Sullivan, H., M. Barnes and E. Matka (2002), 'Building collaborative capacity through theories of change: Early lessons from the evaluation of Health Action Zones in England', *Evaluation*, **8** (2), 205-226.

Sullivan, H. and C. Skelcher (2002), *Working across Boundaries*, Basingstoke: Palgrave.

5. A Learning Network Approach to Community Empowerment

Derrick Purdue

INTRODUCTION

Collaboration is central to the role of community organisations in contemporary Britain, and it takes two principal forms: horizontal networking to develop cohesion out of fragmented and divided communities; and vertical partnership working to connect to powerful local stakeholders, such as authorities, agencies and funders. The Joseph Rowntree Foundation (JRF) Neighbourhoods Programme is an experimental learning network, which models both these types of collaboration. The Neighbourhoods Programme brings together 20 neighbourhood-based community organisations and offers them a partnership with a large charitable foundation with professional facilitators and evaluators as well as encouraging horizontal networks between the member organisations. This chapter is work-in-progress based on the evaluation of the three-year Programme against its aims to improve community organisations' knowledge of 'what works', their networks and their access to local power holders. The evaluation is intended to contribute to inter-organisational learning within the Programme and the evaluation team has adopted an action learning methodology, exploring the 'theories of change' (Connell and Kubisch, 1998) that underpin the JRF approach to community empowerment. The Programme offers opportunities for learning through evaluation of individual community organisations, of collaboration between organisations and of the effectiveness of the JRF contributions (credit, facilitation, brokerage and increased profile of the Programme) in supporting community organisations to develop in terms of a community empowerment framework (See Table 5A.1). The evaluation draws on fieldwork conducted at the programme's national networking events and regional workshops, as well as interviews held with key individuals both in JRF and in the community organisations.

The chapter falls into two parts. The first explores the different elements of the JRF Programme and their success in delivering community empowerment. Do the opportunities within the Programme – facilitation, networking and other support available from JRF – add up to a package that empowers community organisations? The second part moves beyond the evaluation and begins to use the material gathered in the Programme and the literature on trust and defensiveness in organisations to reflect on the psychological dynamics of learning in community organisations and in inter-organisational networks and partnerships. Tackling community empowerment requires not just practical and technical solutions, but also emotional change not only in power holders, but also in the community organisations themselves. Hence the learning within this network consists not only of transfers of information, but also increases in emotional reflexivity (King, 2005).

THE JRF NEIGHBOURHOODS PROGRAMME

Theories of Change: The Emergence of a Rationale for the Programme within JRF

The Joseph Rowntree Foundation is a charitable foundation set up in 1904 and has a long history of trying to influence social policy through research and lobbying government. Interviews with key members of JRF reveal the kind of shift in work that was envisioned and the underlying 'theory of change'. One respondent claimed that every JRF research project has to be policy relevant, so the JRF Neighbourhood Programme indicates a shift from JRF's usual pattern of policy research to become a 'practice change organisation as well as a policy change organisation'. A key finding of the evaluation would be whether this new orientation is effective and sustainable as a way of delivering community empowerment.

JRF has produced a lot of research on community development and regeneration. The Neighbourhoods Programme may be portrayed as a way of testing whether those ideas are getting through to community practitioners or to local policy makers and whether they actually work in practice. In the words of a JRF staff member:

> Consistent messages have come from the research about the centrality of communities, playing a part in regeneration and the need to start with the communities own agenda: 'What do you want to do?' And 'what do you need to know to help you bring about your aims?'

The JRF staff member explained that in this programme:

> JRF is operating with its own theory of change, which is that a small amount of information and support can have a big impact. The evaluation of this theory of change will depend on the communities' views of how well the programme works in delivering this change.

The Programme's 'learning network' model was driven by three perceptions within JRF. First, that a lot of knowledge exists in community organisations, but that it is scattered widely, and so bringing organisations together with each other in horizontal networks would lead to sharing experience and joint problem solving. This is also empowering as it does not rely on experts. Second, community development and other professionals have accumulated knowledge about organisational and inter-organisational change which is not directly available to community organisations. Third, JRF itself is well-connected into national and local decision-making elites. It was envisaged that these connections could be used to change the position of community organisations in relation to their local elites and develop more positive vertical networks. In fact, a rationale for modelling a positive form of the horizontal and vertical collaborative relations that community organisations encounter in their work was never clearly developed.

Selection of Community Organisations

The process of selecting community organisations to participate in the Programme went through several stages, guided by the project advisory group. First JRF used their own networks to nominate 60 community organisations, of which 40 were then asked to apply and finally 20 were accepted. Ten of these were to be nominated as core community organisations, which were to get significantly more help than the other ten associated community organisations, which would get no credit or facilitation, but would be able to take part in the networking events. This was overturned at the first joint meeting of the facilitators and evaluators. Instead all 20 community organisations were accepted as full members, with variable amounts of credit and facilitation time. The applications were reviewed and feedback was given to the community organisations. Access to credit and further use of facilitation time was dependent on production of an action plan.

The 20 community organisations were intended to provide enough cases for a national programme (within resource constraints), with a wide regional spread, four community organisations in each of five regions – Scotland, Wales, Yorkshire and Humber, and South West England. This distribution also allows for some comparison between the new national/regional structures in Scotland and Wales and the more centralised English regions. The Programme includes a range of community organisations at different stages of development and based in different types of neighbourhood. However, the rationale underpinning the selection of the particular community organisations does not appear to be very clear to the evaluators or the facilitators.

Action Planning

The facilitators had the job of approaching the community organisations to get them to write a three-year action plan to be submitted to JRF. JRF intended the action plans to have two purposes. On the one hand the action plans were to have an intrinsic value as a useful exercise for the community organisations to get their staff teams/committees together to think about the major issues facing their neighbourhoods and develop four – five key strategic aims, which could help them to 'raise their game'. On the other hand, the action plan was also intended to have an instrumental value, in that, by completing them, community organisations would demonstrate their commitment to the programme and JRF would then release their credit to them. JRF appeared to conflate both of these purposes which led some community organisations to feel JRF was sending mixed messages about their relationship to the community organisations – was JRF offering support or control? Feedback from some community organisations via the facilitators suggested that JRF was behaving like a 'typical funder', requiring a lot of effort from the community organisations for very little return. There had been no discussion with the community organisations about whether starting with an action plan was the most useful way to develop the community organisations and their new partnership with JRF. Some of the community organisations responded to their perception of ambivalence on the part of JRF by viewing one of the major intended benefits of the JRF Programme – developing an action plan with external support – as a hoop they were obliged to jump through.

Some common problems emerged at this stage. First, many of the action plans were mainly work plans, setting targets for getting things done (often only covering the first year) rather than a more strategic approach. Second, others attempted to fit too many inappropriate ideas into the action plan. Third, some of the community organisations, often those in the latter category, dragged on for months without being able to complete their action plan.

JRF feedback was kept fairly light to prevent the community organisations feeling that they had yet more work to do in order to 'keep the funder happy'.

Reservations were noted but the community organisations were encouraged to get on with it. Nevertheless in a later questionnaire seven out of 13 community organisations felt action planning had helped them. The main ways in which the action planning helped was to suggest ways forward, to develop a clearer focus on aims, goals, priorities and outcomes and to provide a structure for measuring progress.

Role of the Facilitators

The JRF programme provided an external consultant in each country or region to work as a facilitator with the community organisations in the country or region for five or ten days each per annum. The role of the facilitators was defined as experts who were 'on tap, not on top' – available to help the community organisations to define their aims and to carry them out, not to define issues for the community (see Table 5.1). So the community organisations were to use the facilitators as they saw fit, for example, to mentor the leader, give technical advice, facilitate day events on subjects such as team building or strategic business planning. However, the relationship began with a more directive approach, insofar as JRF defined the initial task – the development of an action plan. This combination of roles caused two problems for some of the facilitators. First, they were used to being called in by a client to do a particular job, so they know (a) that they are wanted and (b) what it is they need to do. The flexible funder-led initiative left them confused – according to one facilitator 'I don't know what product I am selling'. Second, those facilitators who usually act in a responsive mode felt that the directive approach of forcing community organisations to produce an action plan meant that the period of gaining trust and developing an effective working relationship with the community organisations was lengthened.

The external consultant role played by the facilitators, however, is slightly more complicated. They also know that the 'presenting problem' is seldom the 'real problem' – indeed in this view moving from the presenting problem offered by the organisation to the real problem is a key task for the facilitator – and so a fundamental role was to 'broaden their horizons'. According to this point of view, there is a necessity for the facilitators to contribute towards problem definition and not just work towards solutions for problems already clearly known to the community organisations.

Facilitation styles have varied from very hands on and proactive to much more responsive. Several community organisations were slow to start using the facilitator time available to them. In answering a questionnaire at the second national networking event in March 2004, on the broad categories of how they used facilitators, nine out of 13 community organisations used the facilitators to work on strengthening their organisation, eight on improving their partnership working and two on increasing community involvement.

Table 5.1   Facilitator roles

	Client-Initiated	Funder-Initiated
Responsive	Provide solutions to 'presenting problems' (training)	Experts on tap, flexible but undefined, (mentoring)
Directive	Identifying 'real problems', requires high trust (development)	Developing strategy (action planning)

Credit, JRF Name and Knowledge Resources

Community organisations were allocated a credit line of either £5000 or £10,000 (or zero), depending on their perceived need. Credit appears to be the most straightforward benefit of the programme and could have been the motivating factor for some of the applications, yet credit remains underspent. For some of the small community organisations, this was their first funding, or as large as they could comfortably manage. Consequently, some of these have used the money successfully where clear purposes emerged, but others appear to have lacked the capacity to handle the credit effectively. Similarly, some larger well-funded community organisations have found it difficult to identify what the programme is offering them and so what it is suitable to spend the small amount of credit on. Most of the community organisations have used their membership of the Programme by referring to the JRF name in one way or another, either on funding applications, or in discussion with partner agencies. In four cases community organisations have taken up the offer of having an official letter from JRF outlining their interest in the community organisation through the programme sent to agencies active in their neighbourhood. JRF also encouraged the community organisations to use JRF publications where the research was relevant to issues they faced and to access both the general JRF website and a specific password-protected site for internal communication within the programme. Take-up of the website has been at best uneven and the publications have not been widely referred to.

Networking Events

The programme came together for the first time in May 2003 for a two-day national networking event and again for a second time in March 2004. Networking events were seen favourably, especially because they gave time for meeting others who face similar issues and problems. The community organisations felt it was important to 'know we are not alone', and were inspired by ideas and inputs from speakers and workshop presenters, as well as from other participants. Most of the regions have also held regional meetings. At this stage the agendas have largely been defined by the regional facilitator, but have also begun to act as inter-organisational visits, exposing others in the region to the success stories of the host group. Six community organisations out of 13 surveyed had participated in regional workshops. Ways in which these workshops were found to be useful included: discussing practical issues, problems and solutions; networking; sharing good practice and information. In one region the ability to relate to similar problems in similar areas with similar structures was important. In another region there was a desire for a regional identity with JRF support, which could develop a perspective on regional renewal/regeneration.

The idea of joint working between community organisations on substantive issues such as youth was raised by JRF at the first national networking event and a list of topics was agreed, around which thematic workshops were organised at the second national event. However, while community organisations appeared interested, they have not taken much initiative in getting together, which led JRF to propose replacing joint working with a new format. JRF will appoint a researcher to interview a number of community organisations interested in a topic, to produce a briefing and to call a meeting of the community organisations involved to discuss the short paper. 'Engaging people' and 'funding' were chosen as the two first topics.

Brokerage

JRF has undertaken or is preparing to play an 'honest broker' role in five of the neighbourhoods. The problem in hand is usually strained relations with the local authority over recognition of the organisation as a significant local actor, with resource implications in terms of funding and/or assets. There have been two models of intervention – low profile, where the brokering is undertaken by the regional facilitator alone, or high profile, where it is led by JRF staff and Advisory Group members. The low profile facilitator model is being successfully used in one case, where the issue was to bring together the established neighbourhood organisation with newly funded strategic organisations that had by-passed them, in order to develop a code of practice to regulate their interactions. This is progressing through a number of meetings brokered by the regional facilitator, with a similar, but more conflictual process starting in another neighbourhood. The high profile model has been used in conflicts with the local authorities. In one case, a joint meeting was held including the local authority that led directly to a payment being made to the community organisation. However, the community organisation felt that there needed to be a way of following up the brokering action or the increased profile could be short-lived. In another community organisation JRF brokered a meeting with the Chief Executive of the local authority to improve working relations on Neighbourhood Renewal Funding. The NRF money was released to community organisations across the city shortly before the meeting, which allowed the local authority to shift the meeting on to less challenging issues. An inherent danger with brokering is that a major national organisation like JRF can be seen by the local power holders as an easier organisation to deal with, diverting them from directly engaging with the community organisation itself. However, in the former case the brokering process and feedback from the other local stakeholders involved has led to the community organisation accepting criticism, re-assessing their defensive posture and opening up to engage afresh, and they have gone on to set up further meetings without JRF.

Role of the Evaluation Team

In the original bid the evaluation team saw themselves supporting core community organisations self-evaluations through individual visits pulling together learning on specific themes through inter-organisational workshops. When the distinction between core and associated community organisations was abandoned, the evaluation team chose ten community organisations to work more closely with. However, as the effort of getting community organisations to work with the facilitators on the action plans appeared quite daunting, a general feeling developed within the JRF staff and Advisory Group that there were already too many top-down relationships developing in the programme. It was agreed that the evaluation team should adopt a 'light touch' and not complicate relations with premature meetings with the community organisations, let alone collective thematic meetings. This has led to a decision to visit all the community organisations equally for evaluation interviews. Overall, the evaluation team has adopted a responsive mode of evaluation, participating in networking events and annual action plan reviews rather than duplicating these with further meetings, but in the final year of the programme they are leading specific research on 'diversity' and 'engaging with power holders'.

The Impact of the JRF Programme on Community Empowerment

The early stages of the evaluative research within the JRF Programme have generated findings on the levels of empowerment of a range of community organisations and their capacity to act strategically in their neighbourhoods which may be considered to reflect wider experience beyond the programme.

- First was a lack of organisational capacity and sustainable leadership structures. Many community organisations remain extremely fragile and overreliant on individual leaders, with inadequate support systems. Most of their time is spent on responding to immediate demands and funding bids, so their capacity for strategic action is usually severely limited. Even large and comparatively powerful community organisations are vulnerable to external influences such as funding crises, policy shifts and they can easily cease to be 'flavour of the month' with funders and local power holders.
- Second was the relative lack of horizontal networking among community organisations, so that they often feel isolated from others like themselves across the country. Some community organisations also struggle to bring together competing groups from across their own divided neighbourhoods in ways that make effective collaboration possible.
- Third is the weak position they hold within vertical partnerships with statutory authorities and agencies. They still tend to lack influence in partnerships and are frequently ignored by local decision-makers and power holders, who often take decisions over their heads. This power imbalance can make partnership working in the neighbourhoods an uphill struggle.

Working in this challenging environment, the Programme has been slower to engage the community organisations than was expected. As it is a low intensity programme, with small inputs spread over three years, community organisations can forget it is there between bouts of activity. There has been uneven take up of the small amounts of funding available, even though this is the most readily understood part of the programme, as well as relatively low use of some other resources. The facilitators have had to win the trust of the community organisations and define a role, while also working to the action planning agenda defined by JRF. Action planning and internal capacity building were the main focus of facilitation work in the earlier stages of the Programme. Where the initiative was left to the community organisations there has been little action at all, for example in organising visits to each other. Difficulties in engaging with the Programme were felt at both ends of the spectrum of the scale of organisations: while some more established groups have found it hard to work out a way of working that is of significant benefit to them, some small fragile groups had not developed the capacity to engage with the programme to any significant degree at all, within the first 18 months of its life time.

National and regional networking events are highly valued by the community organisations. Visits to each other, as well as joint working of various sorts, have been mooted but by and large fail to take place for a variety of reasons including: the intermittent nature of the programme; the tight time constraints on the leaders of most community organisation; lack of confidence and cover for those in small groups. Brokering by JRF has raised the profile of the organisations involved, although this is still at an early stage, and has in some cases shown evidence of contributing to increasing trust between organisations where relationships were previously log-jammed. The evaluation itself has been a bit tentative as the team worked out a role for itself in the changing pattern of the programme.

PSYCHOLOGICAL DYNAMICS OF INTER-ORGANISATIONAL LEARNING

As a learning network, the JRF Neighbourhood Programme is dedicated to promoting a number of versions of inter-organisational learning, through the various aspects of the programme. Action planning and facilitation have been effective ways of producing knowledge transfers, with JRF publications and website proving minor contributors. Developing action plans (and business plans) is one way in which the facilitators help the community organisations to make the tacit knowledge about their own communities and organisations more explicit and therefore more possible to share across the organisation and to present to outside agencies. The networking events, with their emphasis on sharing experience have provided space for cooperative multi-directional knowledge transfers, while collaborative knowledge creation (innovation) has so far been most obvious in the brokering processes (Hibbert and Huxham, 2005). In each case of brokering JRF and a single community organisation came together with local stakeholders external to the JRF Neighbourhood Programme to explore new ways of working together. The programme evaluation is in the process of drawing together and making more explicit the learning or knowledge that is scattered across various organisations, and the various collaborative research projects between community organisations are another potential point at which practice may be shared and potentially innovative ideas generated.

The capacity of community organisations in general to engage with and learn from other groups, networks and partnership structures is not a purely rational issue of knowledge and strategy, but also an issue of individual and group emotions. While emotions are central to mobilising communities, emotions can also take a destructive form, or at least develop patterns which cause individuals and the organisations they are active in to lose flexibility and get stuck in negative emotional patterns which prevent learning and innovation. These common problems that community organisations in general tend to face were likely to be reflected in the JRF Programme, given the range of size and circumstances of the 20 organisations in the Programme.

Theories of Emotions in Inter-organisational Learning

I will look at three theories of emotions and psychological dynamics: Argyris and Schön (1996) on the psychological positions involved in single and double loop learning; Mindell (1995) on the strong emotions rooted in the experience of power relations; and the Tavistock School psychoanalytic theories on defensiveness in groups (Halton, 1994; Stokes, 1994).

Inter-organisational learning may be conceptualised in terms of single and double loop learning (Argyris and Schön, 1996). Single loop learning refers to operational change, improving techniques for reaching accepted goals, changing strategies but staying in the same paradigm. Double loop learning, by contrast, goes further in changing the way of learning and typically involves a much more open and negotiated approach to problem solving. Learning to work with new partners in new institutions around new agendas is always going to be a challenge. Yet the literature on organisational learning suggests that acknowledging the difficulties is part of the solution. Argyris and Schön (1996) ground single loop learning and double loop learning in contrasting emotional positions of defensiveness and trust, which they call Model I and Model II respectively. Model I behaviour consists of evaluating how others behave and attributing motives to them. This takes the form of defensive thinking where the main motivation is for individuals or organisations to 'cover their backs'. Threatening or embarrassing issues are kept out of the discussions, with a tendency to rigidity and suppression of emotion and trust of others.

Double loop learning (ibid.), on the other hand, requires individuals, organisations or partnerships to change their basic psychological approach to a Model II attitude to learning, which is more open and trusting. Communication is kept open and ideas on why the other person or organisation is behaving in a particular way are tested in discussion, with an openness to reframing problems (Gray, 2003), which depends on taking emotional risks and requires 'learning with others' and consequently 'learning about yourself and your own organisation' (Hoggett, 2003).

While Argyris and Schön are happy to focus on the learning involved in a shift from defensiveness to trust, others use approaches that attempt to link the internal world of these emotional states with the external world of politics and power. One such approach traces the impact of external power and conflict on shaping emotions, and takes as its model the experience of childhood abuse and minorities' experience of harassment and oppression (Mindell, 1995). Thus Mindell relates the presence of strong emotions such as fear and anger in groups to power differentials between diverse social groups (e.g. differences in class, race and gender). Oppressed and marginalised groups feel abused by more powerful mainstream groups and this can result in having feelings of revenge towards their oppressors. When repressed, these emotions may appear as numbness or despair. While anger can be, and frequently is, a motivating force for community political engagement, fear is less productive and despair disempowering. The response of powerful groups to the vengeful feelings of the oppressed is often to treat them as pathological (ibid., 1995) and attempt to suppress them. Mindell argues that in order to create good collaborative relationships these strong emotions need first to be acknowledged.

An alternative to this political approach grounding emotions in histories and biographies of oppression is the psychoanalytic approach of the Tavistock School, in which group emotions are treated as grounded in early psychological processes. These are considered to be fairly universal and, following Melanie Klein, they distinguish two emotional positions – the 'paranoid-schizoid position' and the 'depressive position' (Halton, 1994) – and claim that the emotional life of an organisation, or a group within an organisation, may be dominated by one or other of these. The 'paranoid-schizoid position' is characterised by feelings of distrust, control, hostility and blame (i.e. defensiveness). This position derives from two early psychological processes; 'splitting' emotional objects (usually the mother) into 'good' and 'bad'; and projection of one's own 'bad' elements onto outsiders (e.g. other organisations or groups). The contrasting 'depressive position' is more psychologically advanced where objects (people, groups, organisations) are recognised as having both positive and negative elements and reparative work is undertaken to mend relationships and move forward.

Bion, the leading theorist of the Tavistock School, identified three defences (which he called 'basic assumptions') that groups use to contain anxiety (Stokes, 1994). The first is dependence on a leader, who takes care of the emotional needs of the group, rather than challenging them to make changes and face challenges. The second is to operate in fight-or-flight mode, identifying enemies without or within. This comes closest to the paranoid-schizoid position, or defensiveness. The third defence, pairing, is where the group colludes in the unfounded hope that a pair of individuals coming together within the group will produce a solution to all their troubles, organisational or emotional. The overall thrust of this argument is that to undertake the primary task of an organisation will generally involve the vulnerability of trusting others and coping with ambivalent feelings, as well as the anxiety of uncertainty and change. Groups may switch between these defences to protect the group from such emotional stress. Furthermore, individuals find working at the boundaries of their organisation is innately anxiety provoking (James and Huffington, 2004) and so working in partnerships can be particularly testing. Any two groups that share social space (e.g. separate teams in the same service or organisation) can relate through a 'dynamic of envy and resentment' (Hoggett, 2003) and feel more comfortable indulging in these sorts of mutual blame than taking the risk of opening up to negotiate effective collaboration. While Mindell and the Tavistock School may appear at first glance to be diametrically opposed, the two approaches can be seen as complementary, since the group defences described by Bion would be ways of the group protecting its members from being overwhelmed by the powerful emotional conflicts Mindell describes.

Given these theoretical discussions, it is important to acknowledge that vertical relations of power and dependency between people and organisations tend to bring up strong emotions and a certain amount of irrational behaviour on both sides. Feelings of distrust, control, hostility and mutual blame are common in regeneration partnerships, where organisations of unequal power attempt to work together (Purdue, Hambleton, Razzaque and Stewart, 2000). It is not uncommon for community (and statutory) organisations to get stuck in the 'paranoid-schizoid position' (Halton, 1994), or what is less alarmingly known as 'Model I behaviour' (Argyris and Schön, 1996). Interventions by action researchers and external consultants are often aimed at moving organisations on from the 'paranoid-schizoid position' to the 'depressive position' (Halton, 1994) which involves integrating problematic feelings rather than blaming others or burying emotional problems. Or again, they attempt to move from Model I to Model II behaviour (Argyris and Schön, 1996) with an emphasis on trust, openness and negotiation.

Learning in the sense used here consists not only of acquiring new information and new technical skills, but also involves undergoing an emotional change which develops greater reflexivity – emotional as well as cognitive (King, 2005). Argyris and Schön argue that, while this psychological learning occurs in individuals it is also a collective learning of the organisation. A lot of the examples they work with are of learning to trust others across boundaries within organisations. In the literature on multi-organisational partnerships, trust is defined as consisting of the acceptance of risk and vulnerability deriving from the action of others and an expectation that the other will not exploit this vulnerability (Humphrey, 1998: 216-217). Trust can take the form of trust in the 'competence' of the other or 'goodwill' towards the other (Humphrey, 1998), with the latter including an emotional acceptance of the other. Trust is the opposing emotional position to defensiveness. The problem of learning new patterns of trust between collaborating organisations is an extension of organisational learning, often within less clear authority structures. A learning network such as has been set up for this JRF Programme still involves individuals and groups, as well as organisations; and it still involves the need for finding ways of developing trust and reflexivity in conditions of psychological uncertainty. This will be demonstrated below in the examples of four different organisations' relations with the different aspects of the network.

Trust and Defensiveness in the JRF Programme

The focus of the Programme was on practical help for the organisations, and so dealing with emotional issues fell outside the 'psychological contract' of mutual expectations (Guest and Conway, 2002) under which the Programme was set up. While the evaluation did not set out to test psychological models through action research, this section aims to explore some of the dynamics of group emotions in community organisations as represented in the Programme. Facilitators' reports are used to reflect on what are, in fact, common patterns of behaviour in community organisations engaged in urban regeneration work, which frequently requires inter-organisational collaboration.

While the majority of the community organisations have maintained positive relations with their facilitators, there has been some evidence of gate-keeping behaviour, where leaders of community organisations blocked contact between the Programme and other staff. There are community organisations where key individuals appear to have resisted involvement in the Programme, and this suggests that they may be adopting a defensive pattern which minimises the potential change impact of the Programme on their organisations. Emotional defensiveness is widespread through many organisations in the community as well as in other sectors, and the JRF community organisations are in no way exceptional. The emotional issues that community organisations within the JRF Programme have encountered in attempting to engage with the Programme are indicative of these emotional patterns within community organising and inter-organisational working more generally. Four cases of defensiveness are explored.

Community leaders frequently articulate or channel vengeful feelings of having been abused by the local powers, while the community more widely tends to the numbness Mindell associates with repressed revenge – often noted as the apathy of local communities. This appears to have been case in community organisation A, where its leaders felt that they had been badly treated by the local authority over years and have developed a dislike of statutory organisations and a pervasive negative attitude. When JRF suggested brokering a deal, the regional facilitator undertook a series of interviews with stakeholders and found that they considered the organisation negative and ineffective. The facilitator fed this back and the community organisation agreed that they had to change and start again in their relations with the outside world. This move towards greater trust led to successive meetings and some sense in which local problems could be addressed. However, after a while they moved back to a more defensive attitude, more concerned with blaming external agencies than mobilising their own capacity to act and to negotiate with the outside world. Breaking out of such defensive patterns is a difficult journey to make, which most community organisations would find difficult.

In the second case, community organisation B took up the JRF offer of brokering over a funding crisis. The community organisation had been struggling with a failing council and a defensive civic culture and had become very isolated in a funding battle. The organisation had begun to see enemies everywhere in the council, government office and in the wider community structures. JRF took part in two brokering meetings. In the second round of negotiation JRF sought legal support and was successful in gaining a reprieve on funding cuts. However, the community organisation was unable to make any allies within the Local Strategic Partnership or to break through the Council's own defensive posture. There has since been a new round of cuts with little prospect of victory.

Both these cases may be interpreted as Bion's 'fight–flight' response (Stokes, 1994), a sort of defensiveness, which is concerned with protecting against external (and sometimes internal) enemies. While it is difficult to deal with abusive power relations, a fight–flight response, casting the council as 'the enemy', leaves an organisation isolated in the environment in which they have to operate. Having external enemies can create a unity of purpose. However, this can have the downside of deflecting attention from internal problems rather than addressing them. Alternatively, the process of splitting and projecting bad feelings can be repeated within an organisation and be played out through internal splits and conflicts.

In the third case of community organisation C, the responsibility for leading the organisation appeared to have been left to two key people, and there was very low staff morale. The organisation requested an audit from the facilitator, but when this brought to the surface tensions which the organisation had been avoiding, the relationship with the facilitator deteriorated. It seems that the facilitator's wake up call when reporting these tensions to the board set off a strong defensive reaction; that is, protecting against the emotions associated with change by 'projecting' (Halton, 1994) the resentment that had been uncovered in the organisation on to the facilitator. However, after a long period of letting the facilitator hold these feelings for them, the organisation was able to carry through the changes the facilitator had suggested and move forward (although the facilitator's influence has never been acknowledged). This may be interpreted as an example of another of Bion's defence mechanisms, 'pairing', (Stokes, 1994), which is the collusion between two or more in a group who are entrusted by the others to produce an apparent solution, which prevents the necessity of facing the real challenges, and thus contains the group's anxiety. This collusion was evident accompanied by fight–flight, with the outside facilitator being blamed for the uncomfortable feelings aroused by bringing conflict and uncertainty to the surface.

In the fourth case, the facilitator has found it very difficult to engage with community organisation D. All connections with the facilitator were 'bottle-necked' by being referred to a single leader, who did not respond to outside approaches from the Programme. Little use was made of resources on offer; there were frequent low-level complaints and negativity about the Programme. The absent leader appears not to understand what the Programme may have to offer. This case may be interpreted as an example of 'leader dependence', Bion's third defence mechanism (ibid.), which can include leaders that are significant by their absence rather than their presence. It has already been noted that many community organisations suffer from low organisational capacity, which often takes the form of excessive dependence on individual leaders. However, in Bion's theory (ibid.) there is a big difference between organisations where a dynamic leader creates opportunities for the group to take up challenges and achieve results on the one hand and dependent organisations on the other where the leader's role is to contain anxiety or challenge the members, usually preventing change. In the case of organisation D, this passive sort of defensiveness appears to be evident in relation to the Programme, though not necessarily in other parts of the organisation.

Leaders are highly significant in the relations between the Programme and the organisation, acting as either a positive champion or a negative gate keeper. This is part of a wider role of connecting the inside to the outside both organisationally and emotionally. Leaders are therefore the focal point in all three of the defence mechanisms as well as in positive trust and learning. The JRF Programme contains a number of positive and dynamic community leaders who are able to work in a Model II fashion, in open collaboration. They learn fast about building creative alliances, such as neighbourhood-based forums of frontline workers, seek out other effective local actors, cross boundaries with public agencies as well as other community organisations.

However, these dynamic community leaders may well still come up against defensive emotional barriers raised by public agencies (see also previous work commissioned by JRF, Purdue et al., 2000). Community groups often have good reasons for resenting some of their potential partners. Defensiveness is by no means the sole preserve of the community sector. Indeed local authorities in many areas are deeply rooted in the defensive position. Community organisation E is led by a highly effective and flexible learner, but has struggled against the local authority housing department, which has never trusted organisation E or its leader. The housing department, which is supposed to work in partnership with organisation E, has made their indifference and contempt for the local community quite clear and just launched a major redevelopment of the estate without any consultation whatsoever. Community organisation F, similarly dynamic, found its relations with other organisations in the neighbourhood going sour as a rival local leader began to work in a competitive and undermining way, using a power base in the council. The JRF facilitator undertook a lengthy brokering process through the JRF Programme, which repaired the damage and established civil inter-organisational relationships in the neighbourhood, but organisation F has again fallen foul of defensiveness in the surrounding organisational environment.

CONCLUSION

Overall, community organisations do lack access to knowledge, networks, money and power as the original programme brief claimed. The light touch approach embodied in the programme design has delivered significant benefits to some of the community organisations involved, while others have struggled to engage. Trust is the oil of effective inter-organisational learning, and we found that success was most likely where an organisation has already developed a relationship with the facilitator, or where a strong champion existed in the community organisation who felt able to trust the facilitators and the rest of the Programme. So if trust was the key to success, defensiveness formed a major social psychological barrier to inter-organisational learning. With the benefit of hindsight, the JRF model could have provided a way of exploring the 'shadow side' of partnerships (Prins, 2002). Some of the misgivings expressed by the facilitators made it apparent that there was a lack of clarity about the 'psychological contract' (Guest and

Conway, 2002) underpinning the engagement between JRF and the community organisations. Cast in a role of practical community development, the facilitators were not granted the role of consultants able to challenge the psychological patterns of the organisations and work through difficult emotional issues. They could, therefore, be kept at arms length to protect ineffective but cherished defensive patterns in some organisations, at the expense of reflexive emotional learning. With hindsight, the Programme could have tackled these issues more directly, but it requires a relationship of trust between the community organisations and their facilitators in order to do so. Practical help may be the way in which trust is built up so that deeper issues can be tackled. It also takes time for an organisation to confront emotional issues, and it may require a facilitator to hold the feeling of anxiety for the members of the organisation, until they are able to act on the problem, as happened in organisation C.

The wider context within which the organisations operate is also important. A tricky aspect of trying to develop trust between a community organisation and a more powerful statutory organisation or funder is that the trust has fairly quickly to become a two-way process of mutual trust. If community activists feel they have to trust their local authority, but that this trust is not being reciprocated (Purdue et al., 2000), then the unequal relationship quickly starts to feel abusive. Community organisations exist in an environment replete with more powerful actors that they have to engage with to achieve their own ends. Building trust, openness and negotiated learning (that is, Model II behaviour) therefore becomes a constant but necessary struggle, and defensiveness remains a tempting, if ultimately destructive, option.

ACKNOWLEDGEMENTS

Thanks to the Joseph Rowntree Foundation for funding this research and to the members of the Evaluation Team of the JRF Neighbourhood Programme, Mandy Wilson (COGS) and Pete Wilde (COGS), for their help and support, and particularly to the evaluation project leader, Marilyn Taylor (UWE), for her advice on drafts of the chapter.

REFERENCES

Argyris, C. and D. Schön (1996), *Organizational Learning II: Theory, Method and Practice*, Reading MA: Addison Wesley.

Connell, J. and A. Kubisch (1998), 'Applying a Theory of Change Approach to the Evaluation of Comprehensive Community Initiatives: Progress, Prospects and Problems', in K. Fullbright-Anderson, A. Kubisch and J. Connell (eds), *New Approaches to Evaluating Comprehensive Community Initiatives (Volume II)*, Washington DC: Aspen Institute, pp. 15-44.

Gray, B. (2003), 'Framing of Environmental Disputes', in R. Lewicki, B. Gray and M. Elliot (eds), *Making Sense of Intractable Environmental Conflicts: Concepts and Cases*, Washington: Island Press, pp. 11-34.

Guest, D. and N. Conway (2002), *Pressure at Work and the Psychological Contract*, London: CIPD.

Halton, W. (1994), 'Some Unconscious Aspects of Organizational Life: Contributions from Psychoanalysis', in A. Obholzer and V. Zagier Roberts (eds), *The Unconscious at Work: Individual and Organizational Stress in the Human Services*, Hove and New York: Brunner Routledge, pp. 11-18.

Hibbert, P. and C. Huxham (2005), 'Interorganizational Learning: Intentions and Consequences', in T. Gössling, R.J.G. Jansen and L.A.G. Oerlemans (eds), *Coalitions and Collisions*, Nijmegen: Wolf Publishers, pp. 161-172.

Hoggett, P. (2003), 'Overcoming the desire for misunderstanding through dialogue', *Local Government Studies*, **29** (3), 118-127.

Humphrey, J. (1998), 'Trust and the Transformation of Supplier Relations in Indian Industry', in C. Lane and R. Bachman (eds), *Trust Within and Between Organisations: Conceptual Issues and Empirical Applications*, Oxford: Oxford University Press, pp. 214-240.

James, K. and C. Huffington (2004), 'Containment of anxiety in organizational change: A case example of changing boundaries', *Organizational and Social Dynamics*, **4** (2), 212-233.

King, D. (2005), 'Sustaining Activism through Emotional Reflexivity', in H. Flam and D. King, *Emotions and Social Movements*, London: Routledge, pp. 150-169.

Mindell, A. (1995), *Sitting in the Fire: Large Group Transformation using Conflict and Diversity*, Portland: Lao Tse Press.

Prins, S. (2002), 'Helping and Hindering Dynamics in Multiparty Collaboration: Designing Psychodynamic Action Research', in D. Purdue and M. Stewart (eds), *Understanding Collaboration*, Bristol: UWE, pp. 163-166.

Purdue, D., R. Hambleton, K. Razzaque and M. Stewart (2000), *Community Leaders in Area Regeneration*, Bristol: Policy Press.

Stokes, J. (1994), 'The Unconscious at Work in Groups and Teams: Contributions from the Work of Wilfred Bion', in A. Obholzer and V. Zagier Roberts (eds), *The Unconscious at Work: Individual and Organizational Stress in the Human Services*, Hove: Brunner Routledge, pp. 18-27.

Taylor, M, D. Purdue, M. Wilson and P. Wilde (2005), *Evaluating Community Projects: A Practical Guide*, York: Joseph Rowntree Foundation.

Table 5A.1   *Community empowerment evaluation framework*

Problem	What would make change happen? *rationale for the project*	How you plan to make change happen? *aims and objectives*	What results do you want to see? *outcomes of the project*
Analysis			
No one has analysed local problems and assets. Lack of direction – activity tends to be reactive rather than proactive	Consultation is needed with local communities to identify their needs and plan action	Profile community needs and assets. Draw up an action plan with short- and medium-term objectives to guide your work	A plan of action which local communities feel a part of
Engagement			
People are not engaged, little activity is going on locally to tackle problems	Community development is needed to encourage people to engage with the project	Set up community development and outreach projects. Develop a strategy to communicate with people and tell people what your project is all about	Local communities are engaged in a variety of activities and tackling local problems
Capacity			
Lack of leadership; lack of organisational ability; low level of skills; low level of resources	Sustainable leadership and organisational ability are needed to plan and co-ordinate action and raise funds	Provide opportunities to develop: • leaders and organisations • management skills • team building and accountability • fundraising skills	Effective and sustainable organisations and accountable leadership. Sustainable funding and assets

Table 5A.1   *Community empowerment evaluation framework (continued)*

Problem	What would make change happen? *rationale for the project*	How you plan to make change happen? *aims and objectives*	What results do you want to see? *outcomes of the project*
Cohesion			
The community is divided and fragmented	Common ground, mutual respect and understanding between communities and individuals	Develop negotiating, mediation and conflict resolution skills. Hold events and meetings to bring different groups together	Local communities acting effectively together
Power and influence			
Those who have power ignore the needs of the community; policy is not geared to local need and the community not involved in decision-making	People in power need a greater understanding of the needs of the community and the skills to communicate effectively with local people. Confidence and community-owned assets, rather than local authority-owned assets, can give the community greater power	Develop political, promotional and negotiating skills. Develop greater understanding and rapport with statutory bodies and other partners. Capacity building with statutory bodies and other partners so that they engage more effectively with communities. Develop the skills and resources to build up community-owned assets and services	Be taken seriously by power holders; work more effectively with them; make changes in policy and practice Effective management of community assets and services

Source: Developed by the JRF Neighbourhood Programme Evaluation Team (see Taylor, Purdue, Wilson and Wilde, 2005).

PART II

Learning in Partnerships and Networks

6. Collaboration, Knowledge and Learning: Integrating Perspectives

Paul Hibbert and Chris Huxham

INTRODUCTION

Learning is often claimed as an explicit aim of, or potential benefit from, collaboration and learning through collaboration is at the heart of many government policies. It is perhaps not surprising therefore that there has been much research addressing issues relating to learning in collaborative relationships. Our own interest in the area is in its potential as a theme in the theory of collaborative advantage (Huxham, 2003a; Huxham and Vangen, 2005). Ultimately we are concerned with determining whether theoretical conceptualisations relating to learning in collaboration can usefully inform practitioners about how to act in collaborative situations.

Literature on learning in the context of collaboration covers a wide range of perspectives, but where significant bodies of research output are evident they tend to take a particular focus on the issue. The role of industry networks in promoting learning and the nature of inter-partner learning in strategic alliances and joint ventures are examples. Whilst these are important contributions, our interest is to investigate whether taking a broad view of the literature in the area can lead synergistically to new and useful insights about the nature, role and impact of learning as it relates to inter-organisational collaborations.

This review serves three purposes. First, it provides a mapping of the terrain that can function as a loose guide for data collection, in empirical research aimed at supporting emergent theory development (Huxham, 2003b) – for example, action research of the sort characterised by Eden and Huxham (1996). The second and third purposes of the review relate to the power gained from synthesising the literature into a conceptual framework. The second potential purpose of the review is thus to support broader emergent theorising that combines both literature-driven and data-driven theorising (Hibbert and Huxham, 2005; Huxham and Hibbert, 2005). The third potential purpose is the main focus of this chapter: the possible use of the synthesis in its own right as an interim tool for supporting collaborative practice. In this sense, as with other frameworks in the theory of collaborative advantage, we are interested in its potential to be used by managers to guide an exploration of aspects of the collaborative situations that face them and so construct appropriate responses.

METHODOLOGY: REVIEW, SYNTHESIS AND INFERENCE

The methodology used for constructing this review and synthesis reflects its three purposes. We consulted a wide range of material on inter-organisational learning, collaborative learning and (potentially) related group learning processes. We also included material that seemed likely to relate to learning in collaboration, which related to discussions of knowledge 'creation' and 'transfer'. Our only criterion for inclusion was that material had potentially to relate both to collaboration (that is, any multi-party/multi-organisational project or form, relating to any sector) and to issues that might be connected with learning. We were thus not concerned with literature on learning *per se* (although some key elements of debates in the organisational learning and knowledge literature are touched upon, where these help to highlight key questions), nor, at this stage of the research, with literature on collaboration *per se*.

We systematically scanned a wide range of business, public administration, non-profit, management, strategy and policy research journals for the years 1998-2004, looking for articles at the learning collaboration interface. Earlier articles were also included where they appeared to be key foundation pieces referred to by many authors. We also scanned around forty books relating to collaboration, looking for references to learning or related topics. The bounds of the review were largely set within literature on collaboration but a broad, cross-disciplinary view was taken, which encompassed a range of theoretical perspectives, application areas and inter-organisational forms, as well a small number of chapters from outside the collaboration area which address key issues in the fields of organisational learning and knowledge. The review therefore steps across public, private and non-profit studies of learning activities – and research approaches from hypothesis testing to collaborative inquiry. This process identified around one hundred articles and twenty book sections, of which in total around eighty proved to be relevant. Although it has not been possible to include all of these here, they have each influenced the arguments that follow.

The process of deriving the review and synthesis can be considered as an iterative procedure which consisted of several steps, as discussed below:

1. *Extracting key concepts and relationships from the articles.* Here we were concerned with collating key terms that were explicitly used in the existing literature on inter-organisational learning, and understanding how to use them as 'handles' for grappling with the literature. That is, key terms such as 'knowledge transfer', 'knowledge creation', 'exploration', 'exploitation' (and so on, were identified, as were the explicit relationships between them, as argued in the literature.

2. *Grouping these into collections of related concepts.* This grouping was considered at two levels. First, the connection of relatively closely connected terms – 'diversity' and 'culture', for example – that often appeared in the same works. Second, through the development of higher level terms – for example 'partner complexity' as a grouping for notions of culture and diversity – and the grouping of these higher level terms into major groups.

3. *Considering ways in which the concept groups might relate to each other.* The connections between (and ordering of) major groups of concepts were considered and explored in a number of ways. That is, we sought to explore, in a very broad way, how the concepts might provide a general understanding of the process of learning in collaborative contexts.

4. *Considering how specific concepts within each group might relate to specific concepts in other groups.* By focusing on the different plausible connections between specific concepts within the groups we further developed our broad understanding of the process of learning in collaborative contexts, by seeking to identify possible detailed variants within the general conceptualisation.

5. *Trying out alternative methods for representing these relationships diagrammatically.* An important part of the development of our understanding of the possible learning processes, from our synthesis of the literature, was to represent the conceptual groupings, connections and processes in a number of diagrammatic forms which could be critically examined by us and others.

6. *Testing out our ability to articulate the essence of the diagrams verbally and in writing to both academic and practitioner audiences and noting their reactions.* Through critical engagement of a variety of views on our diagrams, we continued to reshape and develop our conceptualisations. In doing so we sought to generate a summary picture of extant research on learning in collaborative contexts that

was both meaningful and useful for both academic and practitioner audiences.

Steps (1) and (2) aimed to provide the overview of extant research that is needed to guide future data collection (i.e. for the first purpose described above). Steps (2) and (3) aimed to provide the basic conceptual framework that could be integrated with data-driven theory in the future (i.e. for the second purpose described above). Steps (3) and (4) aimed to provide the conceptual framework in a way that can be useful in practice (i.e. for the third purpose described above).

In moving from step (1) to step (4) we have used an increasing amount of interpretive reasoning. In step (1) we have aimed to be faithful to our understanding of what the original researchers have actually stated. By step (4) we are considering relationships that might be inferred on the basis of logical or experiential reasoning but, in the main, have not been explicitly identified by others. Not surprisingly, therefore, the key concepts of step (1) have remained fairly stable, while several iterations of (2) to (6) have already taken place. We have thus explored several versions of the conceptual framework before arriving at the one to be described in the following sections.

COLLECTING CONCEPTS: SITUATION CHARACTERISTICS, ATTITUDES AND OUTCOMES

From this process, three broad groups of concepts have currently emerged as key strands in the literature. These relate to the characteristics of situations in which learning takes place, attitudes to learning in these situations, and the kinds of outcomes relating to learning sought (or at least gained) through collaborating. In this section we discuss each of these in turn.

Situation Characteristics

Five groups of characteristics of collaborative situations emerge from the literature as having a bearing on the development of learning although, as we discuss later in the chapter, the boundaries between these categories are blurred and inter-relationships can be identified between the elements. Before addressing – later in the chapter – the complexity that is apparent when considering these groups as a whole, we discuss each of them in turn below, in the following order:

- Partner complexity – diversity, culture.
- Structural characteristics – network and/or partnership forms.
- Management style/stance – participative or controlling.
- Knowledge characteristics – explicit and tacit.
- Understanding and experience – learning, the field of enquiry, collaboration.

Partner complexity – diversity and culture. We begin our consideration of the situatedness of inter-organisational learning at the broadest level; the complex social nature of partners in cases reported in the literature. Palmer (2001) has suggested that the diversity of interacting partners is an important contributor to learning, helping collaborations to draw upon the knowledge and understanding of different communities; these may be communities in the broadest sense, or communities of practice (Lave and Wenger, 1991; Mohrman, Tenkasi and Mohrman, 2003). Communities of practice in particular support different kinds of knowledge within and across organisations, accounting for knowledge 'stickiness' and 'leakiness' which can be problematic learning issues (Brown and Duguid, 2001). Diversity, therefore, leads to the possibility that certain tensions will be developed (Huxham and Beech, 2003; Lunnan and Kvålshaugen, 1999), for example between accommodating and assimilating a breadth of knowledge, and progress towards narrower, well-defined learning objectives. Diversity amongst partners also makes the situation less amenable to control. The literature suggests that an important factor influencing learning possibilities is culture – including institutional (Reason, 1999), but more particularly regional and national (Nonaka, Ray and Umemoto, 1998; Simonin, 1999), conceptions. Calling upon diversity may thus give rise to unintended (or unspecifiable) outcomes. On the positive side these outcomes may desirable, innovative conceptions – knowledge creation. On the negative side, cultural matters may introduce incompatibilities in collaborative situations; for example, Milliman, Taylor and Czaplewski (2002) highlight culturally derived misunderstandings in multi-national team situations. Paradoxically, cultural 'incompatibilities' may therefore introduce barriers to harnessing the external knowledge which diversity provides (Faulkner and de Rond, 2000).

Structural characteristics – network and/or partnership forms. The structure within which interactions take place may also have an important bearing upon the learning outcomes. Many authors focus on particular structural forms; often these are either relatively goal-defined partnership forms, or broader, enabling or capacity-building network forms. Examples of the partnership form range from project-focused collaborations with a small number of contributing organisations (Hennestad, 1998), to large international research consortia (Mothe and Quélin, 2000). Examples of network forms include communities of practice and best practice networks, as described by Rosenkopf, Metiu and George (2001), Hartley and Allison (2002) and Breu and Hemingway (2002).

The choices that are made about the kind of structure that may be appropriate to the particular collaboration's objectives also implicitly introduce variations in the types of connections between actors that are developed and drawn upon. Granovetter's (1982) conception of strong and weak ties is important here, as is DeFillippi, Arthur and Lindsay's discussion (see Chapter 7 in this volume) of intra-community and inter-community dynamics; their treatment helps to provide traction on the links between the scope and depth of appropriate collaborative interaction and the alternative tasks that may be at hand. That is, on the one hand, goal-defined partnership forms are most reliant upon a relatively small number of strong ties, within a narrow group of actors, to facilitate action (whatever the size of the total group may be (Reagans and McEvily, 2003; Elliot and Homan, 1999). The defined project goals in such cases might include the fulfilment of learning objectives (of the 'knowledge transfer' type). Alternatively, broader capacity building or innovative goals are argued to be more likely to also involve weak ties, bridging communities and integrating diverse knowledge resources to support knowledge creation (Lazerson and Lorenzoni, 1999; Assimakopoulos and Macdonald, 2003). It seems, therefore, that these possibilities for inter-organisational structure are also related to the issues of diversity, culture and tensions (Lunnan and Kvålshaugen, 1999) that we touched on earlier; essentially these are matters that cannot be considered separately.

Management style/stance – participative or controlling. In the preceding discussion we have seen how partner complexity and the structural characteristics of inter-organisational learning situations are linked. Research also suggests that the management style adopted by partners involved in the collaboration is connected too. The principal area of decision relates to the closeness of control (Tsang, 2002) – whether actors from organisations actively aim to control processes and aims or operate in a more exploratory, participative mode. At the relatively 'closely controlling' end of the spectrum, partners choose to undertake explicit management functions such as defining goals, specifying processes and evaluating progress (Palmer, 2001; Boddy, Macbeth and Wagner, 2001). At the relatively 'loosely controlling', participative end, networks are constituted through 'reflexive social practices' (Sydow and Windeler, 2003) and practitioners are 'learning by participating in, creating and continuously recreating a particular community of practice' (Bouwen, 2003: 340). Decisions about management style therefore have a potentially important role in influencing what kinds of learning outcome are most likely in a given collaborative situation.

Knowledge characteristics – explicit and tacit. Where learning is a deliberate focus of managerial decision-making, the nature of the knowledge involved is also argued to be a relevant matter. There is an irreducible tacit dimension to all knowledge (Polanyi, 1966; Nooteboom, 1999), but for the purposes of inter-organisational learning a key distinction is whether: tacit knowing may be common to the participants, in situations where shared national or technical languages exist (Chikudate, 1999); or whether problematic inter-disciplinary discourses are likely to be involved, which highlight partner differences (Jevnaker, 1998). If the inter-organisational situation is to be designed to accommodate the tacit dimension of knowledge (that is, support participation in a tradition or point of view that enables tacit knowing – Tsoukas and Vladimirou, 2002), then it has been suggested that mechanisms such as loose social relationships (Ingram, 2002) or informal interactions (Powell, 1998) will need to be enabled – requiring a negotiated stance to interaction (Geppert and Clark, 2003). This emphasises the point made in the previous section discussing management styles in collaboration; high levels of control are likely to increase the risk that sharing at a tacit level, and the potential for creativity, are reduced. That is, the nature of the knowledge which is important to any defined learning objectives ought perhaps to inform choices about the level of control that is exercised. High levels of control seem to be most appropriate for situations in which the unshared knowledge is thought to be largely explicit in character.

Understanding and experience – of learning, of the field, of collaboration. It has been suggested that collaborative (shared) learning approaches – especially where creativity and tacit knowing are important – are most effectively supported by 'people centred processes', such as staff transfers and relationship developments (Almeida, Song and Grant, 2002) whereas the more competitive approaches, focused upon explicit transfers (acquisitions) are related to the competencies and intent of the acquiring organisation (Inkpen, 2000). The work of a number of authors allows us to suggest that the whole spectrum of attitudes to learning, and process choices that organisations can make decisions about, is dependant upon capacities for *understanding*. (Cohen and Levinthal's 1990 term 'absorptive capacity' is perhaps one such notion). These are based upon the prior experience of the organisations (or individuals within them); Lave and Wenger suggest that 'understanding and experience are in constant interaction – indeed they are mutually constitutive' (1991: 51-52). In the inter-organisational setting in particular, the literature suggests three types of experience that help to support the capacity for understanding:

- Experience of learning (Alter and Hage, 1993).
- Experience of the relevant knowledge domain(s) (Inkpen, 2000).
- Experience of collaboration (Lehrer and Asakawa, 2003; Khanna, Gulati and Nohria, 1998).

The kinds of learning outcomes that might be supported by such experience and the role of understanding in particular learning situations are discussed later in this chapter. Before we reach that discussion, however, we consider the *attitudes to learning* that partners in collaboration may have. These can influence the ways in which capacities for understanding are employed (or suppressed) and may therefore have a significant effect on the possibilities for learning.

Attitudes to Learning

We have suggested above that a consideration of the kinds of attitudes to learning collaborators have may have an effect on the possible learning outcomes. Participants may have definite attitudes to learning related to participation in a collaboration – to allow knowledge to be taken from or shared with partners, or to develop attitudes that allow some kind of innovative transformation of it. A kind of 'spectrum' of sharing is suggested, ranging across the following kinds of intention:

- To 'selfishly' acquire knowledge exclusively for the participant's own organisation, thus exploiting a partner.
- To share knowledge with specific organisational partners, in a relatively controlled fashion, thus exchanging with a partner.
- To share knowledge in a broad, open manner amongst a range of partners, thus exploring innovative solutions to problems-at-hand collaboratively.

These distinctions have been discussed in the work of a wide range of authors, for example March (1991), Oliver (2001), Schuler (2001), Lunnan and Kvålshaugen (1999), Faulkner and de Rond (2000); Yan and Child (2002). There is also a fourth kind of stance that is worthy of discussion:

- To exclude or sideline the consideration of learning: either implicitly, because the collaborative agenda is focused elsewhere; or explicitly, because it is regarded as unimportant.

As Beamish and Berdrow (2003) have suggested, lack of consideration of learning as an aim does not preclude the emergence of learning outcomes. A fuller exploration and empirical development of attitudes to learning in collaboration, which shows a complex and fine grained range of stances within four broad categories explored above, is presented in Huxham and Hibbert (2005).

Having reviewed the characteristics of the collaborative situations in which learning may occur, and the attitudes of partners operating in such situations, we can now consider the possible learning outcomes that may obtain.

Learning Outcomes

Many authors focus upon the kinds of learning outcomes that occur within inter-organisational situations. Ingram's (2002: 642) definition of inter-organisational learning highlights the kinds of learning possibilities which might be evidenced in practice: 'Inter-organisational learning occurs when one organisation causes a change in the capacities of another, whether through experience sharing, or by somehow stimulating innovation', suggesting the possibility of both planned learning outcomes and unplanned, emergent outcomes. This reflects strands in the literature which report both cases in which planned learning outcomes were achieved and cases in which unplanned or uncontrollable learning outcomes occurred (Norman, 2001; Nooteboom, 1999; Assimakopoulos and Macdonald, 2003).

Vera and Crossan (2003) note that there is considerable overlap between concepts related to organisational learning and organisational knowledge. 'Knowledge' *itself* is a rather broad and problematic term (Easterby-Smith and Lyles, 2003a); it may be related to understanding, insight, skills, expertise, and so on, and can be considered to have both personal and collective aspects (Tsoukas and Vladimirou, 2002). When considering *knowledge* in this chapter, we are therefore mindful of the issues it raises about the extent to which the world – and *knowing* – is socially constructed in practices (ibid.). However, we find that a common classification of learning outcomes, looking across the collaboration literature, is into the categories of '*knowledge transfer*' and '*knowledge creation*'. Bearing in mind our previous discussion of the problematic nature of knowledge, we feel that it is important to acknowledge that these 'outcome terms' are open to debate – in particular knowledge transfer as a metaphor for a learning outcome is imprecise, since it might be more usefully regarded as mirrored through participation in practices (Brown and Duguid, 2001). As Knight and Pye (see Chapter 8 in this volume) suggest, the content, process and contexts for learning are mutually related; learning is therefore more socially constructed, interpretive and complex than linear notions like 'knowledge transfer' suggest. We have reached similar conclusions from our work in a variety of different collaborative contexts (Hibbert and Huxham, 2005). The term knowledge creation is also open to some discussion in terms of its precise meaning, especially around the kind of social structural processes which are involved (Berends, Boersma and Weggeman, 2003) and alternative concepts such as recombination and reuse (Majchrzak, Cooper and Neece, 2004) may be more helpful. However the terms 'knowledge transfer' and 'knowledge creation' are widely used in the literature we reviewed and are 'practitioner friendly', for which reasons it seems useful to retain them, acknowledging the debates set out above.

Knowledge transfer outcomes may be thought of as unidirectional, bidirectional, or more complex multidirectional flows (Hardy, Phillips and Lawrence, 2003). Within this fluid complex of possibilities, equity of outcomes can be an issue; Spekman, Isabella and McAvoy (2000) have related differences in learning outcomes to competitive or collaborative learning intentions. In particular, knowledge transfer outcomes of a unidirectional nature have been linked to competitive learning behaviours in which one partner seeks to take knowledge from another whilst limiting reciprocation (Ingram, 2002). Such outcomes arise at the organisational level, for example through deliberate acquisition of knowledge by one organisation from another or 'spillover' (Mothe and Quélin, 2000). Broader bidirectional and multidirectional knowledge transfer outcomes may occur not only at the organisational level but also at the inter-organisational level. At the inter-organisational level these outcomes include, for example, network participants learning new ways to interact and structure collaborations (Benson-Rea and Wilson, 2003) and improved performance of collaborative entities (Zollo, Reuer and Singh, 2002).

The different knowledge transfer outcomes discussed above reflect approaches based upon organisations learning *from* each other (Bergquist, Betwee and Meuel, 1995). There is another mode to consider – organisations learning with each other. In the context of the collaborative entity this is effectively knowledge creation, either by innovative reconfiguration or by exploring broader cultural connections to import knowledge that is new to all of the collaborators. Knowledge creation is of course an important outcome for collaborations (Mothe and Quélin, 2000) and organisational communities (Lazerson and Lorenzoni, 1999), but we would argue that creation is not an alternative outcome to transfer. Rather we suggest that aspects of each may be entailed in the other. For example, it has been suggested that learning outcomes for individuals can be significant in complex partnerships – particularly in terms of developing competencies for dealing with ambiguity and complexity (Elliot and Homan, 1999) or in crossing paradigms to develop capabilities for collaboration (Reason, 1999). Thus even at an individual level, given suitable structures and motives, aspects of transfer and creation of knowledge in inter-organisational settings are both suggested. This reconnects with the work of Hardy et al. (2003); they have linked multidirectional knowledge flows, in particular, with the possibility of knowledge creation.

THEORISING TRAJECTORIES: FROM ATTITUDES TO OUTCOMES

Our discussion to this point is summarised in Figure 6.1. As discussed in the methodology, we have so far aimed to describe the main ideas emerging from the literatures as faithfully as possible, diverging from the original sources only to the extent that we have extracted ideas from their original contexts and combined them in new ways; but we still consider this to be, in effect, a mapping of the terrain.

In this section we go further, to explore some possible implications of these concepts in combination, focusing in particular on how they may help to explain the ways in which planned or unplanned learning outcomes arise in practical situations of collaboration. By reviewing evidence from empirical studies and theoretical reviews, we consider the ways in which attitudes to learning, and particular *patterns of engagement* with the characteristics of the collaborative situations, are connected to outcomes. This leads to a consideration of possible learning trajectories. In developing these we begin to move from the concern with *theory* and *process* to the issues of *process* and *practice*. This connects with the need for further research in *organizational learning across boundaries* identified in the review conducted by Easterby-Smith and Lyles (2003b). Our interest in the inter-organisational setting as a *specific context for learning* is also consistent with the process and practice areas for research identified in their review.

The patterns of process and practice which we begin to explore naturally draw upon the previous discussions of theory, and include possible ways in which a partner may actively *work* with some situation characteristics and *encounter* others; they also highlight interconnections between the various situation characteristics. Our discussion is presented in three parts; in each we consider learning from the perspective of a single organisation, with a certain attitude to learning in a collaborative setting, engaging in either a '*selfish*', '*sharing*' or '*sidelined*' learning trajectory. Each of these is presented as an exploration of the explanatory potential of the literature – and is therefore very much open to debate and development through further research.

Figure 6.1   *Aspects of learning in collaborative situations*

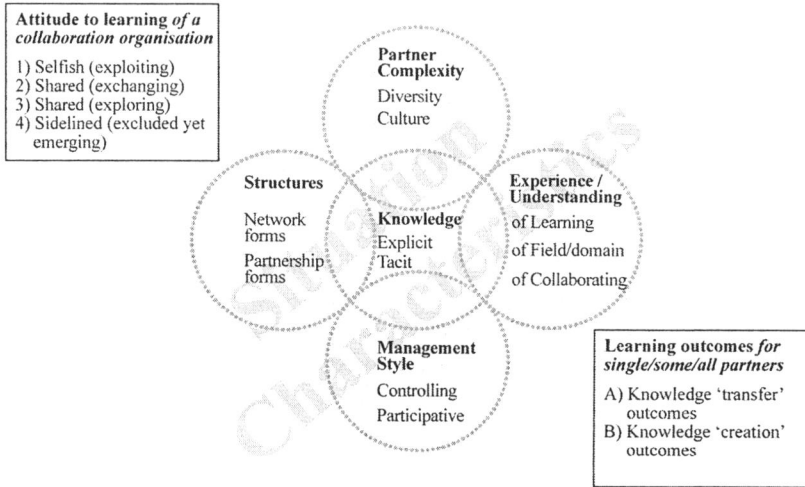

'Selfish' Learning Trajectories

Cases in which an organisation has a 'selfish' or 'competitive' (Soekijad and Andriessen, 2003) attitude to learning in a collaborative setting – that is, where a focal organisation intends to support learning exclusively for itself – have commonly been associated, in the literature, with knowledge transfer outcomes (Nooteboom, 2000; Mothe and Quélin, 2000).

The adoption of a 'selfish' or competitive attitude to learning suggests particular patterns of engagement with certain of the situation characteristics. Typically it makes learning a hidden aim (Huxham and Vangen, 2005) within collaborations ostensibly formed for other project purposes (Spekman et al., 2000), in which the 'selfish' partner seeks to control the processes in a way that preserves the learning opportunity. This requires formal project objectives of another sort; in order to be credible, this is likely to require a partnership form rather than a network form, and therefore the use of strong ties. Through these strong ties, barriers to interaction and learning, related to the different social contexts of organisations (Faulkner and de Rond, 2000), may come to the fore. This is because more collaboratively minded (less 'competitive') partners will be attempting to explore the diversity of the collaboration, whilst the competitive partner(s) – the focus in this case – will be secretive. Ultimately, the nature of the game must become apparent; in such cases, it is therefore unsurprising that 'selfish', competitive learning attitudes can have negative consequences and affect the fate of collaborations (Schuler, 2001; Ingram, 2002). If this leads to a premature breakdown in the collaboration, this may limit or prevent the desired knowledge transfer outcome (Soekijad and Andriessen, 2003). To obtain their desired learning goals, 'selfish' organisations must therefore *understand* learning; that is, they should have a competency which enables them to win the 'learning race' (Ingram, 2002) before the collaboration is dissolved.

Figure 6.2   Selfish learning trajectories and (possibly) relevant situation characteristics

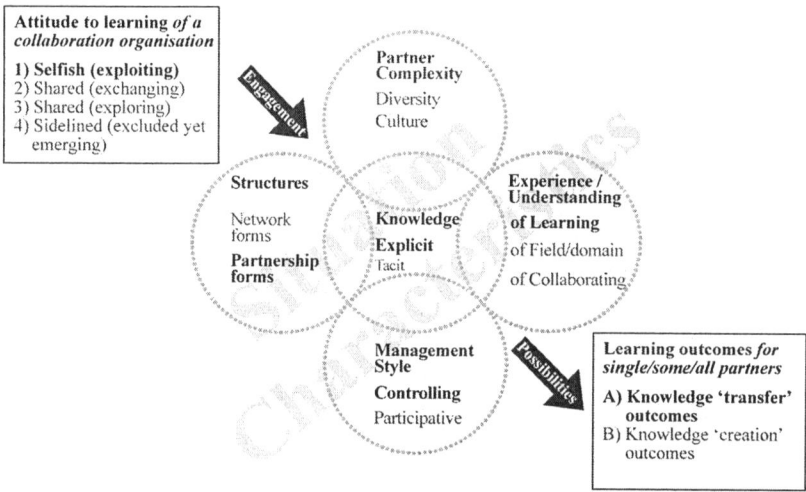

This analysis would suggest that the most likely results of a 'selfish' attitude to learning would either be the abstraction of some useful knowledge by the 'selfish' partner, or the collapse of the collaboration before this can take place. If the 'selfish' partner is concerned to limit spillover, the depth of engagement in the collaboration will be limited (Norman, 2001; Simonin, 1999) and tacit exchange (or more correctly, the mirroring of tacit knowing – dependant upon extensive and open social interaction) would not be a likely outcome. The interactions and possibilities are suggested in Figure 6.2.

'Sharing' Learning Trajectories

Sharing attitudes have been associated in the literature with both knowledge transfer outcomes (Khanna et al., 1998) and knowledge creation (Lehrer and

Asakawa, 2003). As with the selfish learning attitude, they suggest particular patterns of engagement with the situation characteristics.

Cooperative learners may be more likely than 'selfish' learners to be open to the diversity that a collaborative structure can bring (since they are likely to be more open in their engagement); however, since they are therefore likely to take a more loosely-controlling, partnering stance, the diversity is likely to create tensions between exploring the breadth of knowledge available within the situation and the focus upon task objectives (Reagans and McEvily, 2003). Many authors suggest that this greater openness to diversity might, in fact, expose cultural differences that become barriers to progress (for example, Palmer, 2001; Faulkner and de Rond, 2000; Reason 1999). The degree to which active engagement with diversity is intrinsic to the collaboration's learning aims dictates the kinds of structures and connections that may be most appropriate. That is, there might need to be a choice between tightly structured partnership forms in which knowledge may be most efficiently exchanged, and more open network forms which support knowledge creation. The latter form – open network structures – permit bridging 'weak ties' to link disparate communities and bodies of knowledge (Granovetter, 1982), but there must also be some 'action-focused' strong ties which help the network to progress towards desirable outcomes, even if these are not specified in advance (Mohrman et al., 2003). It is possible that there may be combinations of such types of collaboration aims, with combinations of requisite ties involved – supporting learning and other aims – which could add to the collaborative tensions.

It can be seen that there is, therefore, a great deal of potential complexity to be dealt with in such situations. All three of the previously identified kinds of learning histories have been found to be useful in supporting the complexity of shared learning, that is experience: of the particular knowledge domain (Nooteboom, 2000); of learning (Nathan and Misra, 2002); and of collaboration (Child and Yan, 2003). In practice, given the potential complexity, different outcomes may be dependant upon different combinations of experience at different times in the life of the collaboration. In the simplest cases, a 'sharing' attitude to knowledge exchange, allied to experience of the knowledge domain and experience of learning, might be expected to help support the transfer of explicit knowledge. In going beyond exchange, to learn with as well as from partners – for example to address the challenges of innovation such as research and development (Lehrer and Asakawa, 2003), or intractable public concerns (Gray, 1989) – having experience of collaborating becomes important. This is because innovative outcomes have been associated with the need for combining some disparate areas of knowledge from a variety of domains, including some tacit exchange (or mirroring of tacit knowing) to support the transformation of explicit information into new forms of usable knowledge (Beamish and Berdrow, 2003).

To summarise, it seems that a 'sharing' approach to learning in collaborations could possibly be associated with a variety of knowledge 'transfer' and/or creation outcomes, partially dependant upon the particular pattern of engagement with the characteristics of the collaborative situation. Such trajectories are conceptualised in Figure 6.3.

Figure 6.3   Shared learning trajectories and (possibly) relevant situation characteristics

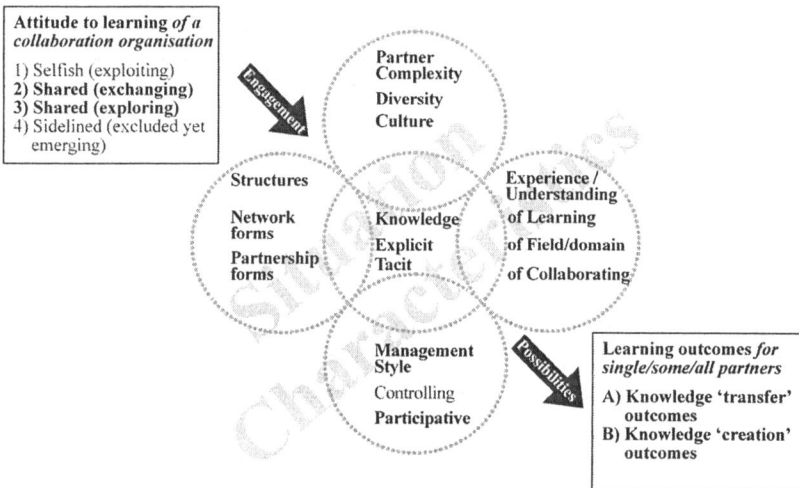

Attitude to learning *of a collaboration organisation*

1) Selfish (exploiting)
2) **Shared (exchanging)**
3) **Shared (exploring)**
4) Sidelined (excluded yet emerging)

Engagement

Partner
Complexity
Diversity
Culture

Structures

Network forms

Partnership forms

Knowledge
Explicit
Tacit

Experience /
Understanding
of Learning
of Field/domain
of Collaborating

Management
Style
Controlling
Participative

Possibilities

Learning outcomes *for single/some/all partners*

A) Knowledge 'transfer' outcomes
B) Knowledge 'creation' outcomes

Situation Characteristics

'Sidelined' Learning Trajectories

In cases where the issue of learning has been sidelined, although the partner's attitude initially excludes learning, it seems that the processes of collaboration can still result in emergent learning outcomes. For example, involvement in collaboration(s) may lead to the development of understandings about how to 'do' collaboration or manage relationships (Boari and Lipparini, 1999; Rosenkopf et al., 2001). There may also be a variety of unintended opportunities for participants to learn about a partner's particular area of competency. That is, those able to take advantage of the potential for 'knowledge spillovers' (Nooteboom, 1999), may acquire new understandings. As might be expected, the literature is less explicit about these unintended outcomes, but there does seem to be some connection between the depth and breadth of engagement and the possibility for unplanned or opportunistic learning, as suggested in Figure 6.4.

Figure 6.4 *Sidelined learning trajectories and (possibly) relevant situation characteristics*

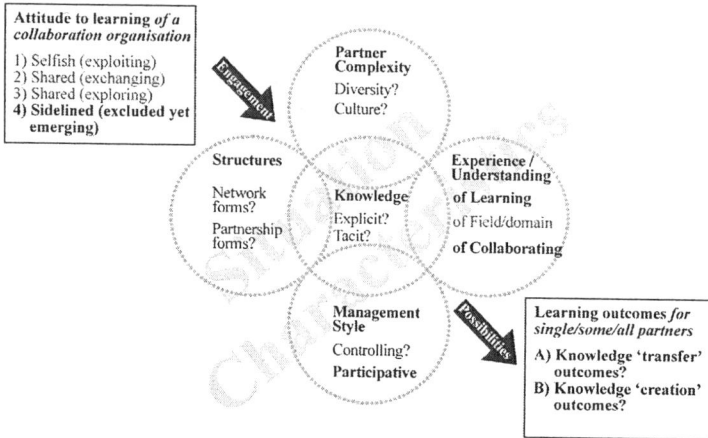

CLOSING COMMENTS

In the previous section connections between attitudes to learning and possible learning outcomes have been described. We have also outlined how these might be linked to patterns of engagement with the characteristics of the collaborative situations through collating inferences from the literature. To conclude, we revisit the three purposes of this review process that we intended in the introduction of this chapter.

In conducting the review, the first of our purposes was to provide a mapping of the terrain, as a possible loose guide for data collection in action research situations. We suggest that this is achieved in assembling the literature thematically as lens(es) for 'parsing' data, but we also suggest that any such thematic mapping is always partial and provisional and open to new insights arising from the data.

The second potential purpose of this review was to support broader emergent theorising that combines both literature-driven and data-driven theorising; the frameworks that we have outlined here provide lines of argument with which emergent theorising can be compared, if the rich context of action settings – and thus the data – is given full attention and priority in such comparisons. That is, collaborative situations in practice will exhibit further degrees of complexity than those addressed in this chapter. For example, learning attitudes amongst partners may not be compatible

(Huxham and Hibbert, 2005) and there are usually other goals, in addition to learning, in collaborations.

The third of our purposes in conducting the review has been our central focus in this chapter, as we noted in the introduction: to provide frameworks which may have some merit as interim tools for supporting collaborative practice. We suggest that the learning trajectories discussed in this chapter, and summarised in Figures 6.2-6.4, do indeed provide some possible utility for reflective collaborative practice. The trajectory discussions suggest that an organisation's attitude to learning may inform the mode of its engagement in a collaborative learning situation. That is, they may help to inform choices about those kinds of characteristics which are amenable to manipulation, and provide some purchase on those entailed consequences, associated with those characteristics, which are less malleable. In this way certain learning possibilities may be enabled – and others suppressed. Reflecting on the learning processes as *engagement* and *possibility* in Figures 6.2-6.4 also helps to highlight the indefinable and interconnected aspects of learning; it is seen as a 'flow of reflective moments [...] organised around trajectories of participation' (Lave and Wenger, 1991: 54); in some cases this may embed the knowledge in the collaborative situation, reflecting the participative nature of knowing.

To conclude, we suggest that providing frameworks that help practice to have a better grasp of the complex nature of (organisational) learning *processes* – and see knowledge transfer or creation as *shorthand terms for outcomes* – is itself helpful. We suggest that this view is consistent with the view of organisational learning as the development of knowledge through and within social practices. In particular it accords with the structuration perspective of Berends et al. (2003), which circumvents polarising trends in the debate tending to favour either individualist or cultural perspectives; such integrative conceptualisations help to support an exploration of the issues in collaborative contexts. In addition, learning situations are always expected to involve *change*, being more about transformation than transfer (Lave and Wenger, 1991); indeed communities of practice, important in participative conceptualisations of knowing, may be sources of *both* change and resistance (Brown and Duguid, 2001). Explorations of the suggested trajectories in collaboration might therefore reveal interesting links between learning and the dynamics of collaborative situations.

REFERENCES

Almeida, P., J. Song and R.M. Grant (2002), 'Are firms superior to alliances and markets? An empirical test of cross-border knowledge building', *Organization Science*, **13** (2), 147-161.

Alter, C. and J. Hage (1993), *Organizations Working Together*, London: Sage.

Assimakopoulos, D. and S. Macdonald (2003), 'Personal networks and IT innovation in the Esprit program', *Innovation Management, Policy and Practice*, **5** (1), 15-28.

Beamish, P. and I. Berdrow (2003), 'Learning from IJVs: The unintended outcome', *Long Range Planning*, **36** (3), 285-303.

Benson-Rea, M. and H. Wilson (2003), 'Networks, learning and the lifecycle', *European Management Journal*, **21** (5), 588-597.

Berends, H., K. Boersma and M. Weggeman (2003), 'The structuration of organizational learning', *Human Relations*, **56** (9), 1035-1056.

Bergquist, W., J. Betwee and D. Meuel (1995), *Building Strategic Relationships*, San Francisco: Jossey Bass.

Boari, C. and A. Lipparini (1999), 'Networks within industrial districts: Organizing knowledge creation and transfer by means of moderate hierarchies', *Journal of Management and Governance*, **3** (4), 339-360.

Boddy, D., D. Macbeth and B. Wagner (2001), 'Implementing Cooperative Strategy: A Model from the Private Sector', in D. Faulkner and M. de Rond (eds), *Cooperative Strategy: Economic, Business and Organizational Issues*, Oxford: Oxford University Press, pp. 193-210.

Bouwen, R. (2003), 'Relational Knowledge and North-South Discourses on Development Projects', in W.M. Scott and W.E. Thurston (eds), *Collaboration in Context*, Calgary: Institute for Gender Research and Health Promotion Research Group, University of Calgary, pp. 339-347.

Breu, K. and C. Hemingway (2002), 'Collaborative processes and knowledge creation in communities-of-practice', *Creativity and Innovation Management*, **11** (3), 147-153.

Brown, J. and P. Duguid (2001), 'Knowledge and organization: A social practice perspective', *Organization Science*, **12** (2), 198-213.

Chikudate, N. (1999), 'Generating reflexivity from partnership formation: A phenomenological reasoning on the partnership between a Japanese pharmaceutical corporation and Western laboratories', *The Journal of Applied Behavioral Science*, **35** (3), 287-305.

Child, J. and Y. Yan (2003), 'Predicting the performance of international joint ventures: An investigation in China', *Journal of Management Studies*, **40** (2), 283-320.

Cohen, W.M. and D.A. Levinthal (1990), 'Absorptive capacity: A new perspective on learning and innovation (technology, organizations and innovation)', *Administrative Science Quarterly*, **35** (1), 128-152.

Easterby-Smith, M. and M. Lyles (2003a), 'Introduction: Watersheds of Organizational Learning and Knowledge Management', in M. Easterby-Smith and M. Lyles (eds), *Handbook of Organizational Learning and Knowledge Management*, Oxford: Blackwell, pp. 1-15.

Easterby-Smith, M. and M. Lyles (2003b), 'Organizational Learning and Knowledge Management: Agendas for Future Research', in M. Easterby-Smith and M. Lyles (eds), *Handbook of Organizational Learning and Knowledge Management*, Oxford: Blackwell, pp. 639-652.

Eden, C. and C. Huxham (1996), 'Action Research for the Study of Organizations', in S. Clegg, C. Hardy and W. Nord (eds), *The Handbook of Organization Studies*, Beverly Hills: Sage, pp. 526-542.

Elliot, M. and G. Homan (1999), 'Collaborative Partnerships: Enabling Organizational Learning', Chapter presented to the British Academy of Management.

Faulkner, D.O. and M. de Rond (2000), 'Perspectives on Cooperative Strategy', in D.O. Faulkner and M. de Rond (eds), *Cooperative Strategy: Economic, Business, and Organizational Issues*, Oxford: Oxford University Press, pp. 3-39.

Geppert, M. and E. Clark (2003), 'Knowledge and learning in transnational ventures: An actor-centred approach', *Management Decision*, **41** (5), 433-442.

Granovetter, M. (1982), 'The Strength of Weak Ties: A Network Theory Revisited', in P.V. Marsden and N. Lin (eds), *Social Structure and Network Analysis*, London: Sage, pp. 105-130.

Gray, B. (1989), *Collaborating: Finding Common Ground for Multi-Party Problems*, San Francisco: Jossey Bass.

Hardy, C., N. Phillips and T.B. Lawrence (2003), 'Resources, knowledge and influence: The organizational effects of interorganizational collaboration', *Journal of Management Studies*, **40** (2), 321-347.

Hartley, J. and M. Allison (2002), 'Good, better, best? Inter-organizational learning in a network of local authorities', *Public Management Review*, **4** (1), 101-118.

Hennestad, B.W. (1998), 'A constructive triad for change learning', *Journal of Management Inquiry*, **7** (1), 40-52.

Hibbert, P. and C. Huxham (2005), 'A little about the mystery: Process learning as collaboration evolves', *European Management Review*, **2** (1), 59-69.

Huxham, C. (2003a), 'Theorizing collaboration practice', *Public Management Review*, **5** (3), 401-423.

Huxham, C. (2003b), 'Action research as a methodology for theory development', *Policy and Politics*, **31** (2), 239-248.

Huxham, C. and N. Beech (2003), 'Contrary prescriptions: Recognizing good practice tensions in management', *Organization Studies*, **24** (1), 69-94.

Huxham, C. and P. Hibbert (2005), 'More or Less than Give and Take: Manifested Attitudes to Inter-partner Learning in Collaboration', in K. Weaver (ed.), *Proceedings of the Sixty-fifth Annual Meeting of the Academy of Management* (CD), ISSN 1543-8643.

Huxham C. and S. Vangen (2005), *Managing to Collaborate: The Theory and Practice of Collaborative Advantage*, London: Routledge.

Ingram, P. (2002), 'Interorganizational Learning', in J. Baum (ed.), *Blackwell Companion to Organizations*, Oxford: Blackwell, pp. 642-663.

Inkpen, A. (2000), 'Learning through joint ventures: A framework of knowledge acquisition', *Journal of Management Studies*, **37** (7), 1019-1043.

Jevnaker, B. (1998), 'Absorbing or Creating Design Ability: Hag, Hamax and Tomra', in M. Bruce and B.H. Jevnaker (eds), *Management of Design Alliances: Sustaining Competitive Advantage*, Chichester: John Wiley and Sons, pp. 107-135.

Khanna, T., R. Gulati and N. Nohria (1998), 'The dynamics of learning alliances: Competition, cooperation, and relative scope', *Strategic Management Journal*, **19** (3), 193-210.

Lave, J. and E. Wenger (1991), *Situated Learning: Legitimate Peripheral Participation*, Cambridge: Cambridge University Press.

Lazerson, M. and G. Lorenzoni (1999), 'Resisting organizational inertia: The evolution of industrial districts', *Journal of Management and Governance*, **3** (4), 361-377.

Lehrer, M. and K. Asakawa (2003), 'Managing intersecting R&D social communities: A comparative study of European "knowledge incubators" in Japanese and American firms', *Organization Studies*, **24** (5), 771-792.

Lunnan, R and R. Kvålshaugen (1999), 'Acquiring Knowledge in Alliances: The Impact of Individual Characteristics', Chapter presented to the 1999 EGOS conference.

Majchrzak, A., L.P. Cooper and O.E. Neece (2004), 'Knowledge reuse for innovation', *Management Science*, **50** (2), 174-188.

March, J. (1991), 'Exploration and exploitation in organizational learning', *Organization Science*, **2** (1), 71-87.

Milliman, J., S. Taylor and A.J. Czaplewski (2002), 'Cross-cultural performance feedback in multinational enterprises: Opportunity for organizational learning', *Human Resource Planning*, **25** (3), 29-43.

Mohrman, S.A., R.V. Tenkasi and A.M. Mohrman Jr. (2003), 'The role of networks in fundamental organizational change: A grounded analysis', *The Journal of Applied Behavioral Science*, **39** (3), 301-323.

Mothe, C. and B. Quélin (2000), 'Creating competencies through collaboration: The case of Eureka R&D consortia', *European Management Journal*, **18** (6), 590-604.

Nathan, M.L. and S.K. Misra (2002), 'No pain, yet gain: Vicarious organizational learning from crises in an inter-organizational field', *The Journal of Applied Behavioral Science*, **38** (2), 245-266.

Nonaka, I., T. Ray and K. Umemoto (1998), 'Japanese organizational knowledge creation in Anglo-American environments', *Prometheus*, **16** (4), 421-439.

Nooteboom, B. (1999), *Inter-Firm Alliances: Analysis and Design*, London: Routledge.

Nooteboom, B. (2000), 'Learning by interaction: Absorptive capacity, cognitive distance and governance', *Journal of Management and Governance*, **4** (1-2), 69-92.

Norman, P.M. (2001), 'Are your secrets safe? Knowledge protection in strategic alliances', *Business Horizons*, Nov-Dec, 51-60.

Oliver, A.L. (2001), 'Strategic alliances and the learning life-cycle of biotechnology firms', *Organization Studies*, **22** (3), 467-489.

Palmer, D. (2001), 'Learning is top priority and major challenge for more alliances', *Strategy and Leadership*, **29** (3), 35-36.

Polanyi, M. (1966), *The Tacit Dimension*, New York: Doubleday.

Powell, W.W. (1998), 'Learning from collaboration: Knowledge and networks in the biotechnology and pharmaceutical industries', *California Management Review*, **40** (3), 228-241.

Reagans, R. and B. McEvily (2003), 'Network structure and knowledge transfer: The effects of cohesion and range', *Administrative Science Quarterly*, **48** (2), 240-267.

Reason, P. (1999), 'General medical and complementary practitioners working together: The epistemological demands of collaboration', *The Journal of Applied Behavioral Science*, **35** (1), 71-86.

Rosenkopf, L., A. Metiu and V. George (2001), 'From the bottom up? Technical committee activity and alliance formation', *Administrative Science Quarterly*, **46** (4), 748-774.

Schuler, R.S. (2001), 'Human resource issues and activities in international joint ventures', *The International Journal of Human Resource Management*, **12** (1), 1-52.

Simonin, B.L. (1999), 'Ambiguity and the process of knowledge transfer in strategic alliances', *Strategic Management Journal*, **20** (7), 595-623.

Soekijad, M. and E. Andriessen (2003), 'Conditions for knowledge sharing in competitive alliances', *European Management Journal*, **21** (5), 578-587.

Spekman, R.E., L.A. Isabella and T.C. MacAvoy (2000), *Alliance Competence: Maximizing the Value of Your Partnerships*, New York: Wiley.

Sydow, J. and A. Windeler (2003), 'The Reflexive Development of Inter-firm Networks', in A.F. Buono (ed.), *Enhancing Inter-Firm Networks and Interorganizational Strategies*, Greenwich, Connecticut: Information Age Publishing, pp. 169-186.

Tsang, E.W.K. (2002), 'Acquiring knowledge by foreign partners from international joint ventures in a transition economy: Learning-by-doing and learning myopia', *Strategic Management Journal*, **23** (9), 835-854.

Tsoukas, H. and E. Vladimirou (2002), 'What is organizational knowledge?', *Journal of Management Studies*, **38** (7), 973-993.

Vera, D. and M. Crossan (2003), 'Organizational Learning and Knowledge Management: Toward an Integrative Framework', in M. Easterby-Smith and M. Lyles (eds), *Handbook of Organizational Learning and Knowledge Management*, Oxford: Blackwell, pp. 122-141.

Yan, Y. and J. Child (2002), 'An analysis of strategic determinants, learning and decision-making in Sino-British joint ventures', *British Journal of Management*, **13** (2), 109-122.

Zollo, M., J.J. Reuer and H. Singh (2002), 'Interorganizational routines and performance in strategic alliances', *Organization Science*, **13** (6), 701-713.

7. Brokerage, Closure and Community Dynamics: Implications for Virtual Knowledge Work Collaborations

Robert DeFillippi, Michael Arthur and Valerie Lindsay

It is hardly possible to overrate the value ... of placing human beings in contact with persons dissimilar to themselves, and with modes of thought and action unlike those with which they are familiar.
John Stuart Mill (1987/1848: 581)

INTRODUCTION

The coordination of knowledge work – work involving the acquisition, creation, combination, transfer and storage of knowledge – in virtual space presents new challenges. Knowledge work frequently involves both intra-community and inter-community dynamics, both of which have been subject to theoretical scrutiny. Meanwhile, virtual space – where workers regularly communicate across separate physical locations – is still a relatively new phenomenon. How can recent ideas about both kinds of community dynamics be applied to knowledge work in virtual space? How is knowledge work facilitated by ties that either bind people to or provide links between separate communities? How can social capital and social network theories provide insights into how people and their knowledge are connected in virtual space?

Our chapter begins with a brief review of literature on networks and the social embeddedness of learning, both of which relate directly to community dynamics. We then examine how individuals build social capital by bridging (making connections with) and bonding (building deeper relations with) other individuals. Next, we discuss how knowledge work reflects connections within and between communities of knowledge workers. We introduce the concept of community social capital and relate community social capital to Burt's concepts of brokerage and closure. Based on these concepts we examine two forms of knowledge-based community work: knowledge work that arises within a community and knowledge work that spans or bridges two or more communities. We illustrate the argument through an example on independent film-making.

The next section of the chapter applies the same underlying theory to a range of examples involving virtual collaboration. These examples cover a range of alternative situations and challenges in terms of the kind of work being done and the virtual collaboration sought. The final section of the chapter reflects back on these examples and offers ideas for future research.

NETWORKS AND THE SOCIAL EMBEDDEDNESS OF LEARNING

Social network theory (Granovetter, 1982) proclaims the paramount importance of social relationships in knowledge exchange among individuals. Social embeddedness theories have reinforced the co-location arguments of economic geographers for effective knowledge exchange among firms in industrial districts (e.g. Barnes, 1999). In particular, social relationships have been shown to increase the speed with which knowledge travels among firms that lie inside the same geographic region (Maskell, 2001).

More broadly, insights into the flow of knowledge are suggested in three network perspectives, concerning social networks, internal networks and external networks (Van Wijk, Van den Bosch and Volberda, 2003). First, social networks are seen as characteristic of all social organizations, whereby an organization's environment is 'a network of other organizations' (Van Wijk et al., 2003: 430). Social network analysis examines relations among and between individuals, groups, organisations and regions, that is, among traditional 'levels of analysis'. Social networks need not be bound to geographic proximity, and many examples of virtual linkages built around social relations exist (a prominent example is that of the Linux operating system programmers, to be discussed later).

Second, internal networks refer to intra-organisational networks, most often researched in the context of the multinational organisation (Ghoshal and Bartlett, 1990). Otherwise referred to as 'new organisational forms', 'heterarchies' (Hedlund, 1994), or 'differentiated networks' (Nohria and Ghoshal, 1997), internal networks, which generally span national boundaries, require integration mechanisms to ensure that knowledge flows between an organisation's individual members and their departments. Third, external networks are organisational forms taxonomically located 'between markets and hierarchy' (Powell, 1990) and are typically seen as arrangements for inter-organisational cooperation in joint ventures and strategic alliances. External networks provide the opportunity for organisations to gain and pool knowledge, for example, in the development of new products. Examples are evident in many of the Japanese corporations' network links with their suppliers, such as Toyota and its keiretsu.

More recent arguments challenge the neatness of the preceding inter-organisational approach. Hedberg and Holmqvist (2001) and Lewin and Volberda (1999) argue that knowledge and learning in inter-organisational forms such as networks, industrial districts or clusters, is not simply the aggregate of the knowledge and learning of its component actors. Rather, joint learning occurs at the interstices of the organisational elements (Powell, Koput and Smith-Doerr, 1996) – in other words, between single organisations (Allen, 2001; Hedberg and Holmqvist, 2001) and their boundary-spanning representatives.

How learning at the interstices actually happens, however, is still a subject of ongoing research. Knowledge creation at the interstices between organisations (Hedberg and Holmqvist, 2001) is similar to Burt's (2004) notion that brokerage across structural holes between organisations produces more ideas and new knowledge. This relates to the idea of 'collective invention' noted by Allen (1983) in a study of the UK blast furnace industry (Dahl and Pedersen, 2004). Hedberg and Holmqvist (2001) propose that 'inter-organisational knowledge consists of mutual knowledge, which is unique to collaboration and independent of any single organisation's knowledge'. This kind of knowledge is seen as 'a set of mental models shared by organisations' (ibid.: 737).

Much can be learned about inter-organisational learning from the pioneering work of Granovetter (1982) and (Uzzi, 1997) on social networks and the embeddedness of actors within networks of relationships. Gilsing and Nooteboom (2005) examine Granovetter's 'strength of weak ties' as applied to inter-organisational networks in the Dutch multimedia and biotechnology industries. They find that the relative importance of density and strength of ties in these industries depends in part on whether the focus of the network's knowledge work is knowledge exploration or knowledge exploitation.

Social embeddedness models help to explain how and why organisations in a network interact. They suggest, for example, that strong interactions among geographically close firms will lead to lower transaction cost exchanges (Barnes, 1999), as well as to the transfer of both tacit and explicit knowledge (Uzzi, 1997). Trust among individuals, developed through their socialisation across boundaries (a key feature of embeddedness), is essential to inter-organisational learning, and this is influenced by an attitude of high transparency and openness of the focal firm's leadership (Friedman, Lipshitz and Overmeer, 2001; Hedberg and Holmqvist, 2001; Lichtenstein, 2000).

The paramount role of the individual and the individual's relationships are noted by Maskell, Eskelinen, Hannibalsson, Malmberg and Vatne (1998), who suggest that the creation of informal networks of contacts starts from relations between two individuals and progresses to entire networks. For example, informal managerial networks enhance the flows of knowledge, particularly tacit knowledge, among the firms inside a cluster or network (Uzzi, 1996). A similar phenomenon may now be emerging between clusters. In such a situation, people occupying separate clusters may be linked through relational, rather than geographic, proximity (Cowan and Jonard, 2000). In turn, dispersed but connected groups may have the capacity to act like 'small world networks', reflecting relations between people spread across different clusters (Watts and Strogatz, 1998). Here we see global linkages arising from individual relationships and spanning firms, communities, industries and nations.

Ideas about the density of ties, strong interactions between representatives of adjacent firms, networks growing from relations between two individuals, the flow of tacit knowledge, and 'small worlds' stemming from global networks all invite a question about how social relations grow from the self-organising behaviour of individual knowledge work participants. These ideas also invite a further question about the extent to which this self-organising reflects shared interests, and if so what kind of groups emerge to reflect these interests. It is to these questions that we turn next.

BRIDGING, BONDING AND SOCIAL CAPITAL[1]

The preceding literature on networks and embeddedness has found distinctive expression in the research and theorising of Burt (2000, 2004, 2005) whose perspectives on social capital underlie the conceptual framework utilised in this chapter. We begin our analysis at the micro level of personal ties and then expand our framework to include increasingly macro forms of network relationships.

Networks among people are commonly represented as a set of points or nodes (representing individuals) and a series of links or ties between pairs of nodes (representing relationships between individuals). These networks typically involve both bridging and bonding (Putnam, 2004). Bridging, as we use the term here, involves one individual making a new tie or sustaining an existing tie with another individual across what would otherwise be a 'hole' in the overall social structure. It is bridging by particular individuals that connects groups of people who would otherwise have no connections to other groups. Bridging does not require strong ties between the connected individuals (Burt, 2005). In contrast, bonding, as we use the term here, involves one individual developing strong ties with another individual. This bonding can be based on the time spent, trust built and degree of reciprocal services established between the two individuals. Both bridging and bonding can contribute to a person's social capital, which may be defined simply as 'the advantage created by a person's location in a structure of relationships' (ibid.: 4).

Bridging thus connects people who are not otherwise connected. In other words, the creation of a bridge spans what would otherwise be a structural hole in the surrounding network of actors in a social system. Social capital theory implies that certain people have advantages because they are better connected to other people within social systems. These basic observations provide a conceptual starting point for our examination of how learning and knowledge acquisition is facilitated by the connections some actors have to other actors in knowledge work.

Let us begin with an example of two individuals (Ann and Liz) and their social networks. Figure 7.1 illustrates both bridging and bonding activities. Ann is an employee of a large software company working closely with one of her employer's corporate customers. Ann has several bridges into two main groups, one of fellow software programmers in her own company, the other of software users at the customer site. Ann also provides a medium for communications between these two groups. Liz, in contrast, performs similar work to Ann and is connected to her fellow employees and customers. However, Liz also has bridges to other groups, to other local professionals, to an online group of software writers, and to a friendship group representing a range of companies and occupations. Let us assume for the sake of illustration that Liz and Ann both invest equally in the overall set of five relationships represented for each of them (Raider and Burt, 1996).

The contrast between Ann and Liz invites certain questions regarding the respective patterns of their relationships. Ann has multiple contacts in each of only two groups, while Liz has single contacts in five groups. Does this mean that Ann has bonded better with people in her two groups than Liz? If so, can Ann benefit from the more trusting relationships she has built? Or are the bonds so strong, and the communications lines so repetitive, that there is a risk of 'groupthink' among members in her tight network? In contrast, do Liz's bridges into five different groups provide her with access to a wider range of information? If so, is the level of trust between Liz and her contacts sufficient for her to rely on what she hears? These questions point to the distinctive network configurations, involving both bridging and bonding, that people develop, and the consequences of these network configurations for accessing and sharing knowledge.

Figure 7.1   Example network maps for two knowledge workers

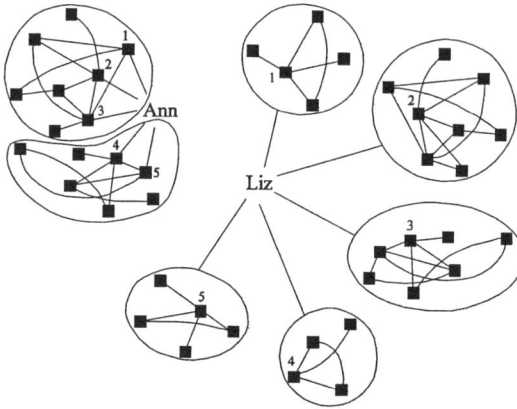

Source: Raider and Burt, 1996.

Knowledge work – which involves both individual and collective practices for acquiring, creating, combining, transferring and storing knowledge – would appear to require both bridging and bonding behaviour. Bridging allows for the initiation of contacts between individual parties through which knowledge transfer can occur. Bonding allows for the kind of interpersonal trust-building that is likely to sustain the relationships that have been previously initiated. Bridging can span existing 'holes' in the social structure, while bonding can encourage the flow of information and ideas across bridges. Moreover learning – the process through which new knowledge is created or acquired – can occur for individuals or groups of individuals as knowledge generation and transfer activities unfold. The challenge is to seek to optimise both bridging and bonding – that is for the individual to most effectively leverage his or her overall social capital – in contributing to knowledge work activities.

COMMUNITY SOCIAL CAPITAL

We now turn our attention from individual networks to the roles people can play in broader community activities. The communities we are interested in are those involved in knowledge work in some enduring way. We call these 'knowledge work communities' – largely voluntary meeting-grounds where people perform knowledge work and pursue their collective learning agendas.

These knowledge work communities can interact not only with their individual members, but also with other communities, and with host organisations and industries, often with far-reaching consequences. Moreover, this interaction need not reflect any common assumptions about levels of analysis, or about hierarchy between these levels. Rather, the present discussion assumes that such interactions are reciprocally influencing each other and reflect the embedded nature of knowledge work interactions among its various participants (DeFillippi, Arthur and Lindsay, 2006).

Our conception of a knowledge work community is not to be confused with other meanings of the term community, such as those prescribing a place of residency or a formal membership obligation. Some communities can form because of their members' affiliation with a particular organisation. Other communities can reflect a common set of occupational interests. Communities can also form around shared interests in a particular topic or phenomenon. The idea of a knowledge work community relates closely to Wenger's (1998) conception of a community of practice, where members interact along three interdependent dimensions of joint enterprise, shared repertoire and mutual engagement:

- *Joint enterprise* involves a collective response to the situation in which the community finds itself, typically involving common goals and mutual identification and accountability.
- *Shared repertoire* refers to communities' ways of doing things, the stories they exchange, the tools they develop and apply, and the actions and concepts they employ in performing their work.
- *Mutual engagement* refers to the community's interactions in their work, including volitional efforts to get to know one another, exchange experiences, and pursue professional interests.

Previously, we referred to social capital as 'the advantage created by a person's location in a structure of relationships'. We extend this to 'the advantage created by a person's or a group's location in a structure of relationships'. Seen in this way, the concept of social capital provides a link between individual and community activities.

Burt (2005) refers to the two kinds of contribution to social capital described above in terms of brokerage and closure. Brokerage involves the development of a community's ties with outsiders through which knowledge can be usefully gained or traded. Brokerage creates social capital, for example when a software development community enjoys ties with prospective product users. Closure refers to the ties that exist among a community's members, for example the ties among a software development community's own members. The opportunity to maximise community social capital occurs when there are high levels of both brokerage and closure. To continue the example, this would involve a software development community having effective external relationships with potential product users, and close internal relationships among its own members. Alternative combinations of high and low brokerage and closure are shown in Figure 7.2.

We can note that the conversion of high amounts of individual bridging and interpersonal bonding into community brokerage and closure may not be straightforward. Community members may be all talking to the same source, or to different but uninformed sources, and thereby limiting the range of knowledge to which they have access. Community members may also be bonding around issues, such as pay levels or employment conditions, having little bearing on the community's distinctive knowledge base. However, Figure 7.2 does provide a template against which to examine how community social capital may be accumulated.

Figure 7.2   Brokerage and closure in community social capital

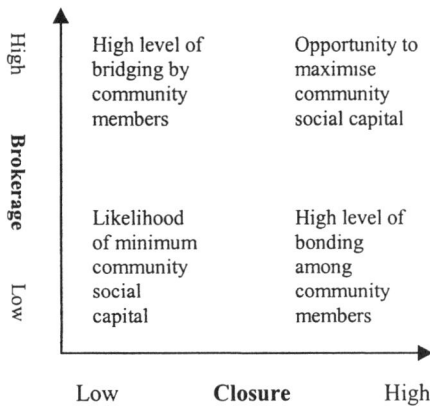

Source: *DeFillippi, Arthur and Lindsay, 2006; adapted from Burt, 2005.*

We can also note that different patterns of community social capital have different implications for patterns of knowledge work collaboration. In the case of low brokerage and low closure, illustrated in the lower left quadrant of Figure 7.2, the knowledge work situation is highly fragmentary and atomistic. There is no coherent knowledge work community reflecting the three dimensions of joint enterprise, shared repertoire and mutual engagement. Nor are there any systematic connections with holders of distinctive but potentially complementary expertise. In these circumstances, knowledge work is likely to be proceed slowly, as knowledge and its possessors are isolated from others holding similar or complementary knowledge. This is essentially the null set of community social capital and as such it is least germane to our discussion in this chapter.

A second situation is where there is a high level of closure and member bonding within a knowledge work community but a low level of bridging to other knowledge communities (lower right quadrant of Figure 7.2). In such communities, members exhibit high levels of joint enterprise and mutual engagement, and develop a shared repertoire for further knowledge work. However, the isolation of such a community from other knowledge work communities can have adverse consequences. Deeply shared community practices may prevent the community's members from being open to new knowledge originating outside their community. Such a 'not-invented-here' syndrome has been observed in communities across a wide variety of business, government and non-profit situations. Such closed communities and their organisations and institutions similarly run the risk of being unable to adapt to changing external circumstances, which call for new sources of knowledge.

A third situation is where there is a relatively low level of closure within a community but a relatively high level of bridging to other communities (top left quadrant of Figure 7.2). Such conditions are likely when the so-called community in question is transitory. Its members are in disarray over the kind of joint enterprise they seek to pursue, and over the joint repertoire and mutual engagement that can serve that joint enterprise. Moreover, there may be obstacles to the community developing stronger ties among its members. For example, networking activities sponsored by local business or civic organisations may bring together people who are deeply committed to the communities from which they came, but who lack any shared commitment to working together. Although people may make some fragmentary connections, the sponsoring organisation may fail to achieve any enduring benefit.

The ideal type of knowledge work community is one characterised by both high closure and member bonding and high levels of community brokerage and member bridging to other communities (top left quadrant of Figure 7.2). Such communities possess deep wells of collective knowledge that all members may share and access. However, such communities are also aware of, and in communications with, other communities possessing diverse but potentially valuable new knowledge. Studies of science-based communities in biotechnology, physics and engineering find that their members are richly connected to each other and to diverse sources of complementary scientific knowledge residing in other scientific sub-communities (Powell et al., 1996; Knorr Cetina, 1999). Here, mutual engagement, shared repertoires and knowledge work through joint enterprise occurs within communities, and task accomplishment and problem-solving through the application of complementary repertoires occurs across communities.

The conception of community social capital as involving components of both brokerage and closure is the one adopted throughout our chapter. We turn next to these distinctions and suggest a conceptual means to incorporate these distinctions as intra- versus inter-community dynamics.

BROKERAGE AND CLOSURE IN PHYSICAL SPACE

A long-standing debate exists on the virtues and vices of community and their associated social practices. Tönnies (1887/1955) made famous the distinction between the 'Gemeinschaft' as a community of shared values, knowledge and local customs such as those found in rural villages versus the 'Gesellschaft' as an association of loosely connected individuals whose impersonal and transitory interactions were most common in the burgeoning urban metropolises of his time. Contemporary sociologists James Coleman (1988) and Robert Putnam (2000) held a similarly idealised vision of community as Gemeinschaft. In particular, Putman (2000) bemoaned the loss of community in America as evidenced by the drop in associational activity and a growing distance from neighbours, friends and family. Putnam's evocative metaphor of 'bowling alone' symbolised his concern with the seeming replacement of Gemeinschaft with Gesellschaft.

However, such an ideal image of community was challenged by Tönnies's sociological contemporary Durkheim (1893/1984), who suggested that the Gemeinschaft vision of community limited individual expression. From a neo-Austrian knowledge perspective, Hayek (1945) later argued in defence of Gesellschaft on the grounds that it was impossible for knowledge to be assembled within a single mind or closed Gemeinschaft-like community. Hayek asserted that it was the sharing (and trading) of knowledge within an open market that made possible the creation of 'spontaneous order' out of widely dispersed 'uncommon knowledge'. Ahuja (2000) suggested the need for both Gesellschaft and Gemeinschaft perspectives, with the relative emphasis contingent on the actions and purpose of the network.

Rather than force a choice between these contrasting visions of community, Lindkvist (2005) has argued for the existence of two complementary forms of community dynamics, each of which harkens back to the original Gesellschaft and Gemeinschaft distinctions of Tönnies. Lindkvist's fundamental point is that intra-community and inter-community dynamics are typically quite different. This can lead us to make sharper distinctions about how one or more communities influence knowledge work processes. Let us illustrate the point with an example of a film-making project, occurring at a single physical location (the film set), to illustrate these contrasting dynamics.

Picture a group of performing actors together on the film set to make a film. Picture in contrast the other groups of workers on the set – production staff, camera operators, set designers, special effects teams, stunt performers, and so on – that make up the crew. For the sake of illustration, let us assume that each member of the film crew maintains a long-term affiliation with a community of similar specialists, so that not only do the actors maintain their own community, but so too do the camera operators, set designers, and so on.

Table 7.1   Characteristics of intra-community versus inter-community knowledge work

Characteristic	Intra-Community Knowledge Work	Inter-Community Knowledge Work
Individual knowledge bases:	Similar	Different
Purpose of knowledge exchange:	Joint enterprise	Task completion
Method of knowledge retention:	Shared repertoire	Complementary repertoires
Basis for individual learning:	Mutual engagement	Problem-solving
Knowledge-generation process:	Paradigm-driven – based on shared understanding	Market-driven – responding to inter-community goals
Emergent process of social capital formation:	**Closure**	**Brokerage**

Source: Adapted from Lindkvist, 2005.

A community of film actors is likely to engage in knowledge work differently on their own than if they are involved with a more diverse film-making crew. The knowledge bases that the actors draw on will be similar, since they are all trained in the same profession. The actors' purpose in exchanging knowledge will emphasise their joint enterprise to promote the acting profession. They will seek to retain knowledge by adding to the shared repertoire about acting they already possess. The basis for individual learning will emphasise mutual engagement with other members of the acting community. The actors' approach to generating new knowledge will be based on the existing assumptions, or paradigms, that guide their profession. The predominant approach to social capital formation will be one of closure, that is, of talking only to other community members.

In contrast, the basis for knowledge-sharing among a mixed crew of actors and other film-making specialists is likely to emphasise different knowledge bases – what actors know about acting, camera workers know about camera work, and so on. The purpose in exchanging knowledge will emphasise task completion – in this case to successfully finish the film. They will seek to retain knowledge by adding to the repertoires of their separate communities. The basis for individual learning will emphasise problem solving, in response to challenges faced in making the film. The approach to generating new knowledge will emphasise market circumstances, such as the budget or intended audience of the film. Their predominant approach to social capital formation will be one of brokerage, that is, of talking across community boundaries.

The above discussion extends the contrast between intra-community closure and inter-community brokerage in Figure 7.2 into a contrast between two sets of five factors. The two sets of factors, covering issues of both knowledge transfer and new learning, are summarised in Table 7.1.

The persistent challenge in community-based knowledge work is to get the balance between closure and brokerage right. This means optimising the extent to which community members on the one hand work with and learn from each other (through closure), and on the other hand interact with different communities (through brokerage). In the preceding film-making example, relevant communities were described as achieving a balance between intra-community and inter-community knowledge work and learning. However, in that example the communities' members were assumed to be together in physical space. The development of intra-community closure and intra-community brokerage faces additional challenges when knowledge work arises among geographically distant community members. It is those challenges to which we now turn.

BROKERAGE AND CLOSURE ACROSS VIRTUAL SPACE

In this section we will consider in more detail the components of Table 7.1. Using examples from a range of community settings, we will illustrate how Table 7.1 can be used to interpret a variety of situations, each of which calls for collaboration involving virtual space (that is, where the knowledge workers are in more than one physical place and need to collaborate over virtual media, such as the World Wide Web). The examples illustrate how both brokerage and closure can occur across a variety of situations within and across community settings. They also involve questions of balancing between, or optimising across the degree of brokerage and closure.

In each of our examples below organisations are involved. However, our intention is not to focus on the organisations themselves, but on the dynamics of both intra-community and inter-community activities from which organisations – as well as participating individuals, communities or host industries – may benefit.

Connecting across Virtual Space: Teltech Experts and their Client Communities

Teltech is a small Minneapolis-based organisation that locates and facilitates expert guidance for its clients on an as-needed basis. Typically, the experts are not Teltech employees, but geographically dispersed authorities in their specialised fields. The clients are one or more groups of an organisation's workers, such as a product design group needing specialised engineering advice. Examples of work supported by Teltech experts include the development of thermal blankets for jet engines, and the establishment of patents for engine heaters.

Teltech's core business is concerned with accessing, managing and maintaining a wide network of experts from a range of technical areas. The company matches individual experts and client needs with little regard for geographic proximity. Rather, the assumption is that the appointed experts and clients will work remotely from one another using a combination of telephone and software-driven computer communications. The Internet allows clients to access and download specific information that technical experts provide, and provides for follow-up conversations leading to modification of client designs, frequently in real time. Clients benefit from the access they have to an outside expert, while the Teltech experts gain new knowledge from exposure to the client's problems (Davenport, 1994).

By reference to Table 7.1, we can envision the typical consulting project as involving a client engineering community and a separate expert community represented by the Teltech-appointed consultant. The consultant acts as knowledge brokers, bridging between the two communities. Each project combines the respective community knowledge bases, drawing on complementary repertoires and using a problem-solving approach to completion of the task. At the same time, the client and expert communities' own knowledge bases are likely to be enriched by new knowledge generated by the project. Teltech's growth has relied largely on the World Wide Web as a key communication and information medium in brokerage between the separate client and expert communities.

Emergence of a Virtual Community: The Linux Community

How do a group of enthusiastic but disconnected software programmers find one another and build community over the Internet? The answer has been dramatically illustrated through the emergence of the Linux community. The community evolved from its members' commitment to collaborate over the development of a new computer operating system.

In 1991, motivated by the desire to build an operating system to handle data complexity, University of Helsinki undergraduate Linus Torvalds developed the first version of Linux. Later that year, in the spirit of open-source programming that had helped him develop his operating system he posted a message about it on the Web. A small community of enthusiastic respondents quickly helped Torvalds develop his prototype. Within four years, however, over 500,000 people joined the Linux virtual community, giving thousands of hours of free time to make improvements to the software (Torvalds and Diamond, 2001). Linux became commercialised through companies like Red Hat, and was incorporated into an increasing number of popular applications. By 2004, the market for Linux applications and software reached US$11 billion (Hamm, 2005). The commercial uptake of Linux by large corporations like IBM resulted in them offering employment and consulting opportunities to 'ace' members of the Linux community, including its founder, Torvalds.

Again we can refer back to Table 7.1. The Linux story reflects an evolution first toward high closure, as the Linux community was formed and the operating system software developed, and then toward high brokerage, as the commercialisation of Linux took hold. The emergent Linux community thrived on a strong sense of joint enterprise, employing a largely shared repertoire of programming skills and involving intense mutual engagement over the Internet. However, beyond this strong intra-community closure, certain Linux developers created bridges to commercial organisations that sought to adopt the Linux system. Thus, a situation of brokerage developed, providing access to Linux and mutual problem-solving opportunities between user communities in commercial organisations and the Linux community. Virtual communication has been central to this brokerage, as it was for the Linux community from the outset.

Promoting a Virtual Community: Clarica Life Insurance Agents

Our next example is of a commercial organisation that built its success on high brokerage, but then recognised the need for increased learning through a heightened sense of closure amongst its independent agents. Moreover, this example is drawn from the insurance industry, where the tradition has been for agents to work competitively and independently, rather than to collaborate and share knowledge.

Clarica Life Insurance Company, a division of Sun Life Financial, provides retail insurance products to Canadian clients. It has a sales force of

3,000 agents, all contracted to sell only Clarica products. For many years, agents were simply expected to work independently with potential customers, and to maximise their commissions. However, the company came to believe it could benefit from greater knowledge sharing among these agents. It therefore took the initiative to encourage the formation of a community of practice, to help the agents develop individual and collective capabilities and new ideas. The company pledged the community could be run 'by agents, for agents', and did not allow Clarica management access to community discussions. Community-based learning began to occur as the agents called on one another to help solve their customer-related problems, and built a database of common information. At the end of the pilot scheme, some 95 per cent of responding agents thought the community of practice should continue (Saint-Onge and Wallace, 2005).

Reflecting back on Table 7.1, we can see how Clarica was able to promote a new community of practice through increased closure among a group of previously disconnected agents. The company recognised the similarity of its agents' knowledge bases around identifying and satisfying client needs, and the potential value of a greater sense of community. By providing a computer-based infrastructure and leaving the agents to explore this infrastructure on their own, Clarica was able to promote a sense of joint enterprise. The agents then began to exchange experiences and ideas, largely through virtual communications, that reflected a growing shared repertoire and continued mutual engagement with one another. As a result, the sponsoring organisation Clarica was able to benefit from the greater shared understanding and new knowledge that the agents generated.

Developing Institutions to Promote Research: Medical Research across Communities

A different kind of example is one about an industry institution, in this case the not-for-profit US National Cancer Institute (NCI). In contrast to established tradition within its industry, the NCI seeks to promote both closure within and brokerage between communities in pursuit of interdisciplinary solutions to the 'big problem' of cancer research. Years of cancer research have led to the view that understanding the causes of cancer and deriving effective diagnostic and therapeutic strategies is a scientific challenge that lies beyond the capabilities of any single research community representing a single scientific discipline.

The emergence of biomedical science and its connections to biochemists around the world, prompted the NCI to develop a strategy that encourages multidisciplinary teams (National Cancer Institute, 2001). These teams represent knowledge in areas such as human genome sequencing, developments in imaging, and the discovery of target-specific treatments. Such a multidisciplinary approach to cancer research requires collaboration among and between communities of biologists, chemists, epidemiologists, imaging scientists, mathematicians, physicians and physicists across a range of clinical and laboratory settings, often though virtual media across different states and countries. In order to facilitate and coordinate this collaboration, the NCI established a Consortia and Networks program, which incorporates databases and computer networks that bring together scientists with the necessary range of knowledge and skills. The NCI's role is to provide the necessary infrastructure and information technology, enabling the linking of its various communities virtually.

This time Table 7.1 suggests that NCI's point of departure was to recognise the separate community investments in joint enterprise, shared repertoire and mutual engagement that each community of specialists – biologists, chemists, epidemiologists, and so on – could contribute to the institute's broader goals. It therefore took on the role of catalyst to encourage greater brokerage between these separate communities on the daunting task challenges of cancer research and on the benefits that complementary repertoires and a problem-solving focus could bring. Moreover the brokerage was market-driven, since it sought to respond to prevailing diseases. This example suggests how an industry institution can sponsor and facilitate virtual collaboration among diverse communities, in order to solve 'big problems' otherwise beyond the capability of a single organisation or scientific discipline.

Developing National Economies: The Case of Singapore

A final example shows how we can widen our lens to consider how communities interacting within close geographic proximity can forge links with virtual communities, or geographically distant communities, as part of a national economic development program. The Singapore government has identified biotechnology as a 'pillar' of its economy for the twentyfirst century (Fingold, Wong, and Cheah, 2004). It plans to build a world-class regional centre of excellence in the biotechnology and biomedical industries.

Geographically-concentrated industry clusters have already been created in both biomedicine and biotechnology, each with impressive links to relevant global corporations. However, an additional strategy is to attract top researchers – including Nobel laureates – from overseas, to join the local communities that contribute to the established cluster. These individuals are expected to also draw on their existing ties to virtual scientific communities, and to physical communities in their previous home institutions, to complement the local talent and knowledge in the Singapore industry. The local Singapore clusters retain the traditional advantage of physical face-to-face communication, while at the same time enjoying links to other sources of expertise through the key individuals that have been attracted to the region. A number of start-up enterprises have already been developed to take advantage of the combination of a developing pool of specialised local knowledge and its connections to a larger pool of world-renowned players.

In this example, we see how the attraction of top researchers from around the globe has complemented the traditional community-building opportunities that regional industries are able to foster. In accordance with Table 7.1, the researchers remain active participants through virtual connections to their established specialist communities, and as such tap into the joint enterprise, shared repertoire and mutual engagement through which they pursue their specialised work. At the same time, the researchers are drawn toward a pattern of physical interaction and interdisciplinary brokerage encouraged by the existence of a geographically-concentrated industry cluster. The city state of Singapore, much like the NCI, has positioned itself as the beneficiary of both global community activities and the local task-centred, problem-solving emphasis that geographically-concentrated industry clusters provide.

PROVISIONAL LESSONS FROM THE CASE STUDIES

The preceding case examples illustrate links between the conceptual framework underlying this chapter (namely Figure 7.2 on brokerage and closure, and Table 7.1 on the factors associated with each of brokerage and closure) and its implications for knowledge work collaborations. In this section we will examine how the cases can be used to inform future practices of knowledge work collaboration. In particular, we suggest three initial lessons that might be drawn.

Brokerage and closure are dynamic features of virtual knowledge work collaborations: Our cases suggest that brokerage and closure are not static states for virtual knowledge work collaborators. Rather, brokerage and closure evolve over time in response to successive actions and interactions among knowledge work collaborators within and across distinct communities. Referring back to Figure 7.2 and Table 7.1, we can interpret our case examples in terms of an evolutionary trajectory; one that takes the participants across multiple states of community social capital and their associated patterns of brokerage and closure.

For example, Linux began as a collective (not communal) response by individuals to Linus Tovalds' technical problems, and over time the problem solvers evolved into a community of Linux system developers. Moreover, the Linux community has steadily expanded its reach to a variety of commercial software user communities and thus has evolved toward a state of high brokerage and high closure. In contrast to Linux, the Clarica Life Insurance company initiative began with high brokerage between its agents and their customers, but low closure among the agents themselves. Community formation and closure came in response to the agents' recognition that they may be able to help one another.

In some cases, there is a need for greater brokerage, for example among separate scientific communities described in the National Cancer Institute (NCI) case, and also in the Singaporean biotechnology example. In summary, knowledge work participants in virtual knowledge work must recognise that their current balance of inter-community brokerage and intra-community closure may need to be adjusted over time to reflect changed circumstances.

Currently, there is increasing concern with intellectual property theft across nations. Our examples suggest this may have a chilling effect on the ability of virtual knowledge work community members to collaborate with one another. However, if nations can tap into successful virtual collaborations, as Singapore has begun to do, this could lead to a loosening of constraints over intellectual property, greater brokerage between communities and more rapid innovation. There will always be a need to weigh the benefits versus risks of brokerage versus closure in knowledge work collaboration, and the balance between the two is likely to change over time in specific situations.

Effective virtual knowledge work collaborations require rich and redundant links between participants: One of the challenges posed in our study of knowledge work collaborations is to understand the interdependent roles played by different types of participants in knowledge work. Our preceding case examples, as well as work beyond this chapter, illustrate the key role to be played by many different types of participants-including individuals, organisations, communities and host industries (DeFillippi et al., 2006).

For example, there is a key role for closure among Linux software developers in safeguarding the integrity of the Linux community. By contrast the story of Clarica illustrates new benefits to the sponsoring organisation from intra-community closure at the same time as the community's members, the agents, continue with separate acts of brokerage toward their clients. The NCI case emphasises the role that professional associations can play in representing separate scientific communities through inter-community brokering. In the case of Singapore's economic development in the biotechnology and biomedical industries, the co-location of biomedical institutions in physical space through industry clustering is complemented by the role of brokerage fostering inter-community brokering.

Our case stories suggest that collaborations in knowledge work can be activated and supported by more than one type of participant (individual, organisation, community or host industry), and that collaborations that are supported by diverse types of participants tend to be more robust. For example, collaborations that are dependent upon one or a small handful of individuals are fragile, should those individuals depart from the collaborative project or enterprise. Similarly, collaborations that are dependent solely upon the brokerage of a community located within a single organisation may be at risk of changing policies within that organisation. Multiple, redundant sources of connections between knowledge work participants within and across community boundaries are likely to be more durable.

IT tools enable but do not guarantee successful virtual collaborations: Our cases all acknowledge the role played by modern information technology in extending the reach for collaboration among geographically-distant participants in knowledge work. While not guaranteeing the success of virtual collaboration, IT tools are particularly important in enabling the development of virtual knowledge work practices that maintain a community by promulgating its joint enterprise, shared repertoire and mutual engagement.

For example, the Linux community has evolved both a set of communications tools (to update the operating system) and supporting practices (regarding member conduct and communication protocols). The Clarica agent community was created through the company's provision of relevant communications software. Both the NCI and Singaporean biotechnology examples are about institutions recognising the need for better tools to support broader collaborations.

Tools are important contributors to a virtual community's ability to develop all three of a strong sense of joint enterprise, an expanding shared repertoire, and a high level of mutual enterprise. However, perhaps more important than the mere existence of IT tools, is the reinforcement of community members' behaviour towards each other. This in turn reflects on the leadership that evolves within a community (for example on the high respect Linux community members held for Linus Torvalds). It also highlights the dangers of alternative approaches, such as community leaders being appointed from outside. This was a danger that Clarica seemed to be aware of in not interfering with the agent community it had inspired.

Who can benefit from the above lessons? One answer is the communities themselves, whose joint enterprise lies behind their closure and brokerage activities. Another answer is the individuals who are motivated to join in community knowledge work activities. A third answer is the organisations who interact with, but frequently may not directly employ, the community members involved. A final answer is the host industry in which interdependent individual, community and organisational knowledge work activities unfold. Moreover, our various examples all point to persistent interdependence among all four potential beneficiaries, rather than to any underlying 'levels of analysis' that might subordinate the individual to the community, the community to the organisation, and the organisation to the industry. All four potential beneficiaries may be seen as interdependent participants in knowledge work activities, and each participant can benefit from a broader appreciation of how knowledge work unfolds (DeFillippi et al., 2006).

CONCLUSION

This chapter has described how social network theory, and in particular Burt's (2005) theory of social capital, can be employed to understand how knowledge work gets accomplished. Burt's (2005) insights can also be combined with those of Lindkvist (2005) to provide a contrast between intra-community closure and inter-community brokerage. An example from the film-making industry was offered to show how these contrasting patterns of closure and brokerage can occur in physical space.

We have examined virtual collaboration through a range of examples reflecting contrasting intra-community and inter-community situations, and where in each case at least some collaboration involved virtual communication. The examples involved providing expert support across virtual space (Teltech), the emergence of a virtual community (Linux), promotion of a virtual community (Clarica life agents), supporting medical research across scientific communities (NCI) and the development of national economies (Singapore biotechnology). All of these examples highlight a shifting balance between closure and brokerage as knowledge transfer processes and new learning take place.

The examples also suggest lessons about the dynamic nature of both brokerage and closure, the benefit of rich links among knowledge work participants, and the significance of IT tools to either help or hinder knowledge work collaborations. These lessons and the utility of our underlying theoretical approach can be usefully tested in further research efforts.

NOTE

[1] The next two sections draw heavily upon chapters two and three of DeFillippi, Arthur and Lindsay (2006).

REFERENCES

Ahuja, G. (2000), 'Collaboration networks, structural holes, and innovation: A longitudinal study', *Administrative Science Quarterly*, **45** (3), 425-455.

Allen, P.M. (2001), 'A complex systems approach to learning in adaptive networks', *International Journal of Innovation Management*, **5** (2), 149-180.

Allen, R.C. (1983), 'Collective invention', *Journal of Economic Behaviour and Organization*, **4** (1), 1-24.

Barnes, T. (1999), 'Industrial Geography, Institutional Economics and Institutions', in T. Barnes and M. Gertler (eds), *The New Industrial Geography: Regions, Regulation, and Institutions*, London: Routledge, pp. 1-21.

Burt, R.S. (2000), 'The Network Structure of Social Capital', in R.I. Sutton and B.M. Shaw (eds), *Research in Organizational Behavior*, Greenwich: CT: JAI Press, pp. 345-323.

Burt, R.S. (2004), 'Structural holes and good ideas', *American Journal of Sociology*, **110** (2), 349-399.

Burt, R.S. (2005), *Brokerage and Closure: An Introduction to Social Capital*, New York, Oxford University Press.

Coleman, J.S. (1988), 'Social capital in the creation of human capital', *American Journal of Sociology*, **94**, Supplement, 95-120.

Cowan, R. and N. Jonard (2000), *The Dynamics of Collective Learning*, MERIT Working Paper Series.

Dahl, M.S. and C.O.R. Pedersen (2004), 'Knowledge flows through informal contacts in industrial clusters: myth or reality?', *Research Policy*, **33** (10), 1673-1686.

Davenport, T. (1994), *Teltech: Making a Business of Knowledge Management*, Unpublished Case.

DeFillippi, R.J., M.B. Arthur and V.J. Lindsay (2006), *Knowledge at Work: Creative Collaboration in the Global Economy*, Oxford: Blackwell.

Durkheim, E. (1893/1984), *The Division of Labour in Society*, London: MacMillan.

Fingold, D., P.-K. Wong, and T.-C. Cheah (2004), 'Adapting a foreign direct investment strategy to the knowledge economy: The case of Singapore's emerging biotechnology cluster', *European Planning Studies*, **12** (7), 921-941.

Friedman, V.J., R. Lipshitz and W. Overmeer (2001), 'Creating Conditions for Organizational Learning', in M. Dierkes, A.B. Berthron, J. Child and I. Nonaka (eds), *Handbook of Organizational Learning and Knowledge*, Oxford: Oxford University Press, pp. 757-774.

Ghoshal, S. and C.A. Bartlett (1990), 'The multinational corporation as an interorganizational network', *Academy of Management Review*, **15** (4), 603-625.

Gilsing, V. and B. Nooteboom (2005), 'Density and strength of ties in innovation networks: an analysis of multimedia and biotechnology', *European Management Review*, **2** (3), 179-197.

Granovetter, M.S. (1982), 'The Strength of Weak Ties: A Network Theory Revisited, in P.V. Marsden and N. Lin (eds), *Social Structure and Network Analysis,* Beverly Hills, CA: Sage, pp. 105-130.

Hamm, S. (2005), 'Linux Inc.', *Business Week*, January 31, 60-68.

Hayek, F.A. (1945), 'The use of knowledge in society', *American Economic Review*, **35** (4), 519-530.

Hedberg, B. and M. Holmqvist (2001), 'Learning in Imaginary Organizations', in M. Dierkes, A.B. Berthron, J. Child and I. Nonaka (eds), *Handbook of Organizational Learning and Knowledge*, Oxford: Oxford University Press, pp. 733-752.

Hedlund, G. (1994), 'A model of knowledge management and the N-form corporation', *Strategic Management Journal*, **15** (5), 73-90.

Knorr Cetina, K., (1999), *Epistemic Cultures: How the Sciences Make Knowledge*, Cambridge: Cambridge University Press.

Lewin, A.Y. and H.W. Volberda (1999), 'Prolegomena on co-evolution: A framework for research on strategy and new organizational forms', *Organization Science*, **10** (5), 519-534.

Lichtenstein, B.B. (2000), 'Self-organized transitions: A pattern amid the chaos of transformative change', *Academy of Management Executive*, **14** (4), 128-141.

Lindkvist, L. (2005), 'Knowledge communities and knowledge collectivities: A typology of knowledge work in groups', *Journal of Management Studies*, **42** (6), 1189-2110.

Maskell, P. (2001), 'Towards a knowledge-based theory of the geographical cluster', *Industrial and Corporate Change*, **10** (4), 921-943.

Maskell, P., H. Eskelinen, I. Hannibalsson, A. Malmberg and E. Vatne (1998), *Competitiveness, Localised Learning and Regional Development: Specialisation and Prosperity in Small Open Economies*, London: Routledge.

Mill, J.S. (1987/1848), *Principles of Political Economy*, Fairchild, NJ: Augustus M. Kelley.

National Cancer Institute (2001), 'Plans and Priorities for Cancer Research', Accessed March 1, 2006 at *http://2001.cancer.gov/promoting.htm#1*.

Nohria, N. and S. Ghoshal (1997), *The Differentiated Network*, San Francisco, CA: Jossey-Bass.

Powell. W.W. (1990), 'Neither Market nor Hierarchy: Network Forms of Organization', in B. Staw and L.L. Cummings (eds), *Research in Organizational Behavior*, Greenwich, CT: JAI Press, pp. 295-336.

Powell, W.W., K.W. Koput and L. Smith-Doerr (1996), 'Interorganizational collaboration and the locus of innovation: Networks of learning in biotechnology', *Administrative Science Quarterly*, **41** (1), 116-145.

Putnam, R.D. (2000), *Bowling Alone. The Collapse and Revival of American Community*, New York: Simon and Schuster.

Putnam, R. D. (2004), Interview, *The Observer*, No. 242, March, pp. 14-15.

Raider, H.J. and R. Burt (1996), 'Boundaryless Careers and Social Capital', in M.B. Arthur and D.M. Rousseau (eds), *The Boundaryless Career: A New Employment Principle for a New Organizational Era*, New York: Oxford University Press, pp. 187-200.

Saint-Onge, H. and D. Wallace (2005), 'Clarica's Agent Network (Canada)', Case 335, *http://www.beepknowledgesystem.org/*.

Tönnies, F. (1887/1955), *Community and Association,* London: Routledge and Kegan Paul.

Torvalds, L. and D. Diamond (2001), *Just for Fun: The Story of an Accidental Revolutionary,* New York: Harper Business.

Uzzi, B. (1996), 'The sources and consequences of embeddedness for the economic performance of organizations', *American Sociological Review*, **61** (1), 674-698.

Uzzi, B. (1997), 'Social structure and competition in interfirm networks: The paradox of embeddedness', *Administrative Science Quarterly*, **42** (1), 35-67.

Van Wijk, R., F.A.J. van den Bosch and H.W. Volberda (2003), 'Knowledge and Networks', in M. Easterby-Smith and M.A. Lyles (eds), *Handbook of Organizational Learning and Knowledge Management*, Oxford: Blackwell Publishing, pp. 428-453.

Watts, D. and S.H. Strogatz (1998), 'Collective dynamics of "small world" networks', *Nature*, **393**, 440-442.

Wenger, E. (1998), *Communities of Practice: Learning, Meaning, and Identity*, Cambridge, UK: Cambridge University Press.

8. The Search for Network Learning: Some Practical and Theoretical Challenges in Process Research[1]

Louise Knight and Annie Pye

INTRODUCTION

Business and public sector leaders and managers are increasingly concerned with how networks of organisations function and can be influenced; organisation theory and management research need therefore to extend into the domain of inter-organisational networks. Building on our experiences of investigating network learning (NL) – learning by a group of organisations as a group (Knight, 2002; Knight and Pye, 2005) – our aim in this present chapter is to elaborate some techniques for capturing and analysing network process data and to evaluate them in the light of others' insights into the process of process research and into (learning) process theorising. Our focus is on the practical aspects of process research but, in reflecting on these, we also attend to more conceptual issues.

The purpose of the investigation of network learning was to assess whether, and if so how, the notion of organisational learning could be translated to the level of inter-organisational networks, in particular to extensive networks – those with many organisations with various types of links (i.e. beyond joint ventures or small groups working collaboratively to specific objectives).

This presented a number of challenges. The first concerned appreciating the implications of the several, highly diverse conceptualisations of organisational learning (OL), for example: OL as information processing versus as a social and political process (Easterby-Smith and Araujo, 1999); OL as individual or group learning within organisations versus an organisation-centred view of OL (Crossan, Lane, White and Djurfeldt, 1995), in which learning outcomes are considered to be evidenced through changes to organisational properties. How might one recognise NL? In a network-centred view of network learning, what changes to network level properties would constitute NL outcomes? Second, there is relatively little empirical research on OL from which one might learn about conceptualising and investigating learning process. A third challenge lies in the practicalities of doing research in inter-organisational networks (Knight, 2004). For example, Van de Ven (1992) elaborates the demands of longitudinal process research in organisations – a relatively simple context compared to networks, which leads to the question of how can one gain 'visibility' of network learning in extensive networks over long periods of time? Fourth, there is relatively little empirical research on processes in extensive inter-organisational networks. Many authors take a structural perspective in their research focusing on measures such as centrality, based on work on social networks (Krackhardt, 1992); in contrast, research on social practice in networks is relatively neglected. Where attention is paid to interaction and process aspects, for example by scholars in the MOPAN and IMP networks,[2] this is often at the level of inter-organisational relationships and 'small' networks with limited numbers of actors.

In this chapter, we focus on approaches which relate to researching network learning processes and the process of process research, and explain the methods adopted as well as what we learnt from the experience which may be of value to future research in this field. The next section presents, in roughly chronological order, several phases of the study, from designing the study to testing results. We describe our approach to our empirical inquiry into network learning, reflecting on our search for useful strategies and methods given the absence of well-established ways of conducting qualitative process research in extensive inter-organisational networks. In the third and fourth sections, the implications of our efforts in investigating and theorising network learning are then considered in the light of previous writing on researching process, and on learning process. Finally, we present our conclusions, with suggestions for further theorising and developing research practice.

Whilst NL outcomes were comparatively easy to distinguish, learning process was much more difficult; we found constructs from prior research did not provide sufficient descriptive or explanatory power. Having identified 'sub-plots' within 'episodes' of network learning, however, we were able then to undertake a comparative analysis of learning process and learning outcomes. From this, we developed a network-centred model of network learning, viewing learning as a social, political and non-linear process. It is a perspective which is distinct from many conceptualisations of learning in organisational and inter-organisational settings that tend to be derived from theories of individual learning. We propose that future theoretical development of learning process would benefit from researchers being more explicit about whether they regard learning as isomorphic across individual, group/collective, organisational and network levels, or whether they are adopting a more data-driven conceptualisation of learning. We expect that many of the issues discussed here in the context of network learning are also highly relevant to other network processes, such as changing and innovating.

INVESTIGATING AND THEORISING NETWORK LEARNING

Designing the Study

Building on Crossan et al. (1995) arguments about levels and perspectives of organisational learning, we believed that greater conceptual clarity about learning at different levels could be achieved by distinguishing the context of learning from the agent that is said to be learning. On that basis, network learning was defined as learning by a group of organisations as a group; in contrast, the term inter-organisational learning was applied to learning in an inter-organisational setting whether by individuals, groups, organisations or networks (Knight, 2002). Further elaboration of a notion of network learning was the objective of the first, conceptual phase of our study.

The second, empirical phase of the study involved three health service networks, but focused most intensively on one of these, the English prosthetics (artificial limb) services network. This network provides a specialist service for some 55,000 users, mostly through 34 NHS Disablement Service Centres (DSC). Some patients receive some care direct from the private sector. All but two centres contract with commercial companies for the provision of prosthetists' and technicians' (P&T) services. Most limb componentry is provided by sister companies of, or separate operating divisions within, the four P&T service companies that serve the NHS. These and some further actors and relationships in the network are illustrated in Figure 8.1.

Compared to other NHS services, the prosthetics network has few actors, which are closely linked, so it should not be regarded as typical for the NHS. Nevertheless it is an extensive network – involving over fifty organisations – and a complex network, in that there is a mix of relations between organisations (e.g. hierarchical between the Department of Health, hospital Trust boards and DSC managers; contractual between DSCs and suppliers; competitive between suppliers; cooperative within trade and professional associations; political between local patient groups and DSC managers, and national groups and the Department of Health). Its relatively well-defined boundaries and the strong sense of community that prevails made it easier to negotiate access and study the network as an entity than one might expect.

Figure 8.1   Illustration of the English prosthetics service

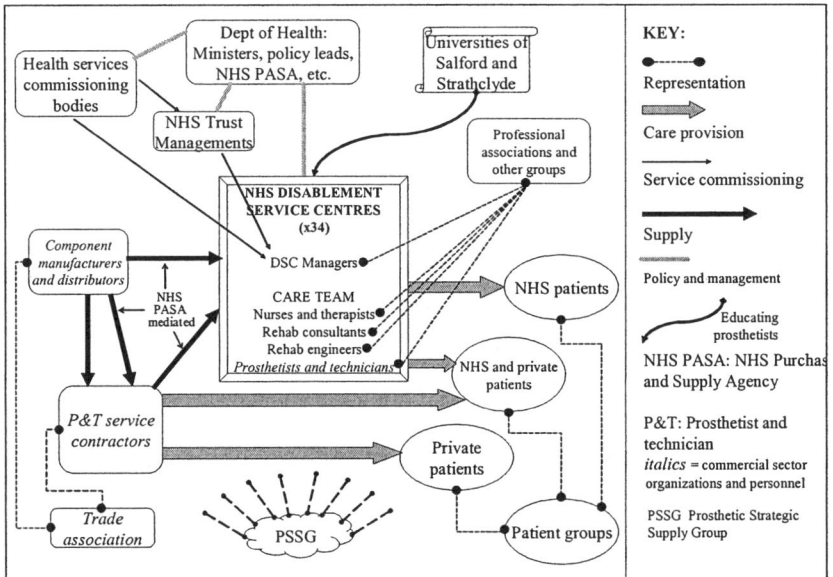

Source: Knight and Pye (2004).

In summary, our research strategy was:

- To explore network learning empirically in three extensive health-related supply networks which included commercial and public sector organisations.
- A comparative case study (Yin, 1994; Numagami, 1998), centred on five in-depth cases of network learning, which we termed learning episodes.
- To deploy methods to provide a historical, contextual and processual perspective (Pettigrew, 1990).
- To use a variety of techniques, 'interviewing, observing, mining available documents and records, taking account of non-verbal cues, and interpreting inadvertent unobtrusive measures' (Lincoln and Guba, 1985: 199), to collect historical and current data. Documentation and interview material provided retrospective data

about the network. Participant-observation, interview material and documentation provided real-time data.

Interview transcripts and other data in electronic form were analysed using NVivo software. The first step was coding data by learning episodes (further elaborated below: see Casing Network Learning). Second, for each episode, a text report was produced which then served as the episode-specific data for further coding with the various aspects of learning identified during the conceptual phase of the study (Knight, 2002: 445-449). Each paragraph of this report was labelled with the interviewee's initials, the date of the interview and the paragraph number from the original transcript, so it was possible readily to take account of the source of the quote, its context and the timing of an interview.

Doing Participant-observation

Data collection through participant-observation was extensive in the prosthetics network, and more limited in the other two networks (electronic assistive technology and pressure area care equipment). Necessarily, participant-observation was more opportunistic than interviewing. Nevertheless, as its value became increasingly apparent, specific efforts were made to generate and exploit opportunities for participant-observation.

Interaction with the prosthetics network pre-dated this study; it arose from a programme of research investigating supply strategy in health service supply networks (Harland and Knight, 2001: 162). This work led to an invitation to help establish a cross-network group – the Prosthetic Strategic Supply Group (PSSG) – in 1997/98. The invitation came from our research sponsor, then the NHS Supplies Authority, which was superseded in 2000 by the NHS Purchasing and Supply Agency (NHS PASA), with which the research partnership is ongoing.

The PSSG wanted to obtain a detailed overview of the network and decided to conduct a survey of senior NHS and contractor personnel at each Disablement Service Centre. One of us (Knight) acted as the research co-ordinator for the survey; a choice which we now recognise as particularly fruitful even though it was highly resource-intensive for a time, as discussed below. So, in addition to attending the regular meetings of the PSSG, we were involved in several working groups, variously as observer, facilitator and participant. The survey led to invitations to present the key findings at a company staff conference and a Centre Managers' conference. These interactions were complemented by attendance at other conferences, and supplier and Centre visits. In all, we estimate that Knight's involvement in the prosthetics network, and work with the NHS PASA Rehabilitation team, averaged out to at least a half-day per week, over a period of nearly five years.

Interviewing

'Qualitative interviewing requires intense listening, a respect for and curiosity about what people say, and a systematic effort to really hear and understand what people say.' This statement from Rubin and Rubin (1995: 17) neatly describes what we aimed for in interviewing. We sought to ask open questions and adopt a reflexive interviewing style (Hammersley and Atkinson, 1983: 112), regarding the interviewees as 'conversational partners' who play an active role in shaping the discussion 'rather than as objects of research' (Rubin and Rubin, 1995: 10-11).

The basic interview guide used provided reminders and prompts, not a rigid structure. In addition to formal, planned interviews, many informal interviews were conducted as and when appropriate, to inquire about current developments in the networks, or to address specific gaps noted during the course of analysing empirical data or to assess tentative interpretations of the data.

Casing Network Learning

Whilst the comparative case study approach seemed appropriate, it was not immediately evident what should constitute a case. Searches for description-rich cases of network learning in published research had led us to identify several cases – the evolution of a new industry recipe (Spender, 1989), reforms of emergency response services (Kouzmin, Jarman and Rosenthal, 1995; McHugh, 1995; Paton, Johnston and Houghton, 1998), the development of an effective coordinated response to a product tampering crisis (Nathan and Mitroff, 1991) and the establishment of the 'Toyota Group's' knowledge-sharing network (Dyer and Nobeoka, 2000) – all of which could be described as episodes of network learning. There seemed to be two choices: to focus on the network as the object of analysis, or to use network learning episodes.

Ragin (1992: 8) suggests 'two key dichotomies in how cases are conceived: (1) whether they are seen as involving empirical units or theoretical constructs and (2) whether these, in turn are understood as general or specific', which he used to construct a conceptual map to answer: 'what is a case?'. The four categories and their key distinctions are summarised in Table 8.1, below.

This categorisation was used to understand the various options and their implications. Whilst strategic networks might be regarded as objects (cell 2 in Table 8.1), it is more difficult to bound extensive inter-organisational networks. Therefore, it is more appropriate to view extensive networks as theoretical constructs; since networks are an established construct, network cases are 'conventions' (cell 4). Network learning episodes are also not clearly bounded, but are not established constructs and therefore are seen as cases that are 'made' (cell 3).

Table 8.1   Conceptual map for answers to 'what is a case?'

	CASE CONCEPTIONS	
	Specific	**General**
UNDER-STANDING OF CASES **As empirical units**	*1. Cases are found.* 'researchers see cases as empirically real and bounded, but specific. They must be identified and established as cases in the course of the research process.' (p. 9). Example of research cited: Harper (1992) identifies 'community' through the individual respondent. 'Community' is not a given.	*2. Cases are objects.* 'researchers also view cases as empirically real and bounded, but feel no need to verify their existence or establish their empirical boundaries in the course of the research process, because cases are general and conventionalised' (p. 9-10). Case designations are based on existing definitions from the research literature. Example cited is of using conventional units (e.g. families and formal organisations) to explore generic processes, e.g. misconduct (Vaughan, 1992).
As theoretical constructs	*3. Cases are made.* 'Researchers in this quadrant see cases as specific theoretical constructs which coalesce in the course of the research. Neither empirical nor given, they are gradually imposed on empirical evidence as they take shape in the course of the research.' (p.10) Example: research on tyranny examines many examples. If important subset emerges this = a case. 'Constructing cases does not entail determining their empirical limits, as in Cell 1, but rather pinpointing and then demonstrating their theoretical significance' (p. 10)	*4. Cases are conventions.* 'researchers see cases as general theoretical constructs, but nevertheless view these constructions as the products of collective scholarly work and interaction and therefore as external to any particular research effort' (p. 10-11). Example: 'industrial societies', 'cases are general theoretical constructs that structure the ways of seeing social life and doing social science. They are the collective products of the social scientific community and thus shape and constrain the practice of social science' (p. 11) and may change over time with shifts in 'intellectual fashions'

Source: Ragin (1992: 8-15).

In this project, the relevant unit for the early stages of data collection – the 'empirical case' – was the network. Early analysis of interview and participant-observation data, to identify significant and current changes taking place in the first network, indicated that there were several useful examples of network learning episodes, and so episodes were selected as the case for subsequent analysis; in other words, episodes are treated as the study's 'analytic case'. For a time, both types of case – empirical and analytic – were in use, as we collected broad-based network data (which provided contextual information, and allowed continued assessment of the initial identification of episodes), but also sought to fill out the episode accounts. The key benefit of this approach is that episodes focus on specific themes of network-level change that network practitioners consider to be important, and the analyst can abstract a learning episode from the stream of experience that is network life, and focus on this. What is routine, stable, or less relevant to the episode can then be regarded as contextual.

In summary, we concluded that the inter-organisational network was the site for data collection – which might be called the empirical case – but our case for the purposes of theory development would be the network learning episode – the analytic case. Within the English prosthetics service network, five episodes of network learning were identified in the early stages of data collection. Two of these, relating to the introduction of a new technology (silicone cosmesis, a life-like cover for an artificial limb) and to the development of the prosthetic profession, have been described in detail elsewhere (Knight and Pye, 2004; Knight and Pye, 2005). For each episode, we identified learning outcomes – actual and prospective changes to network properties which were enduring and widespread, though not necessarily uniform or universal.

Framing the Analysis

Though the data provided much evidence of network learning, the scale and complexity of the episodes made it very difficult to write a narrative for each one, without risk of being overwhelmed by the detail, and inadequate theoretical treatment. Most importantly, we found that early efforts to use analytic themes drawn from the conceptual phase and initial analysis led to an inappropriate divide between structure and action, and an undue focus on learning outcomes at the expense of examining learning process.

A number of established theories, models and techniques from organisation studies were therefore considered as possible frameworks for organising and interpreting network learning episode data: Weick's sensemaking approach (1979; 1995), activity theory (Blackler, 1993; Blackler, 1995; Blackler, Crump and McDonald, 2000; Blackler and

McDonald, 2000; Engeström, 2000) and Pettigrew's context-content-process (CCP) framework (Pettigrew, 1987; Pettigrew, 1990). The latter was selected for reasons set out below.

Usher (1997) writes of seeking to 'dissolve dichotomies', but this can be difficult to achieve whilst providing a coherent structure to a written (and inevitably linear) presentation. Pettigrew's context-content-process framework usefully steers away from dichotomous categories; it emphasises the importance of process, and the recursive influences between the three aspects of the framework. Furthermore, it is derived from substantial empirical work, presenting complex, longitudinal data about 'strategic' change. Compared to others it is more pragmatic, and its relative simplicity makes it more accessible. It is presented as meeting a number of methodological aims and is in the interpretative mode, but does not require the adoption of a firmly defined philosophical/disciplinary base (in contrast to, for example, Blackler's work (1993) using activity theory, based on Vygotskian psychology).

Pettigrew's use of the framework and his contextualist theory of method (Pettigrew, 1985a; Pettigrew, 1990) emphasise vertical and horizontal analysis, considering multiple system levels and processes over time, and their interconnections. It facilitates consideration of learning both as process and outcome/content, and the interaction and integration of multiple levels of actor/unit of analysis – individual, group, organisation and inter-organisational network.

Coping with Process

The analysis and interpretation of learning process proved to be much more problematic than learning context and content. We began by looking for phases in the development of episodes and trying to understand how they interrelated, but this demonstrated the limitations of a linear, staged view of network learning. We also considered the many, varied activities that were leading to the network changes observed in each case. This highlighted what might be termed mechanisms for learning – activities such as communicating and collaborating between network actors. At the level of a whole episode, however, the complexity of the web of activities and their interrelationships meant it was not possible to develop a coherent sense of how network learning unfolded over time, or observe similarities and differences across episodes.

We then considered the activities, roles and influence of different parties more closely, focusing on individual network learning outcomes, or sub-sets of linked outcomes, identified for each episode. From this, we recognised that each of the episodes could be broken down into what we termed 'sub-plots' –

stories-within-a-story. This phase of the analysis yielded ten or so sub-plots for each episode.

Working with sub-plots, it was possible to compare episodes effectively, looking for common, consistent and critical patterns; we identified three types of sub-plot (Knight and Pye, 2005). Broadly: developing meaning sub-plots are about how network-level change occurs through shifts in values and culture; developing commitment sub-plots address the choices and contributions of different actors which cumulatively shape network-level change; in developing method the sub-plots cover the enactment of these choices, that is how changes are reflected and embedded in network operations.

There are two important features of the analysis and interpretation process. First, it was iterative. For example, after initially identifying the three types of episode sub-plots, we returned to the episode data to assess their fit across all episodes. This revealed some gaps in the sub-plots, so these were added in. Then the process categories were assessed once again. This might be regarded as a self-fulfilling approach to analysis since, by this approach, the sub-plots and learning process categories become increasingly aligned. However, the second feature of the analysis and interpretation is that we sought to maintain a sceptical stance, employing tactics advocated by Miles and Huberman (1994: 263-277), notably seeking disconfirmatory evidence and rival explanations, and obtaining respondents' feedback on the initial findings.

Describing and Modelling Network Learning

To illustrate the results of the research process described above, network learning outcomes and network learning sub-plots for the silicone cosmesis and professionalisation episodes are shown in Tables 8.2 and 8.3 (see Knight and Pye, 2004 and 2005 for narratives of these two cases). The final model is illustrated in Figure 8.2; this shows the descriptive and conceptual elements for each of the three parts of the model and the recursive relations between them.

For the network learning context, we followed Pettigrew's categorisation of outer and inner context, in which the latter also describes the network's purpose, actor, history and operations. Evidently, all five network learning episodes for prosthetics share a common descriptive context. On the conceptual side of the model, however, we draw attention to the key contextual factors that, to different extents and in different ways between episodes, influence the unfolding of an episode.

Learning content is described at two levels – the 'headline' level describing the focal topic of the episode and in more detail through the changed network properties which constitute network learning outcomes. These learning outcomes were categorised into three themes, as shown in the conceptual side of the content cell in the model.

Table 8.2   The outcomes of network learning

Episodes →	Silicone cosmesis	Professionalisation
Outcomes **Changes to network practices**	• widespread provision of high, medium and low definition cosmeses • rationing of high cost products • prescribing and fitting silicone cosmeses	• delivery of training and education for prosthetists • role of prosthetist in prescribing • role of prosthetist in clinical governance (CPD, clinical audit, etc.) • integration in to multi-disciplinary clinical team
Changes to network structures	• private and NHS funding for cosmeses, some from central govt. investment programme • manufacturing facilities and supply chains established • 4 suppliers of P&T services to the NHS involved in cosmeses in 2002 vs. none in 1998	• BIST disbanded; establishment of BAPO; other parties' relations with BAPO • University of Salford, and relations between education providers and other network members • reduction in formal authority of suppliers over prosthetists' professional association and education
Changes to network interpretations	• value placed on limb fit and function versus appearance and comfort • expenditure on non-essential products in the context of scarce resources; need vs. want • whether the service in England is good or poor; coping with adverse media attention	• prosthetics as a profession of similar standing to physiotherapists • reduced mistrust of prosthetists

Learning process is described through sub-plots identified by considering how learning outcomes come about. Conceptually, these sub-plots fit within one of three themes, as shown in the model.

Table 8.3   *Summary of learning sub-plots categorised by the three learning process conceptual themes*

Episodes →	Silicone cosmesis	Professionalisation
Processes developing meaning	• developing the view that limb appearance matters, not just limb fit and function • developing the view that the NHS might/could/should fund better limb appearance	• developing view of prosthetist as core member of clinical team (clinicians vs. craftsmen) • developing views about allied health professions • reconciling the above developments with traditional suspicion of preferential prescribing by prosthetists
Developing commitment	• at local and national levels, choosing to make limb appearance an improvement priority, including allocating funds • suppliers deciding to invest in cosmesis production	• designating prosthetics a Profession Allied to Medicine (PAM) • establishing BAPO • making prosthetists' training and education independent of suppliers • setting up the PSSG sub-group on prosthetist career structure
Developing method	• developing silicone cosmesis, and other appearance-related technologies • suppliers setting up production in the UK • (not) distributing central funding • setting up national contract • service providers at centres organising themselves for providing and, especially, rationing the provision of silicone cosmesis and related products	• developing BAPO's 'place at the table' and others learning to accommodate it • suppliers implementing new HR systems • developing training and education • clinicians and Centre Managers adapting contracts, local clinical governance arrangements etc. to reflect changes and fostering new working practices

Complex, recursive relations between and within aspects of network learning context, content and process were apparent. There is not a one-to-one correspondence between learning outcomes and learning sub-plots, or between the conceptual themes (e.g. 'network practices' to 'developing method') (Knight and Pye, 2005: 383).

Figure 8.2   Key elements for describing and analysing network learning

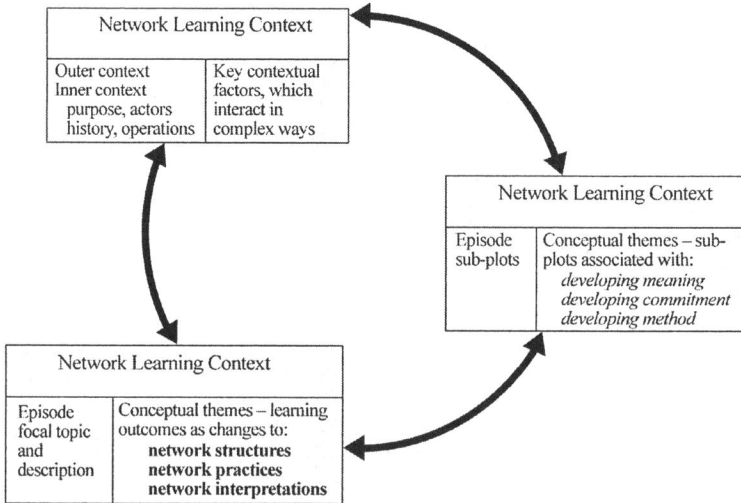

Network Learning Context	
Outer context Inner context purpose, actors history, operations	Key contextual factors, which interact in complex ways

Network Learning Context	
Episode sub-plots	Conceptual themes – sub-plots associated with: *developing meaning developing commitment developing method*

Network Learning Context	
Episode focal topic and description	Conceptual themes – learning outcomes as changes to: **network structures network practices network interpretations**

Source: Knight and Pye, 2005.

Testing the Results

In some qualitative research projects, it is possible to defend the analysis on the basis that it represents a widely shared view or position among interviewees. However, given that: (a) there is no common language among respondents for describing the notions of network learning and network learning episodes and (b) network learning episodes can be seen as collages abstracted from network data, it seemed important to find a way of testing the findings. This was done by consulting practitioners in the prosthetics network. A summary of the early findings on network learning context, content and process was sent to 33 people working in the field of prosthetics, with guide questions to elicit their feedback on the choice of episodes and the conceptual model; 13 responded.

Network participants' responses and the value of this exercise exceeded our expectations. Overall, comments were favourable and very constructive. Generally, it was easier to obtain comments specific to the network context and the episodes, than about the conceptual model of network learning. This does not seem surprising, given the interviewees' familiarity with the prosthetics service and the novelty of the network learning concept. Five people commented however that it was not an easy document to comprehend, which indicates the challenge of translating the study findings into a suitable form for communicating with practitioners. Updates on the development of the episodes and the network context were integrated into the case descriptions and the analysis reviewed.

IMPLICATIONS FOR RESEARCH PROCESS

Participating in Networks

Whilst recognising the demands this places on researchers' methods, skills and commitment and organisational access, Van de Ven (1992) argues for the 'real-time study of strategic change processes as they unfold in their natural field settings'. Regularly scheduled data collection such as surveys and interviews 'identify if and what changes occurred, real-time observations are needed to understand how these changes occurred' (ibid.: 181).

We recognised the potential difficulty of achieving a balance between participation and distance (Hammersley and Atkinson, 1995: 99-109) and actively sought to maintain an approach that combined independence and openness with proximity. Dopson (2003) writes about challenges of negotiating access and how this is neglected in texts on process. In this study, it was not the key challenge; instead, developing relationships across the wider network and remaining sensitive to the potential effects of the main link with NHS PASA on other relationships, were more critical.

Pettigrew (1973; 1985b; 1990) provides rich descriptions of undertaking participant-observation in firms to examine strategic change, addressing in particular the challenges of engaging with and becoming accepted by the firm's employees whilst retaining the distance necessary to be an effective researcher. In the context of inter-organisational networks, these challenges are even greater, in part because of the greater scope and complexity, but also because there is no single geographical location such as an office building where one's presence necessarily signals participation in the network. Furthermore, the opportunities for attending useful meetings (i.e. those attended by a wide cross-section of actors to discuss a matter of importance, and which therefore help to reveal more about actors' interests and relationships with others in the network) could be very limited.

Organising the survey for the PSSG had many benefits including: direct relations with many network members, no longer mediated by NHS PASA colleagues; recognition of our role as professional researchers; formal acknowledgement that we would treat data confidentially; a sense of reciprocity – we had done work that was for the benefit of the network, not just the NHS PASA; contact with network members beyond the PSSG. The high level of interaction with members of the prosthetics network provided a rich source of insights that probably would not have been reached through interviewing alone. The many informal conversations and observations of people in action at and around meetings and events were vitally important in helping us to evaluate what they said and what was said about them (as individuals or concerning roles such as prosthetist) in formal interviews. Participant-observation proved essential for appreciating the social dynamics and politics of the network.

Improving Interviewing

The value of informal interviewing became increasingly apparent as the study progressed. Future research could systematically exploit this through an 'informal interviewing strategy' as an integral part of the research design. When first interviewed, research participants could be asked whether they would be willing to be contacted by 'phone on an occasional basis during the course of the study. This approach would be a resource-effective way of maintaining contact with a broad range of network actors, including those who are less central in the network, so extending the benefits derived from participant-observation. Furthermore, with careful planning, these informal interviews could be timed to precede or follow (or both) events such as conferences which are so important to sub-plots categorised in developing meaning.

Though we sought to do reflexive interviews, the questioning tended to concentrate on the present and past, and steered away from asking questions which might be regarded as encouraging the interviewee to speculate about other network actors. The elements of data that were future-oriented came mostly through participant-observation. On reflection, however, we would now advocate that, once relationships with interviewees are established and particularly through informal interviewing, it is possible and appropriate to ask them about their interactions with others and their interpretation of others' beliefs, actions and motives.

Ideally, in future research, we would: first, ask interviewees about their intentions, expectations and predictions in relation to a network learning episode; then, in the next interaction, ask them to describe and explain (a) their understanding of what had actually happened since the previous interaction and their explanations of these developments and (b) their revised intentions, expectations and predictions; and compare data collected over time. This approach could provide much richer descriptions of, and explanations for, the unfolding of a network learning episode, with better insights into the relations between process and outcome than were possible in this study. We realise however that the researcher would need to be mindful that questioning about future intentions and expectations has possibilities of shaping the future. In summary, given our interest in developing an understanding of developments in the network which recognises social and temporal embeddedness, there is a place for 'hearsay' and 'speculation' in interviews.

Writing Process Research

Langley (1999) describes seven strategies for sense-making in studying process, of which two seem most relevant to this investigation of network learning. Narrative strategy predominates, but it is complemented by a bracketing strategy, defining phases bounded by temporal break points. The five learning episodes we identified began at different times between the mid-1980s and the late 1990s; we considered all but one to be ongoing at the time we completed the interviews. Thus bracketing and punctuating (Weick, 1995: 35) was important to distinguish the episodes from one another and from the stream of network life, in a way that was meaningful to network participants, and to effectively differentiate the subject of the inquiry (network learning) from its context (the network). The 'nested' effect is developed a step further as sub-plots are bracketed within an episode. Notably, the temporal bracketing is of an episode as a whole. Sub-plots, and sub-plot categories, are not temporally defined. Different types of sub-plot occur in different orders in different episodes, and within an episode sub-plots may be consecutive or concurrent.

In writing of transforming qualitative data, Wolcott (1994) evokes the agency of the researcher in the analytic process and emphasises the importance of regarding writing as an integral part of the transformation process (Coffey and Atkinson, 1996; Alvesson and Sklödberg, 2000). Pentland (1999) and Hatch (1996) describe various features of narratives, such as narrative perspective (seeing) and narrative voice (saying) (ibid., 1996). We have narrated the story as observers – the narrator is not a character in the story and this is an external analysis of events (ibid., 1996). And yet, as Hatch goes on to discuss, this categorisation can break down on closer scrutiny – though we do not see ourselves as 'insiders' to the specific developments within episodes, we are closer to some episodes (e.g. contracting) than others (e.g. CADCAM), and prolonged engagement with the network and participation in some of its activities (notably the survey) mean one of us (Knight) was an insider to the network, if a marginal one.

Whilst we may be used to reading case narratives in which the focal actor is an individual, a group or an organisation in a network, decentred network narratives are less common. In constructing the narrative, care was taken to consider opposing view points and changing views of over time across the interviews. In interpreting data and, especially, writing case narratives, it is inevitable that some views and voices are silenced or marginalised (Brown, 1998; Pentland, 1999). As a reflexive researcher, it would be useful to consider which voices one is silencing or marginalising, and how and why.

IMPLICATIONS FOR THEORISING LEARNING PROCESS

This section addresses two related questions: could we have made different and/or better use of prior research on learning process? Why did so little of the prior research seem to be useful in guiding our analysis of learning process? These questions relate to the issue raised by Borgatti and Foster (2003: 1001) as to whether theories developed for networks of persons can also apply to networks of organisations. They remark that 'structuralist explanations are much more likely to scale than are individualist or essentialist explanations' (ibid.: 1001). First, we review three aspects of organisational learning theory to provide context for the subsequent discussion of implications.

Organisational Learning

Conceptions of OL, in particular learning outcomes. Crossan et al. (1995) elaborate the distinction between a view of OL as learning within organisations, where the learners might be individuals or groups, and an organisation-centred view of organisational learning. In the latter, organisational learning is not simply the sum of the learning of groups and individuals within the organisation, but is related to changes to properties of the organisation, such as systems, structures and procedures (ibid.: 345). Critics suggest that, in this organisation-centred view of OL, learning is metaphorical rather than substantive, and those who take it are anthropomorphising in applying human traits such as memory to 'inanimate objects' such as organisations (ibid.: 345).

Cook and Yanow (1993: 374) however reject attempts to conceptualise organisational learning in terms of established views about individual learning: 'this phenomenon is neither conceptually nor empirically the same as either learning by individuals or individuals learning within organisations'. They (ibid.: 383-384) detail three reasons why this is so:

> First, intuitively it is a much shorter conceptual leap to see organisations as cultural entities than it is to see them as cognitive ones. Organisations, being human groups, are more readily understood as being like tribes than they are as being like

individuals or brains. Second, because organisational learning here is understood to involve shared meanings associated with and carried out through cultural artefacts, it is understood as an activity of the organisation, that is, an activity at the level of the group, not at the level of the individual... Third, it is also, then, unnecessary to argue that organisations learn in a way that is fundamentally the same or similar to individual learning. The cultural perspective makes it possible to explore the meaning of organisational learning by beginning with empirical observations of group action rather than relying on conceptual arguments about likenesses between theories of individual cognition and theories of organisation.

They argue instead for a cultural perspective, taking culture to be 'the values, beliefs, and feelings of the organisation's members along with their artifacts', such as stories, rituals, metaphors, etc. (ibid.: 453). This more social perspective of organisational learning has been developed in recent years, with increasing attention to power and politics in organisational learning (Coopey, 1995; Coopey and Burgoyne, 2000; Vince, 2001) and a practice/activity-centred perspective (Nicolini and Meznar, 1995; Gherardi, 2000), though there remains a considerable need for more empirical work (Huysman, 1999; Easterby-Smith, Crossan and Nicolini, 2000; Gherardi, 2000).

OL process(es). Easterby-Smith and Araujo (1999: 3-4) distinguish two conceptions of organisational learning – as a technical process, and as a social process:

> The technical view assumes that organisational learning is about the effective processing, interpretation of, and response to, information both inside and outside the organisation... (whereas) the social perspective on organisational learning focuses on the way people make sense of their experiences at work ... learning is something that emerges from social interaction.

As with conceptualising organisational learning outcomes, many researchers derive constructs of OL process from theories of individual learning process (Dodgson, 1993). For example, Garvin (1993) proposes five forms of OL – learning by: doing; using; failing; observing; listening. The notion of learning from 'experience' is widely used (Dodgson, 1993; Levitt and March, 1996; Miner and Anderson, 1999; Holmqvist, 2003), but is highly problematic (Pye, 1994; Prange, 1999). Hedberg's (1981) notion of unlearning is also widely mentioned, in recognition that an organisation changes from one state to another, and that the process of changing may involve both abandoning the initial state and becoming the new state. Cook and Yanow (1993: 385), however, point out that learning is also about preservation and continuity – an organisation may need to learn in order to stay the same.

In a rare example of an article which is focused on OL process, Berends, Boersma and Weggeman (2003: 1042), drawing on Gidden's structuration theory, define organisational learning 'as the development of knowledge held by organisational members, that is being accepted as knowledge and is applicable in organisational activities, therewith implying a (potential) change in those activities', and propose that 'the process of organisational learning is realised in organisational practices, as a specific form of structuration'. From a case of OL in an R&D setting, they identified several activities that contributed to the learning process (ibid.: 1047-1048): constructing hypotheses, preparing materials, executing experiments, observing, measuring, arguing, calculating, drawing conclusions and writing up results, and articulating more fundamental theories and learning to cooperate. In this conceptualisation, OL outcomes are cognitive, but the view of OL process crosses into more social, practice-oriented views of learning.

Two associated articles provide a second, contrasting example of efforts to research organisational learning process. Crossan, Lane and White (1999) proposed the 4i framework of four processes (intuiting, interpreting, integrating, institutionalising) spanning the levels of individual, group and organisation through which OL comes about. Zietsma, Winn, Branzei and Vertinksy (2002) evaluated and extended this framework through applying it to a dramatic case about environmentalism and logging practices in British Columbia. They added two action-based learning processes: 'attending', which complements intuiting but is more active, and 'experimenting' which complements interpreting. This and Crossan et al.'s original model emphasise feedforward and feedback learning, thus drawing attention to the recursive relations between learning outcomes and processes (as does the work of Berends et al., 2003).

Translating OL to the level of inter-organisational networks. Drawing on some of the literature described above, our own prior research of organisational learning (Knight, 2000) and several articles which provided rich descriptions of learning by inter-organisational networks (Spender, 1989; Nathan and Mitroff, 1991; Kouzmin et al., 1995; McHugh, 1995; Paton et al., 1998; Dyer and Nobeoka, 2000), we proposed that network learning could be recognised through changes to network-level properties. Whilst these changes would be grounded in developing knowledge and practice by individuals and groups, the marker that denotes network learning is the institutionalisation of coordinated practices and/or the embedding of shared views and interpretations (Knight, 2002: 446). Learning might be emergent or purposive, and would not necessarily be associated with improved performance.

Some authors have specifically written about learning process, and the examples of work presented above (Zietsma et al., 2002; Berends et al., 2003) make valuable efforts to develop understanding of organisational learning process by taking an integrative perspective, bridging across levels. These conceptualisations do however evoke stages in time, and accumulation 'up' the levels learning. Tsoukas and Chia (2002) have argued that contributions to the change literature which argue for prioritising change over stability have not (yet) gone far enough; those investigating learning face a similar challenge (Elkjaer, 1999). Opportunities for addressing this may be constrained if we construe the task of describing and analysing network learning process as one of understanding how lower-level learning (individual, group and organisational) accumulates, translates and becomes embedded in the network.

Implications for Theorising

In returning to the literature, we have realised that much of it concerns issues *related to* learning process. There is some discussion of learning through institutionalisation and of how individual learning 'accumulates' to the organisation, and OL is often related to learning from experience by individuals and groups. There is much on strategies for improving learning, sources of and triggers for learning, and factors which enable or constrain learning (e.g. Dodgson, 1993; Bapuji and Crossan, 2004). On inter-organisational learning, Larsson, Bengtsson, Hendriksson and Sparks (1998), for example, consider how organisations appropriate learning from collective knowledge developed through inter-organisational alliances. Nevertheless, there is a frustrating lack of rich descriptions of the learning process itself.

Those who take a more social perspective tend to focus on groups and their collective knowledge (e.g. communities of practice). Writers on OL who take a more cognitive or technical perspective of learning tend to couple their conceptualisation of OL tightly to theories on individual learning. Other authors (e.g. Berends et al., 2003) question the relationship between individual and organisational learning and aim to reconcile the constructs; for them, notions of OL and IL are more loosely coupled. Comparatively, in our investigation of network learning, we have un-coupled the notions of organisational and network learning from individual learning. We do not regard IL, OL and NL as isomorphic.

Our theoretical development of the notion of network learning (Knight, 2002) was inspired by organisational, rather than individual, learning. This study was founded on an organisation-centred view of OL, in which we would differentiate OL from learning at other levels through recognising OL outcomes as changes to organisation-level properties. Our aim in this study was to assess whether this conceptualisation could be translated to the network level, so providing a network-centred view of network learning. We can now recognise that, at the beginning of the empirical phase, we had much more robust notions of network learning outcomes than network learning processes. Though we would prefer to label our research overall as abductive (Coffey and Atkinson, 1996), it could be argued that the development of the outcomes elements of our conceptual model of NL was deductive and the development of our understanding of NL process inductive.

Relating this study to other investigations of (organisational) learning process, we note that Berends et al.'s (2003) inquiry into organisational learning took place in an R&D setting which makes it more difficult to clearly distinguish the subject (learning) from its context (a function whose purpose is to innovate/learn). The case description draws out individual and collective activities which are associated with OL. The discussion of the case does not explicitly highlight from the data how practices become embedded at the organisational level, but relies more on the theory of structuration. In contrast, Zietsma et al.'s (2002) War of the Woods case has a clear focal organisation but could, with some changes to the design, readily have been presented as a network learning episode. In this 4i work, individual, group and organisational learning processes are closely coupled; human agency in learning process at the higher levels is seen in terms of individual and collective learning.

We propose that an alternative path in theory development could be very fruitful: one in which human and organisational agency is recognised as vital for network learning, but as something broader as individual, group and organisational learning. We did not aim to explain network learning process in terms of (just) organisational or individual learning processes. This is not to say that we fail to recognise the agency of individuals and role of groups and organisations in shaping the development of the network. On the contrary, we wanted to look beyond the impact of their individual, group and organisational learning on network learning, and consider how a wider range of organising processes generate network learning. Our concept of NL outcomes is tightly linked to well-established (but not uncontested) notions of OL outcomes (as changes to organisational properties), but our concept of NL process is derived from data rather than established learning theory, as advocated by Cook and Yanow (1993).

Our model of learning process echoes notions of OL process as presented by those who take a social, political view of learning but is distinctive from any models we have encountered. It is also consonant with views of change and changing in which change rather than stability is seen as the 'normal condition of organisational life' (Tsoukas and Chia, 2002); we have considered the relationships between network change and network learning in depth elsewhere (Knight and Pye, 2004).

CONCLUSIONS

We have reflected on our experience of investigating network learning and our efforts to develop an understanding of learning process in extensive inter-organisational networks. Through learning-by-doing – conducting the study and writing this chapter – we have developed several propositions which could help in two aspects of future research: research techniques and theorising (learning) process.

Much of the literature on organisational, inter-organisational and network learning provides a good appreciation of factors that influence process but relatively little insight into how organisations and networks actually might be said to learn. Many researchers rely on notions of learning process derived from theories of individual learning to conceptualise learning process at other levels (group, organisation, network). Other researchers deploy terms like institutionalisation without really unpacking the term and revealing a finer-grained view of learning process. More detailed and sophisticated analyses of OL process are rare.

Developing Cook and Yanow's (1993) challenge to assumed relationships between the concept of learning at individual and organisational levels, we propose that researchers of organisational learning process might find their task easier and more fruitful if they are more explicit about whether they are trying to generate theory of organisational learning process primarily from organisational learning data or primarily from individual learning process theory (whether social or technical).

Early analysis highlighted the need to be attentive to the social and political aspects of learning and the importance of working with the temporal interconnectedness of events and actions and social interconnectedness of actors (Granovetter, 1992; Dacin, Ventresca and Beal, 1999). Building on techniques employed, we propose various ways in which processual research in learning might be strengthened:

- Informal data – Participant-observation and informal interviewing are vital complements of more formal interviews. Identifying useful meetings and events to attend is as important as negotiating access to one-to-one interviews.

- Relationships – Effort needs to be directed to accessing a selection of lower profile network actors, not just leaders and change agents. Efforts to develop trust in relations with actors across the network, not just those who have an immediate impact on the study (notably those who control access) can be rewarded by obtaining high quality data from interviews, especially informal ones.
- 'Serial interviewing', that is interviewing network actors more than once (by 'phone if resources are limited) would provide continuity and a dynamic view of how learning unfolds over time in the network. Contrary to what we are taught about the rules of good questioning from a legalistic point of view, we suggest here that we might want to encourage hearsay and speculation. Respondents' predictions, intentions and expectations, the extent to which they are met, and how they change over time all potentially have much to reveal. Focusing each interview on past developments and future expectations in an iterative fashion helps the analyst appreciate the shadow of the past and the shadow of the future (Axelrod, 1984) on actors' actions and interactions.

These suggestions for appreciating social and temporal embeddedness are about 'getting closer' to the network to appreciate better how and why developments occur. Tsoukas and Chia (2002) close their article on organisational becoming with the assertion that organisational scientists must investigate microscopic change if they are to convey a sense of organisational flow. We hope that our data collection techniques and ways of analysing learning process achieve this, at least to some extent. This, however, only seems to be part of what is required.

There is an important tension between achieving a micro-perspective to convey flow in network life/learning and producing the macro-picture necessary to convey the scope and scale of an episode of network learning lasting, say, 20 years in an extensive inter-organisational network of some 50 or more organisations. In our study of network learning, abstracting episodes of learning from the stream of network life/'becoming' (after Tsoukas and Chia, 2002) and disaggregating these into sub-plots was a key sense-making technique which allowed us to organise the data sufficiently to write narratives of the episodes. A notable feature of the model of learning (Figure 8.2) and the way we have theorised network learning process is that it clearly distances our conception of network learning from those views of learning which assert or imply a staged, linear process with a cumulative effect from learning at lower levels (individual/ group/organisational) to learning at higher levels (organisational or network).

Process research is challenging in all domains, but especially so in extensive inter-organisational networks. It seems that much organisational and management research which adopts a social perspective employs micro-level data. Through the various techniques described, we were able to reconcile micro-level data with building a macro-picture of a macro-level process, and so elaborate a new conceptualisation of network learning which is rigorously network-centred, which theorises learning process not just learning outcomes, and which adopts a social and political view of learning. By reflecting on our experiences of investigating network learning and relating them to others' work on research process and learning, we have identified and presented some suggestions for enhancing future learning research and process inquiry in extensive inter-organisational networks.

NOTES

1. This chapter is based on a paper presented at the First Organisation Studies Summer Workshop, Santorini, June 2005.
2. MOPAN – Multi-Organisational Partnerships and Alliances Network: http://www.mop-a-n.net/default.aspx; IMP – Industrial Marketing and Purchasing Group: http://www.impgroup.org/.

REFERENCES

Alvesson, M. and K. Sklödberg (2000), *Reflexive Methodology*, London: Sage.

Axelrod, R. (1984), *The Evolution of Cooperation*, London: Penguin.

Bapuji, H. and M. Crossan (2004), 'From questions to answers: Reviewing organizational learning research', *Management Learning*, **35** (4), 397-417.

Berends, H., K. Boersma and M. Weggeman (2003), 'The structuration of organizational learning', *Human Relations*, **56** (9), 1035-1056.

Blackler, F. (1993), 'Knowledge and the theory of organizations: Organizations as activity systems and the reframing of management', *Journal of Management Studies*, **30** (6), 863-884.

Blackler, F. (1995), 'Knowledge, knowledge work and organizations: An overview and interpretation', *Organization Studies*, **16** (6), 1021-1046.

Blackler, F. and S. McDonald (2000), 'Power, mastery and organizational learning', *Journal of Management Studies*, **37** (6), 833-851.

Blackler, F., N. Crump and S. McDonald (2000), 'Organizing processes in complex activity networks', *Organization*, **7** (2), 277-300.

Borgatti, S. and P. Foster (2003), 'The network paradigm in organizational research: A review and typology', *Journal of Management*, **29** (6), 991-1013.

Brown, A. D. (1998), 'Narrative, politics and legitimacy in an IT implementation', *Journal of Management Studies*, **35** (1), 35-58.

Coffey, A. and P. Atkinson (1996), *Making Sense of Qualitative Data: Complementary Research Strategies*, London: Sage.

Cook, S. and D. Yanow (1993), 'Culture and organizational learning', *Journal of Management Inquiry*, **2** (4), 373-390.

Coopey, J. (1995), 'The learning organization, power, politics and ideology', *Management Learning*, **26** (2), 193-213.

Coopey, J. and J. Burgoyne (2000), 'Politics and organizational learning', *Journal of Management Studies*, **37** (6), 869-885.

Crossan, M., H. Lane and R.E. White (1999), 'An organizational learning framework: From intuition to institution', *Academy of Management Review*, **24** (3), 522-537.

Crossan, M., H. Lane, R. White and L. Djurfeldt (1995), 'Organizational learning: Dimensions for a theory', *The International Journal of Organizational Analysis*, **3** (4), 337-360.

Dacin, T., M. Ventresca and B.D. Beal (1999), 'The embeddedness of organizations: Dialogue and directions', *Journal of Management*, **25** (3), 317-356.

Dodgson, M. (1993), 'Organizational learning: A review of some literature', *Organization Studies*, **14** (3), 375-394.

Dopson, S. (2003), 'The potential of the case study method for organisational analysis', *Policy & Politics*, **31** (2), 217-226.

Dyer, J. and K. Nobeoka (2000), 'Creating and managing a high-performance knowledge-sharing network: The Toyota case', *Strategic Management Journal*, **21** (3), 345-367.

Easterby-Smith, M. and L. Araujo (1999), 'Organizational Learning: Current Debates and Opportunities', in M. Easterby-Smith, J. Burgoyne and L. Araujo (eds), *Organizational Learning and the Learning Organization*, London: Sage, pp. 1-21.

Easterby-Smith, M., M. Crossan and D. Nicolini (2000), 'Organizational learning: Debates past, present and future', *Journal of Management Studies*, **37** (6), 783-796.

Elkjaer, B. (1999), 'In Search of a Social Learning Theory', in M. Easterby-Smith, J. Burgoyne and L. Araujo (eds), *Organizational Learning and the Learning Organization*, London: Sage, pp. 75-91.

Engeström, Y. (2000), 'Comment on Blackler et al. activity theory and the social construction of knowledge: A story of four umpires', *Organization*, **72** (3), 301-310.

Garvin, D. (1993), 'Building a learning organization', *Harvard Business Review*, July-August, 78-91.

Gherardi, S. (2000), 'Practice-based theorizing on learning and knowing in organizations', *Organization*, **7** (2), 211-223.

Granovetter, M. (1992), 'Problems of Explanation in Economic Sociology', in N. Nohria and R. Eccles (eds), *Networks and Organizations: Structure, Form and Action*, Boston: Harvard Business School Press, pp. 25-56.

Hammersley, M. and P. Atkinson (1983), *Ethnography: Principles in Practice,* London: Routledge.

Hammersley, M. and P. Atkinson (1995), *Ethnography: Principles in Practice*, London: Routledge, 2nd edition.

Harland, C. and L. Knight (2001), 'Supply strategy: A corporate social capital perspective', *Research in the Sociology of Organizations*, **18**, 151-183.

Harper, D. (1992), 'Small Ns and Community Case Studies', in C. Ragin and H. Becker (eds), *What is a Case?*, New York: Cambridge University Press, pp. 139-158.

Hatch, M. J. (1996), 'The role of researcher: An analysis of narrative position in organization theory', *Journal of Management Inquiry*, **5** (4), 359-374.

Hedberg, B. (1981), 'How Organizations Learn and Unlearn', in P. Nystrom and W. Starbuck (eds), *Handbook of Organizational Design Volume 1: Adapting Organizations to their Environments*, Oxford: Oxford University Press, pp. 3-27.

Holmqvist, M. (2003), 'A dynamic model of intra- and inter-organisational learning', *Organization Studies*, **24** (1), 95-123.

Huysman, M. (1999), 'Balancing Biases: A Critical Review of the Literature on Organizational Learning', in M. Easterby-Smith, J. Burgoyne and L. Araujo (eds), *Organizational Learning and the Learning Organization*, London: Sage, pp. 59-74.

Knight, L. (2000), 'Learning to collaborate: A study of individual and organizational learning, and inter-organisational relationships', *Journal of Strategic Marketing*, **8** (2), 121-138.

Knight, L. (2002), 'Network learning: Exploring learning by inter-organisational networks', *Human Relations*, **55** (4), 427-454.

Knight, L. (2004), 'Coping with Multiple Meanings: Some Implications for Theory and Research Practice of Various Conceptions of Network', 11th International Conference on Multi-organizational Partnerships, Alliances and Networks, Tilburg University (NL).

Knight, L. and A. Pye (2004), Exploring the relationships between network change and network learning', *Management Learning*, **35** (4), 473-490.

Knight, L. and A. Pye (2005), 'Network learning: An empirically-derived conceptual model of learning by groups of organizations', *Human Relations*, **58** (3), 369-392.

Kouzmin, A., A. Jarman and U. Rosenthal (1995), 'Inter-organizational policy processes in disaster management', *Disaster Prevention and Management*, **4** (2), 20-37.

Krackhardt, D. (1992), 'The Strength of Strong Ties: The Importance of Philos in Organizations', in N. Nohria and R. Eccles (eds), *Networks and Organizations*, Boston: Harvard Business School Press, pp. 216-239.

Langley, A. (1999), 'Strategies for theorizing from process data', *Academy of Management Review*, **24** (4), 691-710.

Larsson, R., L. Bengtsson, K. Hendriksson and J. Sparks (1998), 'The inter-organisational learning dilemma: Collective knowledge development in strategic alliances', *Organization Science*, **9** (3), 285-305.

Levitt, B. and J. March (1996), 'Organizational Learning', in M. Cohen and L. Sproull (eds), *Organizational Learning*, London, Sage, pp. 516-540.

Lincoln, Y. and E. Guba (1985), *Naturalistic Inquiry*, London: Sage.

McHugh, C. (1995), 'Preparing public safety organizations for disaster response: A study of Tucson, Arizona's response to flooding', *Disaster Prevention and Management*, **4** (5), 25-36.

Miles, M. and A. Huberman (1994), *Qualitative Data Analysis: An Expanded Sourcebook*, Thousand Oaks, CA: Sage.

Miner, A. and P. Anderson (1999), 'Industry and population-level learning: Organizational, inter-organisational and collective learning processes', *Advances in Strategic Management*, **16**, 1-32.

Nathan, M. and I. Mitroff (1991), 'The use of negotiated order theory as a tool for the analysis and development of an inter-organisational field', *Journal of Applied Behavioral Science*, **27** (2), 163-180.

Nicolini, D. and M. Meznar (1995), 'The social construction of organizational learning: Conceptual and practical issues in the field', *Human Relations*, **48** (7), 727-746.

Numagami, T. (1998), 'The infeasibility of invariant laws in management studies: A reflective dialogue in defence of case studies', *Organization Science*, **9** (1), 2-15.

Paton, D., D. Johnston and B.F. Houghton (1998), 'Organizational response to a volcanic eruption', *Disaster Prevention and Management*, **7** (1), 5-13.

Pentland, B. (1999), 'Building process theory with narrative: From description to explanation', *Academy of Management Review*, **24** (4), 711-724.

Pettigrew, A. (1973), *The Politics of Organizational Decision-Making*, London: Tavistock.

Pettigrew, A. (1985a), 'Contextualist Research: A Natural Way to Link Theory and Practice', in E. Lawler (ed.), *Doing Research that is useful for Theory and Practice*, San Francisco: Josey-Bass, pp. 222-274.

Pettigrew, A. (1985b), 'Examining Change in the Long-term Context of Culture and Politics', in J. Pennings and Associates (eds), *Organizational Strategy and Change: New Views on Formulating and Implementing Strategic Decisions*, San Francisco: Jossey-Bass, pp. 269-318.

Pettigrew, A. (1987), 'Context and action in the transformation of the firm', *Journal of Management Studies*, **24** (6), 649-670.

Pettigrew, A. (1990), 'Longitudinal field research on change: Theory and practice', *Organization Science*, **1** (3), 267-292.

Prange, C. (1999), 'Organizational Learning – Desperately Seeking Theory?', in M. Easterby-Smith, J. Burgoyne and L. Araujo, *Organizational Learning and the Learning Organization: Developments in Theory and Practice*, London: Sage, pp. 23-43.

Pye, A. (1994), 'Past, present and possibility: An integrative appreciation of learning from experience', *Management Learning*, **25** (1), 155-173.

Ragin, C. (1992), 'Introduction: Cases of "What is a Case"?', in C. Ragin and H. Becker (eds), *What is a Case? Exploring the Foundations of Social Inquiry*, New York: Cambridge University Press, pp. 1-18.

Rubin, H. and I. Rubin (1995), *Qualitative Interviewing: The Art of Hearing Data*, London: Sage.

Spender, J.-C. (1989), *Industry Recipes: An Enquiry into the Nature and Sources of Managerial Judgement*, Oxford: Basil Blackwell.

Tsoukas, H. and R. Chia (2002), 'On organizational becoming: Rethinking organizational change', *Organization Science*, **13** (5), 567-582.

Usher, P. (1997), 'Challenging the Power of Rationality', in G. McKenzie, J. Powell and P. Usher (eds), *Understanding Social Research: Perspectives on Methodology and Practice*, London: Falmer Press, pp. 42-55.

Vaughan, D. (1992), 'Theory elaboration: the heuristics of case analysis' in C. Ragin and H. Becker (eds), *What is a Case?*, New York: Cambridge University Press, pp. 139-158.

Van de Ven, A. (1992), 'Suggestions for studying strategy process: A research note', *Strategic Management Journal*, **13**, special issue, 169-188.

Vince, R. (2001), 'Power and emotion in organizational learning', *Human Relations*, **54** (10), 1325-1351.

Weick, K. (1979), *The Social Psychology of Organizing*, Wokingham: Addison Wesley.

Weick, K. (1995), *Sensemaking in Organizations*, London: Sage.

Wolcott, H. (1994), *Transforming Qualitative Data*, London: Sage.

Yin, R. (1994), *Case Study Research: Design and Methods*, London: Sage.

Zietsma, C., M. Winn, O. Branzei and I. Vertinsky (2002), 'The war of the woods: Facilitators and impediments of organizational learning processes', *British Journal of Management*, **13**, special issue, S61-S74.

PART III

Conflicts and Failures in Partnerships and
Networks

9. Tie Failure: A Literature Review

Leon Oerlemans, Tobias Gössling and Rob Jansen

Failure
is always the best way to learn
Kings of Convenience
('Failure' on the album 'Quiet is the New Loud')

INTRODUCTION

Whenever organisations choose a collaborative setting, they have certain a priori positive expectations about the outcome of collaboration. Given the assumptions about instrumental rationality, actors would not choose to collaborate with other actors if they did not think it would be beneficial for them to do so. With benefits, however, we do not only refer to economic profit. The benefits of collaboration can also be non-pecuniary. Outcomes of collaborations may take different forms: financial, market access, higher levels of interaction, sympathy, reputation, legitimacy, etc. With respect to one or several of these dimensions, actors should have positive expectations in order to have an incentive to start and maintain an inter-organisational relationship. However, success in collaboration seems to be the exception rather than the rule (Park and Russo, 1996; Büchel, 2003). Several studies using various samples of joint ventures, alliances and other inter-organisational relationships showed failure rates at seven in ten (Coopers and Lybrand, 1986; Zineldin and Dodourova, 2005), two in three (Kogut, 1989), and one in two (Harrigan, 1984). However, one has to be aware of the fact that scholars define failure of inter-organisational relationships in different ways, for example as an ineffective collaborative activity, a premature termination of a tie reflecting negative expectation about the future value of an inter-organisational relationship, or a joint effort that generates unsatisfactory outcomes. Such failures, of course, are detrimental for the collaborating organisations, and, especially, for the joint goal. In order to learn from past experiences for the benefit of future collaboration, on the one hand, and learn from the failures of others, on the other, it can be extremely helpful to analyse failure, to look for the possible reasons for failure and to develop approaches for avoiding tie failure. Thus, the research question guiding this chapter is: according to the literature, which factors explain the failure of inter-organisational ties? The goal of this chapter is to review the explanations for tie failure by important theoretical streams in organisation science and then to review the factors explaining tie failure presented in empirical literature. A combination of these two reviews provides a state-of-the-art overview on inter-organisational tie failure.

In order to answer the research question, we will first (a) define the problem of tie failure. Next, we will (b) review major theoretical streams in organisation science as they pertain to tie failure; (c) focus on empirical literature that deals with factors influencing tie failure, and we will finally (d) draw our conclusions and sketch some avenues for future research.

TIE FAILURE: DEFINING THE PROBLEM

Inter-organisational relationships, such as alliances, are an omnipresent phenomenon (Borgatti and Foster, 2003). Their spread has generated a growing stream of research by organisational scholars who have investigated some of the causes and consequences of such multi-organisational partnerships, mostly at a dyadic level. In his review of the state of alliance and network literature, Gulati (1998) identified five key issues on which scholars have focussed: (a) the formation of alliances; (b) the choice of governance structure; (c) the dynamic evolution of inter-organisational relationships; (d) the performance consequences for firms entering inter-organisational relationships; and (e) the performance of inter-organisational relationships.

The performance and outcomes of alliances and other forms of inter-organisational relationships has received less attention (Oliver and Ebers, 1998; Deeds and Rothaermel, 2003) than the other areas mentioned because of some troublesome research obstacles, which concern measuring tie performance and the logistical challenges of gathering the data necessary to research these topics in detail. As a result, it is one of the 'most exciting and underexplored areas' (Gulati, 1998: 306). Interestingly, in studies of social networks, performance and consequences have received much more attention (Borgatti and Foster, 2003). As was mentioned in the introduction of this chapter, many studies have reported extremely high tie failure rates, and several researchers have tried to identify the key ingredients of alliance success (e.g. Bleeke and Ernst, 1995). These include: flexibility in management of the tie, building trust with partners, regular communication, constructive management of conflict (see Chapter 10 by Gray in this volume), continuity of personnel responsible for the inter-organisational tie, managing partner expectations, and so on.

The primary focus of theoretical and empirical studies of the performance of ties is on tie termination. Several studies have generated important insights into some of the main factors that are associated with the termination of ties (see the next sections for overviews). As Gulati (1998) observes, there are two important limitations of these studies. First, studying failure by focusing on terminations fails to distinguish between 'natural' and untimely dissolutions. Many ties terminate because they are intended to do so by the participating actors at the very outset. Moreover, an inter-organisational tie may simply be a temporary arrangement that the partners plan to end once their (joint) objectives have been met or when it is viable to change an alliance into an acquisition. Gomes-Casseres (1987) even argues that, in some cases, the transformation of an inter-organisational venture may actually signal successful adaptation to environmental dynamics. Moreover, not all ongoing inter-organisational ties are necessarily successful, and some may be continuing more out of inertia (Kim, Oh and Swaminathan, 2006) or high sunk costs. Second, studies of tie termination consider performance as an either-or (death or survival) issue. This is obviously not the case, and a more fine-tuned assessment would take gradations of tie performance into account.

A primary problem confronting scholars studying tie performance is measuring performance itself (Anderson, 1990). Since inter-organisational ties can have many different aims, creating an appropriate multi-dimensional measure of tie performance is a difficult task. An additional problem is created by the dyadic nature of organisational ties. In some cases, performance is asymmetrical, for example, one organisation achieves its aims, whereas the other is not able to do so. Another example concerns accepted asymmetrical performance: Chen and Chen (2002) show that, in international alliances between organisations located in developed and emerging economies, uneven outcomes are regarded as 'part of the deal' due to the differing motives the partners have when entering the inter-organisational tie.

Taking the considerations presented above into account, for the purpose of this chapter, we define an inter-organisational tie as an enduring, yet temporary, inter-firm exchange that organisations join on a voluntary basis to jointly accomplish their respective individual or joint goals. Tie failure is defined as the unintended/unplanned termination or (perceived) unsuccessfulness of an inter-organisational relationship. This definition implies that we take a broad view on tie failure, which will include, for example, tie termination, tie instability or unsatisfactory goal accomplishment. The next section deals with the question concerning which insights on tie failure can be derived from a number of organisation theories.

THEORIES ON TIE FAILURE: A REVIEW

Academic literature on industrial economics, organisation theory and strategic management contains theoretical approaches that shed light on the factors influencing the failure of inter-organisational ties. According to Rahman (2006), transaction cost economics, social exchange theory, evolutionary and organisational learning theory are particularly relevant for studying factors explaining tie failure.

Transaction Cost Theory

Transaction cost theory argues that firms exist in order to economise on transaction costs caused by market-based exchanges between economic actors. Examples of transaction costs include screening for trustworthy exchange partners, negotiating business arrangements, and monitoring the behaviour of partners. Transaction costs are especially high under conditions of high transaction specific investments (high asset specificity), limited frequency of interaction between exchanging actors, and a high degree of behavioural uncertainty about the transaction (Williamson, 1975, 1998). These features of transactions are problematic because the exchanging actors could respond by seeking self-interest with guile, and this opportunistic behaviour, as well as other contingencies, may not be anticipated by an actor as a result of the effects of bounded rationality. Firms implement coordination mechanisms (governance structures) to minimise transaction costs.

Williamson (1975) initially viewed markets and hierarchies as opposing forms of organising transactions. Later, he (Williamson, 1985) also recognised intermediate forms of economic organisation (the so-called 'hybrids'). According to transaction cost economics, hierarchical governance structures would be preferred over exchanges through the market when market-based transactions incur high costs. In general terms, given the features of transactions, an actor is able to determine which governance structure (market, hybrid or hierarchy) is the least costly method to do business. Therefore, when an actor chooses to engage in some hybrid form (e.g., an alliance or another form of inter-organisational relationship) rather than engage in market or unified governance, transaction cost theory would argue that this specific hybrid form is the least costly mode of exchange.

How do transaction cost economics explain tie failure, that is, the dissolution of the hybrid governance structure? To answer this question, we have to take a closer look at the effects of changes of uncertainty levels on the choice of governance structures. It is important to note that the famous matrix in which the different governance structures are presented (ibid.: 79) has the assumption that the uncertainty level is moderate. What, then, are the effects of increased levels of uncertainty? For transactions characterised by low levels of asset specificity, the effects are small. In such a case, relationships between actors are not of high importance, as it is fairly easy to transact with many other (new) partners. In other words, market governance is hardy affected by higher levels of uncertainty. However, the higher the asset specificity is, the higher the need to have mechanisms to solve (possible) conflicts between partners. After all, as a consequence of higher uncertainty levels, there is a higher possibility that contractual gaps occur, which result in contractual adjustments. According to Williamson, these transactions are more likely to be organised by market or by unified governance. In sum, hybrid governance structures are likely to be terminated when uncertainty levels increase. Note that transaction cost theory argues that this is especially the case for inter-organisational relationships in which innovation is the primary aim, as innovation is by definition characterised by high uncertainty levels. Therefore, tie failure is caused by increases in uncertainty levels. A devil's advocate might argue that transaction cost theory does not really deal with tie failure, but only with changes in governance structures as a consequence of the features of transactions. We tend to disagree with this position, as this theoretical approach states that instability is an intrinsic characteristic of the hybrid governance structure.

Social Exchange Theory

Social exchanges are 'voluntary actions of individuals that are motivated by the returns they are expected to bring and typically in fact bring for others' (Blau, 1964: 91). The exchange of a wide variety of resources can serve as the basis for this social behaviour. It should be noted that social exchanges are not necessarily economically driven and are in general not governed by explicit contractual agreements. Rather, resource exchange is viewed as a voluntary process based in principles of reciprocity. This means that relationships are regarded as the glue that binds the actions of actors and frames business exchanges (Emerson, 1976). Due to the fact that there is such a strong emphasis on relationship in social exchanges, these exchanges are often labelled relational contracts (Heide, 1994). Homans, who is the initiator of the theory, describes the crux of the theory as follows (1958: 606):

> Social behavior is an exchange of goods, material goods but also non-material ones, such as the symbols of approval or prestige. Persons that give much to others try to get much from them, and persons that get much from others are under pressure to give much to them. This process of influence tends to work out at equilibrium to a balance in the exchanges. For a person in an exchange, what he gives may be a cost to him, just as what he gets may be a reward, and his behavior changes less as the difference of the two, profit, tends to a maximum.

Trust and power, which are relational results of resource dependencies, are at the very core of social exchange theory. As Arrow (1974: 23) states: 'Trust is an important lubricant of a social system. It is extremely efficient; it saves people a lot of trouble to have a fair degree of reliance on other people's word.' Trust is commonly defined as 'a partner's ability to perform according to the intentions and expectations of a relationship (competence trust) or his or her intentions not to defect' (Nooteboom, Berger and Noorderhaven, 1997: 311). Most scholars argue that trust builds as the relationship matures (Klein-Woolthuis, Hillebrand and Nooteboom, 2005; see below for different perspectives) or through positive experiences in repeated ties (Gulati, 1995). Several scholars (Perry, Sengupta and Krapfel, 2004; Zaheer, McEvily and Perrone, 1998) have shown that trust and trust-development in inter-firm relationships have a positive influence on the (positive) outcomes of these relationships.

Second, power influences the way social exchanges develop (Emerson, 1962). The basic premise of social exchange theory is that actors are in need of critical resources, which are not all in their possession or under their control. Therefore, they depend on resources owned and controlled by other actors. This dependence on others is in turn a basis for power. In other words, there is a power relation in an inter-organisational tie if the partner is in need of the resource that the focal actor has.

Trust and power can influence tie failure. A lack of trust or diminishing levels of trust in inter-organisational relationships incurs cost increases, because actors have to implement measures to counterbalance the low trust levels. Once these costs are perceived as too high relative to the yields of the relationship, it is likely that the tie will fail. It has been argued, however, that also high trust levels can also produce tie failure (Granovetter, 1985). As Granovetter recognises, the emergence of trust is not sufficient to guarantee trustworthy behaviour, and it may even provide the occasion for malfeasance and inequity on a scale larger than in the absence of trust. Granovetter (ibid.: 491-493) describes three such occasions: (a) high trust levels create potential opportunities for, and high potential gains from, malfeasance; (b) fraud is most efficiently pursued by teams with high internal trust (Hollis, 1989: 'honour among thieves'); and (c) conflicts amongst parties to a transaction can develop into coalitions of combatants. A combination of both theoretical arguments leads to the conclusion that both low and high trust levels can lead to tie failure, implying a U-shaped relationship between trust levels and the probability of tie dissolution.

A comparable story can be told for power. Power, more specifically the abuse of power, will lead to a high level of asymmetry in a tie. As far as it is possible to acquire resources from a different actor (a monopolistic situation would exclude this option), the tie will be terminated and a new one will likely be established, as the need for the resource is still present. In sum, from the perspective of social exchange theory, tie failure will be fuelled by both low and high levels of trust, diminishing trust levels over time, and the abuse of power that is the result of resource dependence.

Evolutionary Theory of Organisations

Evolutionary theory of organisations stems from the seminal work of Nelson and Winter (1973) and Burgelman (1983), among others, and has found an important application in population ecology (Hannan and Freeman, 1977) and the resource-based theory of the firm (Barney, 1996). Basically, evolutionary theory of organisations argues that organisational forms evolve (grow, survive or fail) in response to different kinds of environmental forces (ecological, competitive and institutional). Basically, the theory holds that variability exits within the features of organisations in populations. When this variability results in different probabilities to survive in an environment, those traits will become dominant in a population. Although the theory does not advocate a deterministic perspective, as organisations do indeed have a role in influencing their outcomes, the theory is nevertheless very reserved concerning the influence an organisation can have in exercising its own strategic choices.

When applied to the failure of inter-organisational relationships, evolutionary theory focuses in particular on the developmental path of their emergence. Ring and Van de Ven (1994) offer a simple model of the evolution of inter-organisational relationships, such as alliances. They theorise that inter-organisational relationships evolve sequentially by going through the stages of negotiation, commitment and execution. These stages follow a cyclical path, so it becomes a continuous process. Ring and Van de Ven name two specific factors, which they see as influencing the dissolution of cooperative inter-organisational relationships. They first point out the influence of time: due to relation-specific investments (e.g. commitment) that take place over time, the probability of tie termination decreases. Reversely, young inter-organisational relationships are the most vulnerable to termination (see also: Levinthal and Fichman, 1988). Second, they point to the balances between formal and informal processes in negotiation, commitment and execution over time. For example, when formal processes (e.g. excessive formal monitoring and control) dominate one or each of the stages, this imbalance can jeopardise the relationship, as it will create conflict and distrust. Consequently, this will impact negatively on tie duration. Doz (1996) points at the occurrence of path dependency in inter-organisational ties and its impact on tie failure. He argues that ties start off with initial conditions that affect tasks, interface structure and partner expectations. Unsuccessful and terminated ties fail to learn, re-evaluate or re-adjust because they have remained trapped in their initial conditions.

Kumar and Nti (1998, 2004) state that inter-organisational relationships have to deal with outcome and process discrepancies in their developmental paths. 'Outcome discrepancies concern the ability of the partners to achieve their economic and learning objectives. Process discrepancies relate to the partners' satisfaction with the pattern of interaction, and affect their feelings of psychological attachment to the relationship' (ibid.: 356). It follows from Kumar and Nti's definitions that the larger the outcome and process discrepancies, the higher the likelihood of tie failure. Arino and de la Torre (1998) argue that partners who are attempting to restore balance to the relationship begin by renegotiating the terms of the contract. These renegotiations themselves are the seeds of the disintegration of relationships.

Table 9.1   Environmental effects on patterns of network change

	Changes in uncertainty	
	Increase	**Decrease**
Increase	**Network expansion** Tie creation: Increase Tie deletion: Decrease Portfolio size: Increase Portfolio range: Increase	**Network strengthening** Tie creation: Increase Tie deletion: Decrease Portfolio size: Increase Portfolio range: Decrease
Changes in munificence		
Decrease	**Network churning** Tie creation: Increase Tie deletion: Increase Portfolio size: Little change Portfolio range: Increase	**Network shrinking** Tie creation: Decrease Tie deletion: Increase Portfolio size: Decrease Portfolio range: Decrease

Source: Koka et al. (2006: 724).

Recently, Koka, Madhavan and Prescott (2006) offered a comprehensive view on the effects of environmental dynamics on network change in general, and on tie deletion in particular. The results of their line of reasoning are summarised in Table 9.1.

The starting point of Koka et al.'s core thesis is the assertion that the environment affects the pattern of observed network change in predictable ways. Environmental dynamics are indicated by two well-known dimensions: munificence and uncertainty. Munificence is defined as the extent to which resources available to the firm are plentiful or scarce, and can be considered the carrying capacity of the environment. Uncertainty is defined as the extent to which the firm's managers have the ability to accurately assess the current and future states of the external environment of the organisation.

As we are interested in factors increasing the possibility of tie failure, two of the cells in Table 9.1 are of importance: network churning and network shrinking. Network churning is the result of an increase in uncertainty and a decrease in munificence leading to tie termination, among other things. Due to higher uncertainty levels, the predictability of the environment decreases, which might lead to the obsolescence of existing routines between partners. On the other hand, a decrease in uncertainty means that there are fewer resources available to maintain all existing inter-organisational relationships. The case of network shrinking is a combination of decreases in uncertainty and munificence. Tie termination (in markets that are inappropriate to the new, less uncertain, environment) is a result of the actions of those firms that want to free up resources in order to compete. These dissolutions may also be accelerated as firms become aware that some of their previous strategic actions are unlikely to be successful.

Evolutionary theory of organisations applies a process view on factors that influence tie failure. The likelihood of tie failure largely depends on the interaction processes between actors tied in a relationship, more specifically on the processes that cause imbalances, renegotiations and path dependencies. The theory also proposes that tie dissolution is a reaction shown by firms as they try to cope with environmental dynamics.

Organisational Learning Theory

In recent years, the organisational learning theory has proliferated substantially (see also the contributions of Hibbert and Huxham (Chapter 6), and Knight and Pye (Chapter 8) in this volume). Some scholars have argued that learning outcomes and the success of inter-organisational relationships are synonyms (Argyris and Schon, 1978; Fiol and Lyles, 1985). However, as Huber (1991) points out, organisations can learn the wrong things or lack the capabilities to learn the rights things. Levitt and March (1988) argue that the learning process is complex and that there is a time lag between learning and organisational outcomes, which makes it very illogical to equate learning and organisational outcomes.

Table 9.2   Theoretical explanations of tie failure

Theory	Major contributors	Fundamental premise	Explanation of tie termination
Transaction Cost Economics	Williamson (1975, 1985); Hennart (1988); Oxley (1997, 1999)	Firms select governance structures on the costs incurred by characteristics of transactions. Minimising transaction costs, maximising economic efficiency	Higher uncertainty levels increase the likelihood of tie termination, due to the occurrence of contractual 'holes' and bounded rationality
Social Exchange Theory	Blau (1964); Gulati (1995); Das and Teng (2002)	Firms engage in socially bound exchanges to access and share resources. Social norms replace the need for formal governance, allowing for efficient resource transfer	Both low and high levels of trust and power abuse increase the likelihood of tie termination
Evolutionary Theory of Organisations	Burgelman (1983); Doz (1996); Koza and Lewin (1998); Nelson and Winter (1973)	Environments set the context for firms; ties evolve as firms interact with the environment	Initial conditions set the stage for the entire evolution of the tie. Imbalances between formal and informal processes increase the likelihood of tie termination
Organizational Learning Theory	Hamel (1991); Inkpen and Beamish (1997); Levitt and March (1988)	Learning leads to better performance. Learning abilities vary from firm to firm	Inter-organisational ties are breeding grounds of learning races, which create power imbalances and damage the tie

Source: Adaptation of Rahman (2006: 307).

A key concept within the learning perspective that has important implications for the functioning of inter-organisational relationships in general, and tie dissolution in particular, is the race to learn (Hamel, 1991). It is suggested that in inter-organisational relationships in which learning is the focus, firms often race to learn, because greater disparity in learning will lead to less dependence on a partner. Thus, an inter-organisational tie that is stable in the beginning of the collaboration may soon become unstable as a consequence of unequal learning outcomes for the respective partners. Inkpen and Beamish (1997) argue that unequal learning outcomes lead to a change in bargaining power, putting one of the partners in a dyad in a vulnerable position.

Khanna, Gulati and Nohria (1998) further specify the learning race argument, and propose that a distinction be made in this context between common benefits, which are benefits that can only be applied within the context of the tie, and private benefits, which are benefits that can be applied by one of the partners outside the context of the collaboration (see Lavie (2006) for a comparable argument). They suggest that organisations tend to acquire private benefits of learning first before realising common benefits of learning through the inter-organisational relationship. Consequently, a high private to common benefits ratio would add to the instability or risk of termination of inter-organisational ties.

Clearly, the learning perspective has a process view on tie instability and failure. Learning races between actors, which develop over time, create imbalances between actors that increase the likelihood of tie terminations. Although this is very similar to the evolutionary explanation, there is an important difference in the exclusive focus on learning and outcomes of learning. Moreover, note that over time, process instabilities generate tie failure, which is another variation within the context of tie failure.

The four theoretical approaches reviewed so far have helped to distinguish major factors and mechanisms influencing the termination of inter-organisational ties. These insights are summarised in Table 9.2 and will guide our understanding and framing of the results of the empirical research on tie failure discussed in the next section of this chapter.

TIE FAILURE: A SEARCH FOR EXPLANATORY FACTORS IN EMPIRICAL LITERATURE

While the previous section discussed explanations for tie failure put forward by four influential theoretical perspectives, this section concentrates on empirical studies dealing with failure among inter-organizational relationships. The aim of this part of the chapter is to present an overview of factors influencing tie failure as found in the empirical literature. To realise this aim, a limited literature search was performed using ABI Inform and the Web of Science as data sources and using (combinations of) 'collision', 'failure', 'dissolution', 'inter-organisational relationship(s)', 'tie(s)', 'alliance(s)' and 'joint venture(s)' as key words for our search activities. As was mentioned in a previous section, different studies use different definitions of tie failure. As this chapter aims to sketch a broad picture of the factors that, according to the literature, have an impact on different forms of tie failure, we do not distinguish between these different definitions in the following section.

From the definition of an inter-organisational relationship presented in the first section of this chapter, it follows that any such relationship encompasses at least three elements: organisations (collaborating actors) and their characteristics, interaction (transactions, flows and linkages), and an environment (e.g. market, sector, region, country). Here, we argue that (combinations) of the features of these three building blocks of inter-organisational relationships can contain sources of failure. An explanatory factor qualifies as an organisational feature when the specific feature still exists in the absence of an inter-organisational relationship. The size of one of the partners is a good example. An explanatory factor qualifies as a relational factor when the factor ceases to exist if an inter-organisational tie were terminated. The flow of resources between partners is a good example of this, as it is impossible for resources to flow between partners in the absence of a relationship. Lastly, a factor is labelled an environmental factor when it is out of the scope of influence of the collaborating parties, i.e., if a factor can be regarded as exogenous. A clear example of this is the cyclical development of an economy, which can have an impact on the outcomes of inter-organisational relationships, but, in most cases, cannot be influenced by them. Moreover, we tried to determine which theoretical approach informed the research presented in an empirical paper.

In Tables 9.3 to 9.5, we present the results of our literature search. We then briefly discussed the most eye-catching findings. The sources of failure are described in such a way that in all cases they increase the probability of tie failure.

Environmental Factors Influencing Tie Failure

Three of the five environmental factors presented in Table 9.3 refer to features of an economy. Beamish (1985) argues that collaborative efforts in the developing world are generally viewed as less stable compared to efforts in industrialised countries. The political uncertainties that often exist in such economies tend to have a negative impact on the stability of relationships. The paper is inspired by Harrigan's 'Dynamic model of joint venture activity', which basically argues that the external environment in part influences the initial configuration and the stability of a joint venture. Blodgett (1992) points at another dimension of an economy, namely, its level of openness. Her argument runs as follows: an unrestricted economy allows companies greater freedom to alter terms of agreements than is the case in economies that are characterised by high levels of restrictions. This greater freedom provides partners the latitude to engage in strategic breaching, which impedes partnership stability.

Table 9.3   Environmental factors influencing failure rates

Factor	Author(s)	Theoretically informed by	Impact on failure rates
State of development of an economy	Beamish (1985)	Although not explicitly stated, the paper takes an EP	Joint efforts in developing countries have higher failure rates.
Level of concentration in an industry	Kogut (1988)	TCT; SBP	Higher levels of industry concentration increase failure rates
Industry growth rates	Kogut (1989)	TCT.	High growth rates in an industry increase failure rates
Openness of an economy	Blodgett (1992)	No explicit theoretical perspective used	Collaborative efforts in an open economy have higher failure rates
Country risk	Meschi (2005)	TCT; ETO, RDT	A high level of economic risk in a country increases failure rates

Notes: TCT = Transaction cost theory; ETO = Evolutionary theory of organisations, SBP = Strategic behaviour theory; RDT = Resource dependence theory.

Kogut's (1989) assumption that high growth rates in an industry increase partnership failure rates is comparable to an argument found in the evolutionary theory of organisations. Given resource scarcity, higher growth rates in an industry imply that there is an increased competition for these resources. Since it is harder for partnerships to acquire the necessary resources, tie failure rates are higher. Interestingly, his findings argue for a shift away from viewing the transaction as a unit of analysis and towards viewing the whole relationship between partners.

Meschi's paper (2005) distinguishes between two sources of environmental uncertainty: political and economic risk. Political risk is seen as a country's governmental and institutional stability, its social situation, and its level of corruption, amongst others. Economic risk is indicated by a compound measure comprising of GDP per capita figures, the risk of non-payment of goods, loans and dividends, and debt indicators. It turned out that only the economic risk variable impacted on tie failure, that is, high levels of economic risk increased the likelihood of tie termination.

Organisational Features Influencing Tie Failure

The factors presented in Table 9.4 all represent features of organisations or organisational behaviours of (one of the) partners, which impact on the probability of a tie failure.

Table 9.4   Organisational features influencing failure rates

Factor	Author(s)	Theoretically informed by	Impact on failure rates
Partner is a competitor	Park and Russo (1996)	TCT	Direct competitors increase failure rates
Level of experience a partner has with collaboration	Park and Russo (1996); Zollo, Reuer and Singh (2002); Pangarkar (2003); Kale, Dyer and Singh (2002); Reuer and Zollo (2005)	TCT TCT, ETO Not clearly stated ETO, OLT TCT, ETO	Lower levels of past experience with collaboration increase failure rates
Size of one of the partners	Levinthal and Fichman (1988)	TCT, SET	Smaller size of partners increases failure rates
Bounded rationality of actors	Park and Russo (1996)	TCT	Higher levels of bounded rationality increase failure rates
Diversity of activities of one of the partners	Levinthal and Fichman (1988)	TCT, SET	Growth of the diversity of the activities of one of the partners increases failure rates
Political behaviour of one of the partners	Shenkar and Yan (2002)	Not explicitly stated, but qualifies as SET given the emphasis on political issues	Increase of political behaviour of one of the partners increases failure rates
Opportunistic behaviour of one of the partners	Gulati, Khanna, Nohria (1994) Park and Ungson (2001)	ETO, OLT Mainly TCT	Higher levels of opportunistic behaviour of one of the partners increases failure rates
Cultural background of the partners	Gill and Butler (2003)	Not explicitly stated, but qualifies as SET given the emphasis on trust, conflict and dependence	Higher levels of cultural distance between collaborating partners increase failure rates
Alliance capability	Kale, Dyer and Singh (2002)	ETO, OLT	The absence of a specific alliance function increases the likelihood of tie failure

Note: TCT = Transaction cost theory; SET = Social exchange theory; ETO = Evolutionary theory of organisation, OLT = Organisational learning theory.

Park and Russo (1996) state that coalitions between partners who are direct competitors have a higher probability of failure because parental goals often conflict directly. Together with Zollo, Reuer and Singh (2002), Pangarkar (2003), and Reuer and Zollo (2005), they also argue that a lack of past experience in collaborating with external partners is a potential pitfall. Past experience in collaboration (if it is regarded as positive) signals a positive reputation and the fulfilling of relation obligations in the past.

Moreover, Park and Russo (1996) theorise that bounded rationality and failure rate are connected. Given bounded rationality, it is impossible to contractually specify every possible contingency involved in managing the cooperative effort. Combined with higher levels of uncertainty, this increases failure rates. Although applied in a specific setting by Levinthal and Fichman (1988), namely in auditor–client relationships, one could argue that a growth in the diversity of the business activities of one of the partners impedes on the quality of the relationship, as there is a growing possibility that goal misalignment in the partnership will occur with growing diversity.

Furthermore, empirical research established a relationship between opportunistic behaviour and failure rate. Park and Ungson (2001) propose that ties fail because of opportunistic hazards when each partner tries to maximize his own individual interests instead of the collaborative interests.

Recently, a new body of literature has emerged pointing at the importance of the concept of alliance or collaborative capability (also see Chapter 4 by Sullivan et al., this volume) for the survival of inter-organisational ties (Kale et al., 2002; Draulans, De Man and Volberda, 2003). Alliance capability refers to the capabilities firms can develop over time to manage inter-organisational relationships. In their research, Kale et al. (2002) found that firms lacking a specific alliance function, which acts as a focal point for learning and is responsible for internal coordination, resource allocation, monitoring and evaluation of the tie, experience tie dissolution more often.

Relational Features Influencing Tie Failure

Table 9.5 describes features of relationships and the interaction between collaborating partners, which impact on the failure rates of ties. Killing (1983) argued that dominance of one partner in a relationship lends stability to the collaboration. There is growing empirical evidence (Beamish and Banks, 1987), however, that shared (equal) decision-making may in fact be a more stable arrangement. The reasoning is that unequal division of ownership, and thus of decision-making rights, gives the majority holder greater possibilities to dictate terms.

Blodgett (1992), as well as Arino and de la Torre (1998) and Reuer and Arino (2002), ascribe value to the idea that renegotiation of a collaborative arrangement, like many acts, is easier if it has been done before. On the basis of this theoretical idea, it is hypothesised that collaborations that have previously experienced renegotiation of collaborative terms will tend to be more unstable than ones that have not. Instability increases the probability of failure.

Table 9.5   Relational features influencing failure rates

Factor	Author(s)	Theoretically informed by	Impact on failure rates
Level of dominance in relationship	Killing (1983)	Unclear	Equality between partners in a relationship increases failure rates
Distribution of decision-making rights	Beamish and Banks (1987)	TCT	Unequal distribution of decision-making rights increases failure rates
Frequencies of renegotiations between partners in a relationship	Blodgett (1992) Arino and de la Torre (1998) Reuer and Arino (2002)	Unclear ETO TCT	Renegotiations of contract terms of a relationship increase failure rates
Organisational form of the relationship	Gomes-Casseres (1987) Bierly and Coombs (2004)	TCT TCT	Hybrid forms have a higher probability of failure; Equity based ties have a higher likelihood of tie termination
Level of (inter)depen-dency in a relationship	Park and Russo (1996) Gil and de la Fe (1999) Gill and Butler (2003)	TCT Unclear SET	Higher levels of (inter)dependencies between partners increase failure rates
Number of multiple ties in a relationship	Kogut (1989) Park and Russo (1996)	TCT TCT	Fewer multiple ties in a relationship increase failure rates
Level of trust	Levinthal and Fichman (1988) Baird, Lyles, Ji and Wharton (1990) Perry, Sangupta and Krapfel (2004) Gill and Butler (2003)	TCT, SET Unclear TCT, SET SET	Lower levels of trust in a relationship increase failure rates
Number of partners engaged in a collaborative effort	Park and Russo (1996)	TCT	Greater number of partners engaged increases failure rates
Task complexity	Levinthal and Fichman (1988)	TCT, SET	Higher levels of task complexity increase failure rates

Table 9.5   Relational features influencing failure rates (continued)

Factor	Author(s)	Theoretically informed by	Impact on failure rates
Level of relation-specific investment	Levinthal and Fichman (1988)	TCT, SET	Lower levels of relation-specific investments increase failure rates
Time dependency of relationships	Levinthal and Fichman (1998)	TCT, SET	An inverted U-shaped relationship between tie duration and tie failure. Same for product development stages
	Park and Russo (1996)	TCT	
	Bierly and Coombs (2004)		
		TCT	
Level of inter-organisational coordination	Park and Ungson (2001)	Mainly TCT	Higher costs of inter-organisational coordination increase failure rates
Level and direction of reinforcements in a relationship	Arino and de la Torre (1998)	ETO	Negative feedback and reinforcement between partners increase failure rates
Extent of alignment of partner strategies	O'Connor and Chalos (1999)	TCT	Lower levels of alignment of partner strategies increase failure rates
Management control structure between partners	Steensma and Lyles (2000)	SET, OLT	Imbalances in management control structure between partners increases failure
Support from (foreign) partners	Steensma and Lyles (2000)	SET, OLT	Lack of support from (foreign) partner increases failure
Presence of termination penalties	Perry, Sengupta and Krapfel (2004)	TCT, SET	Absence of termination penalties increases failure
Focus of the collaboration	Reuer and Zollo (2005)	TCT, EP	The less focused the collaboration, the higher the likelihood of tie failure
Density level	Amburgey and Al-Laham (2006)	ETO	High and low density levels increase the likelihood of tie failure for certain ties
Legitimacy building strategy of a network	Human and Provan (2000)	NI	An outside-in legitimacy building strategy increases failure rate

Note: TCT = Transaction cost theory; SET = Social exchange theory; ETO = Evolutionary theory of organisation; OLT = Organisational learning theory; NI = Neo institutional theory.

As to the pattern of interdependencies between partners in a relationship, Park and Russo (1996) discern two forms. In one form, the contributions to the collaboration by the partners are not integrated, but lie in a sequential path, as when one partner designs a product for the other to manufacture. In the other form of interdependence, the partners' contributions represent a pooling of their knowledge bases and competences, as when partners jointly develop and manufacture a new good. In neither situation do the interests of the collaborating partners necessarily match.

In the case of sequential interdependence, one partner's gain comes at the direct expense of the other partner. Integrative interdependence asks for ongoing (shared) decision-making between collaborative partners, especially if organizational complexity is greater. As a result, partners are guaranteed to clash on occasion. The most serious threat to partnerships in which integrative interdependencies are important is the chance that important know-how, such as knowledge about manufacturing processes and technologies will be leaking to or be appropriated by a partner. This know-how could subsequently be used to undermine the other's competitive advantages. Such a situation, if it should arise, would seriously impact on the probability of failure.

Researchers within both organizational theory and economics have discussed the importance of attachment or commitment between partners. A critical element of these discussions is that one or both partners are making substantial investments to facilitate and improve the effectiveness of the relationship. An important attribute of these investments is the extent to which they are unique to a particular relationship. Williamson (1975) further developed the implications of such relation-specific investments. He states that the attachment between partners is strengthened over time as the two collaborating partners invest in dedicated equipment and develop expertise specific to the organization's need. As relation-specific investments, by definition, lose (part of) their value when applied to other collaborations, parties become locked into their existing relationships. Contrarily, a lack of relation-specific investments by one or both partners signals lack of attachment or commitment, and therefore increases the failure rate of relationships.

There is ample empirical evidence suggesting a relationship between the duration of a relationship and its failure rate. The management of relationships does not end with the consummation of the collaboration, but needs to be viewed as an ongoing task. At the time of completion of a collaborative agreement, expectations for success held by the partners involved are the highest. From this phase onward, much information about the collaboration is released to the participating actors, and learning takes place. The balance of power may shift (Bleeke and Ernst, 1995). Assurance of reciprocal trust may be confirmed or may turn out to be false, as an initial stock of goodwill during this 'honeymoon period' (Levinthal and Fichman, 1988) is expended. Furthermore, outcomes of the collaboration could differ from what was expected at the start, leading to a wish to end the joint effort. For these reasons, scholars hypothesized that the failure rates of ties would initially increase with time. However, in the long run, the failure rates of collaborations are expected to decline. One reason for this is that the longer the inter-organisational relationship survives, the more established its organisation, momentum and legitimacy will become. Another reason could be that the initial levels of reservation and fear decline as the collaboration produces outcomes that are close to the initial expectations of the participating actors. In sum, with regard to the time dependency of relationships scholars (Levinthal and Fichman, 1988; Park and Russo, 1996) expect the failure rate to be non-monotonic, taking an inverted U-shape form. A comparable inverted U-shape relationship was evidenced in research by Bierly and Coombs (2004) in the context of product development. They found that ties are more likely to be terminated if they are initiated in the early and late stages of product development and less likely to be terminated if they are initiated in the mid-stages of product development.

Interesting case study work on the relationship between legitimacy building strategies and tie failure (on a network level) has been published by Human and Provan (2000). They distinguish between three dimensions of legitimacy – network as form, network as entity and network as interaction – and conclude that all three dimensions of legitimacy must be established if the network is to succeed. However, a strong and early inside-out emphasis (building legitimacy inside the network) is more likely to achieve success than an outside-in focus.

Recently, an interesting contribution to the discussion on tie failure was made by Amburgey and Al-Laham (2006). To begin with, these researchers specify different types of tie failure, namely, the failure of a tie that is (a) a bridging tie; (b) a pendant tie; (c) an intra-component tie, and (d) a dyad. Next, they relate these different types of tie failure to structural cohesion (density) of a network component and formulate a number of hypotheses, which can be summarised as follows: the higher the density level of a network component, the higher the likelihood of tie termination of a (a) bridging tie; (b) dyad; (c) pendant tie. However, the likelihood of so-called component thinning terminations increases with the number of intra-component ties. These hypotheses were tested with a longitudinal research design. The study included strategic R&D alliances of biotechnology in the US and Germany. With respect to the hypothesis on the termination of pendant ties, all hypotheses were empirically confirmed. These findings highlight the notion that dimensions of (or changes of) the network structure impact on tie termination rates.

CONCLUSIONS AND DISCUSSION

In this chapter we reviewed theoretical and empirical literature dealing with tie failure. Our investigations give rise to three general conclusions, which are discussed consecutively in this last section.

In the first part of the chapter, we presented four theoretical approaches relevant for the study of tie failure. Next, we reviewed empirical literature on factors explaining tie failure by using the theoretical framework applied in a given paper as one of our search criteria. From these reviews, we can conclude that the study of tie failure is by and large dominated by the empirical application of transaction cost theory. However, the question arises as to whether the transaction cost theory framework is really well-suited for studying alliance failure. Several scholars (Gulati, 1998; Human and Provan, 2000) have questioned its dominance and pointed at important shortcomings. First, the transaction cost framework treats each transaction as a discrete independent event, which leads to temporal reductionism because inter-organisational ties are seen in an a-historical context. Hence, the framework can be seen to use a static approach. Second, by taking the transaction as its unit of analysis (and not the economic relationship), the transaction cost approach 'ignores the possibility of a social structure resulting from repeated ties and the emergent processes resulting from prior interactions between partners that may alter their calculus when they are choosing contract in alliances' (Gulati, 1998: 303). A decrease in temporal reductionism would imply that for example structural and relational embeddedness would matter for the organisation of transactions. Trust-building, for example, is a process that develops over time between partners that cooperate through repeated ties. The level of trust developed could mitigate appropriation concerns and could lead to the implementation of less hierarchical and more flexible governance structures, decreasing the likelihood of tie failure in the process. Therefore, a dynamic extension of transaction cost theory (perhaps the evolutionary organisation theory could be helpful) would further increase its explanatory power.

Our review of empirical literature on the factors influencing the failures of ties revealed that scholars: (a) use different definitions of tie failure, and (b) propose a wide variety of possible failure factors, which can be categorised in three main groups (environmental, organisational and relational); (c) focus primarily on relational aspects influencing tie failure. This last finding is confirmed by Rahman (2006) and stresses the need to focus research on process indicators describing ongoing interactions between partners in collaborations over time. Therefore, we propose a more detailed analysis of failures in inter-organisational relationships, especially with regard to the question concerning different settings of habitual and relational behaviour collide. These aspects are often connected to (inter)organisational culture. The relationship between organisational culture and business performance is an important field of research (c.f. Hofstede, 1997). Recently, there appears to have been an increase in studies dealing with organisational proximity, which is commonly defined as networked actors whose interactions are facilitated by (explicit and implicit) rules and routines of behaviour and that share a same system of representations, or set of beliefs (Torre and Rallet, 2005; for an extensive discussion of the proximity concept see Knoben and Oerlemans, 2006). Organisational proximity is thought to facilitate dyadic and collective learning and the joint creation of new resources and innovation and can be regarded as an interesting field of research in which the insights of a different scientific field can be fruitfully combined.

A third conclusion is that the majority of studies dealing with tie failure take a dyadic perspective. A fruitful extension of this type of research would be to study the impact of the social or organisational network of these partnering firms on the relative performance of their alliances. Here, we can distinguish two avenues of future research. The first one focuses on relational embeddedness. An interesting question could be whether inter-organisational ties, such as alliances that are embedded to a greater or lesser degree in various networks, have a higher or lower likelihood of failure. After all, one can assume that ties which are more strongly embedded in networks benefit from higher trust and confidence levels and more intense flows of information and knowledge. These characteristics could lower the likelihood of tie failure. A second avenue could be to study the consequences of structural embeddedness. Firms in networks characterised by high centrality levels do not only have to manage their individual inter-organisational ties, but are basically confronted with the management of a portfolio of ties, which could have different strategic scopes. This raises a 'span of control' question: to what extent can ties that are part of a highly centralised network be managed by participating partners? Overstretching the network management capabilities of firms in such networks could impact negatively on relative tie performance. A third avenue of future research is a combination of relational and structural embeddedness. An interesting question could be the extent to which there is a different likelihood of tie failure for comparable ties in different networks. For example, the study of comparable ties in different geographic networks could add to the body of literature on tie failure.

We propose a detailed analysis of tie failure. Our systematic approach allows for such an analysis in the different phases of the life cycle of collaboration. Such an analysis would be helpful for understanding failure, and for avoiding failure, as well.

REFERENCES

Amburgey, T.L. and A. Al-Laham (2006), 'Islands in the net: Structural evolution of R&D networks in biotechnology', paper presented at the 22nd EGOS Colloquium, Standing Work Group Business Network, Bergen, Norway.

Anderson, E. (1990), 'Two firms, one frontier: On assessing joint venture performance', *Sloan Management Review*, **31** (2), 19-30.

Argyris, C. and D.A. Schon (1978), *Organizational Learning: A Theory of Action Perspective*, Reading MA: Addison-Wesley.

Arino, A. and J. de la Torre (1998), 'Learning from failure: Towards an evolutionary model of collaborative ventures', *Organization Science*, **9** (3), 306-325.

Arrow, K.W. (1974), *The Limits of Organization*, New York: Norton.

Baird, I.S., M.A. Lyles, S. Ji and R. Wharton (1990), 'Joint venture success: A Sino-U.S. perspective', *International Studies of Management and Organization*, **20** (1/2), 125-134.

Barney, J.B. (1996), 'The resource-based theory of the firm', *Organization Science*, **7** (5), 469.

Beamish, P.W. (1985), 'The characteristics of joint ventures in developed and developing countries', *Columbia Journal of World Business*, **20** (3), 13-19.

Beamish, P.W. and J.C. Banks (1987), 'Equity joint ventures and the theory of the multinational enterprise', *Journal of International Business Studies*, **18** (2), 1-16.

Bierly, P.E. and J.E. Coombs (2004), 'Equity alliances, stages of product development, and alliance stability', *Journal of Engineering and Technology Management*, **21** (3), 191-214.

Blau, P.M. (1964), *Exchange and Power in Social Life*, New York: Wiley.

Bleeke, J. and D. Ernst (1995), 'Is your strategic alliance really a sale?', *Harvard Business Review*, **73** (1), 97-105.

Blodgett, L.L. (1992), 'Factors in the instability of international joint ventures: An event history analysis', *Strategic Management Review*, **13** (6), 475-481.

Borgatti, S.P. and P.C. Foster (2003), 'The network paradigm in organizational research: A review and typology', *Journal of Management*, **29** (6), 991-1013.

Büchel, B. (2003), 'Managing partner relations in joint ventures', *Sloan Management Review*, **44** (4), 91-95.

Burgelman, R.A. (1983), 'A model of the interaction of strategic behavior, corporate context, and the concept of strategy', *Academy of Management Review*, **8** (1), 61-70.

Chen, H. and T. Chen (2002), 'Asymmetric strategic alliances: A network view', *Journal of Business Research*, **55** (12), 1007-1013.

Coopers and Lybrand (1986), *Collaborative Ventures: An Emerging Phenomenon in Information Technology*, New York: Coopers and Lybrand.

Das, T.K. and B. Teng (2002), 'Alliance constellations: A social exchange perspective', *Academy of Management Review*, **27** (3), 445-456.

Deeds, D.L. and F.T. Rothaermel (2003), 'Honeymoons and liabilities: The relationship between age and performance in research and development alliances', *Journal of Product Innovation Management*, **20** (6), 468-484.

Doz, Y.L. (1996), 'The evolution of cooperation in strategic alliances: Initial condition or learning processes', *Strategic Management Journal*, **17**, special issue, 55-83.

Draulans, J., A.-P. de Man and H.W. Volberda (2003), 'Building alliance capability: Management techniques for superior alliance performance', *Long Range Planning*, **36** (2), 151-166.

Emerson, M.R. (1962), 'Power-dependence relations', *American Sociological Review*, **27** (1), 31-41.

Emerson, M.R. (1976), 'Social exchange theory', *Annual Review of Sociology*, **2**, 335-362.

Fiol, C.M. and M.A. Lyles (1985), 'Organizational learning', *Academy of Management Review*, **10** (4), 803-813.

Gil, M.J.L. and P.G. de la Fe (1999), 'Strategic alliance, organisational learning and new product development: The cases of Rover and Seat', *R&D Management*, **29** (4), 391-404.

Gill, J. and R.J. Butler (2003), 'Managing instability in cross-cultural alliances', *Long Range Planning*, **36** (6), 543-563.

Gomes-Casseres, B. (1987), 'Joint venture instability: Is it a problem?', *Columbia Journal of World Business*, summer issue, 97-102.

Granovetter, M. (1985), 'Economic action and social structure: The problem of embeddedness', *American Journal of Sociology*, **91** (3), 481-510.

Gulati, R. (1995), 'Does familiarity breed trust? The implications of repeated ties in contractual choice in alliances', *Academy of Management Journal*, **38** (1), 85-112.

Gulati, R. (1998), 'Alliances and networks', *Strategic Management Journal*, **19** (4), 293-317.

Gulati, R., T. Khanna and N. Nohria (1994), 'Unilateral commitments and the importance of process in alliances', *Sloan Management Review*, **35** (3), 61-69.

Hamel, G. (1991), 'Competition for competence and inter-partner learning within international strategic alliances', *Strategic Management Journal*, **12**, special issue, 83-103.

Hannan, M.T. and J. Freeman (1977), 'The population ecology of organizations', *American Journal of Sociology*, **82** (5), 929-964.

Harrigan, K.R. (1984), 'Joint ventures and global strategies', *Columbia Journal of World Business*, **19** (2), 7-16.

Heide, J.B. (1994), 'Interorganizational governance in marketing channels', *Journal of Marketing*, **58** (1), 71-85.

Hennart, J.-F. (1988), 'The transaction costs theory of joint ventures: An empirical study of Japanese subsidiaries in the United States', *Management Science*, **37** (4), 483-497.

Hofstede, G. (1997), *Cultures and Organizations: Software of the Mind*, New York: McGraw-Hill.

Hollis, M. (1989), 'Honour among Thieves', British Academy Philosophical Lecture, *Proceedings of the British Academy*, **75**, 163-180.

Homans, G.C. (1958), 'Social behavior as exchange', *American Journal of Sociology*, **63** (6), 597-606.

Huber, G.P. (1991), 'Organizational learning: The contributing processes and the literatures', *Organization Science*, **2** (1), 88-115.

Human, S.E. and K.G. Provan (2000), 'Legitimacy building in the evolution of small firm multilateral networks: A comparative case study of success and demise', *Administrative Science Quarterly*, **45** (2), 327-365.

Inkpen, A.C. and P.W. Beamish (1997), 'Knowledge, bargaining power, and the instability of international joint ventures', *Academy of Management Review*, **22** (1), 177-202.

Kale, P., J.H. Dyer and H. Singh (2002), 'Alliance capability, stock market response, and long-term alliance success: The role of the alliance function', *Strategic Management Journal*, **23** (8), 747-767.

Khanna, T.R. Gulati and N. Nohria (1998), 'The dynamics of learning alliances: Competition, cooperation, and relative scope', *Strategic Management Journal*, **19** (3), 193-210.

Killing, J.P. (1983), *Strategies for Joint Venture Success*, New York: Praeger.

Kim, T-Y., H. Oh and A. Swaminathan (2006), 'Framing interorganizational network change: A network inertia perspective', *Academy of Management Review*, **31** (3), 704-720.

Klein-Woolthuis, R., B. Hillebrand and B. Nooteboom (2005), 'Trust, contract and relationship development', *Organization Studies*, **26** (6), 813-840.

Knoben, J. and L. Oerlemans (2006), 'Proximity and inter-organizational collaboration: A literature review', *International Journal of Management Reviews*, **8** (2), 71-89.

Kogut, B. (1988), 'Joint ventures: Theoretical and empirical perspectives', *Strategic Management Journal*, **9** (4), 319-332.

Kogut, B. (1989), 'The stability of joint ventures: Reciprocity and competitive rivalry', *Journal of Industrial Economics*, **38** (2), 183-198.

Koka, B.R., R. Madhavan and J.E. Prescott (2006), 'The evolution of interfirm networks: Environmental effects on patterns of network change', *Academy of Management Review*, **31** (3), 721-737.

Koza M.P. and A.Y. Lewin (1998), 'The co-evolution of strategic alliances', *Organization Science*, **9** (3), 255-264.

Kumar, R. and K.O. Nti (1998), 'Differential learning and interaction in alliance dynamics: A process and outcome discrepancy model', *Organization Science*, **9** (3), 356-367.

Kumar, R. and K.O. Nti (2004), 'National cultural values and the evolution of process and outcome discrepancies in international strategic alliances', *Journal of Applied Behavioral Science*, **40** (3), 344-361.

Lavie, D. (2006), 'The competitive advantage of interconnected firms: An extension of the resource-based view', *Academy of Management Review*, **31** (3), 638-658.

Levinthal, D. and M. Fichman (1988), 'Dynamics of inter-organizational attachments: Auditor-clients relationships', *Administrative Science Quarterly*, **33** (3), 345-369.

Levitt, B. and J.G. March (1988), 'Organizational learning', *Annual Review of Sociology*, **14**, 319-340.

Meschi, P.-X. (2005), 'Environmental uncertainty and survival of joint ventures: The case of political and economic risk in emerging countries', *European Management Review*, **2** (2), 143-152.

Nelson, R.R. and S.G. Winter (1973), 'Toward an evolutionary theory of economic capabilities', *The American Economic Review*, **63** (2), 440-449.

Nooteboom, B., H. Berger and N. Noorderhaven (1997), 'Effects of trust and governance on relational risk', *Academy of Management Journal*, **40** (2), 308-338.

O'Connor, N.G. and P. Chalos (1999), 'The challenge for successful joint venture management in China: Lessons from a failed joint venture', *Multinational Business Review*, **7** (1), 50-61.

Oliver, A.L. and M. Ebers (1998), 'Networking network studies: An analysis of conceptual configurations in the study of inter-organizational relationships', *Organization Studies*, **19** (4), 549-583.

Oxley, J.E. (1997), 'Appropriability hazards and governance in strategic alliances: A transaction cost approach', *Journal of Law, Economics & Organization*, **13** (2), 387-409.

Oxley, J.E. (1999), 'Institutional environment and the mechanisms of governance: The impact of intellectual property protection on the structure of inter-firm alliances', *Journal of Economic Behavior & Organization*, **38** (3), 283-309.

Pangarkar, N. (2003), 'Determinants of alliance duration in uncertain environments: The case of the biotechnology sector', *Long Range Planning*, **36** (3), 269-284.

Park, S.H. and M. Russo (1996), 'When competition eclipses cooperation: An event history analysis of joint venture failure', *Management Science*, **42** (6), 875-890.

Park, S.H. and G.R. Ungson (2001), 'Interfirm rivalry and managerial complexity: A conceptual framework of alliance failure', *Organization Science*, **12** (1), 37-53.

Perry, M.L., S. Sengupta and R. Krapfel (2004), 'Effectiveness of horizontal strategic alliances in technologically uncertain environments: Are trust and commitment enough?', *Journal of Business Research*, **57** (9), 951-956.

Rahman, N. (2006), 'Duality of alliance performance', *Journal of American Academy of Business*, **10** (1), 305-312.

Reuer, J.J. and A. Arino (2002), 'Contractual renegotiations in strategic alliances', *Journal of Management*, **28** (1), 47-68.

Reuer, J.J. and M. Zollo (2005), 'Termination outcomes of research alliances', *Research Policy*, **34** (1), 101-115.

Ring, P. and A. van de Ven (1994), 'Developmental processes of cooperative interorganizational relationships', *Academy of Management Review*, **19** (1), 90-118.

Shenkar, O. and A. Yan (2002), 'Failure as a consequence of partner politics: Learning from the life and death of an international cooperative venture', *Human Relations*, **55** (5), 565-602.

Steensma, H.K. and M.A. Lyles (2000), 'Explaining IJV survival in a transitional economy through social exchange and knowledge-based perspectives', *Strategic Management Journal*, **21** (8), 831-851.

Torre, A. and A. Rallet (2005), 'Proximity and localization', *Regional Studies*, **39** (1), 47-59.

Williamson, O.E. (1975), *Markets and Hierarchies*, New York: The Free Press.

Williamson, O.E. (1985), *The Economic Institutions of Capitalism: Firms, Markets, Relational Contracting*, New York: The Free Press.

Williamson, O.E. (1998), 'Transaction cost economics: How it works; where it is headed', *The Economist*, **146** (1), 23-58.

Zaheer, A., B. McEvily and V. Perrone (1998), 'Does trust matter? Exploring the effects of interorganizational and interpersonal trust on performance', *Organization Science*, **9** (2), 141-159.

Zineldin, M. and M. Dodourova (2005), 'Motivation, achievements and failure of strategic alliances: The case of Swedish auto-manufacturers in Russia', *European Business Review*, **17** (5), 460-470.

Zollo, M., J.J. Reuer and H. Singh (2002), 'Inter-organizational routines and performance in strategic alliances', *Organization Science*, **13** (6), 701-713.

10. Frame-based Intervention for Promoting Understanding in Multiparty Conflicts

Barbara Gray

INTRODUCTION

Multiparty collaboration has been championed as a useful and often necessary method of organising parties within a problem domain (Trist, 1983; Gray, 1989; Huxham and Macdonald, 1992). More and more examples of the utility of collaboration among for businesses, among not-for-profit and public sector organisations, and in cross-sectoral settings have been offered (Faulkner and de Rond, 2000; Wondolleck and Yaffee, 2000; Bouwen and Taillieu, 2004; Huxham and Vangen, 2005). These forms of organising arise because parties in multiparty contexts find themselves interdependent with others whose decisions affect the focal actors and vice versa. What this means is that no single party can take unilateral actions without generating ripple effects for the others, and, in order to accomplish their objectives, organisations need to form alliances with others.

Despite this interdependence, achieving collaborative outcomes is far from easy (Gray, 1995; Oerlemans, Gössling and Jansen, Chapter 9 in this volume). In many cases parties who might profit from reaching consensus on how to coordinate their activities hold vastly different interpretations of the issues about which they both are concerned (Lewicki, Gray and Elliott, 2003). These differing interpretations may have pitted the parties against one another in decision-making arenas and generated long-standing mistrust and even outright animosities among them (Bryan and Wondolleck, 2003; Gray, 2004; Jansen and Knoben, Chapter 11 in this volume). Even when parties agree on the need to pool their efforts, they frequently do not see eye-to-eye on the aims of the collaboration (Huxham and Vangen, 2005) or once they begin to work together, different interpretations about how to proceed may interfere with the smooth sailing of the collaboration (Gray, 1995; Bouwen, Craps and Santos, 1999; Oerlemans et al., Chapter 9 this volume).

The concept of framing has proven a useful tool for understanding why parties in multiparty arenas find themselves at odds with one another and have difficulty finding common ground. 'Framing refers to the process of constructing and representing our interpretations of the world around us. We construct frames by sorting and categorising our experience – weighing new information against our previous interpretations' (Gray, 2003: 12). Frames are both guides to and outcomes of sense-making processes (Goffman, 1974; Weick, 1995; Tannen, 1993). In the context of inter-organisational problem domains, parties use frames to make sense of their experiences and to locate themselves with respect to other actors in a particular domain. More specifically, framing involves developing 'interpretive schemas that bound and order a chaotic situation, facilitate interpretation and provide a guide for doing and acting' (Laws and Rein, 2003: 173).

In this chapter I will explore a variety of frame types that are likely to generate misunderstandings and interfere with attempts to build collaborative relationships in multiparty arenas. Additionally, I will consider how frame analysis can also create opportunities for reframing or for frame enlargement among the parties – processes which may increase civil dialogue among them and increase possibilities for collaborative action. I will describe several frame-based interventions including: (a) self-reflective frame exploration, (b) perspective taking exercises that encourage disputants to begin to hear (without judgment) the ways other disputants experience the conflict, and (c) rewriting of stereotypes. I explore the potential of these interventions for increasing the prospects for better understanding, civil dialogue and problem resolution among potential partners in multiparty arenas.

UNDERSTANDING FRAMES AND FRAMING

Frames are cognitive heuristics that enable us to bracket and catalogue our experiences of the world (Bartlett, 1932), directing our attention to some stimuli and drawing inferences about their meaning. When we frame something, we put it in perspective by relating it to other information that we already 'know'. Thus, parties can encounter the same facts or engage in the same experience but make sense of it differently because they attend to different data and interpret it through the filter of their own past experiences. Framing refers to the representational process of presenting or expressing how we make sense of things. It involves 'imparting meaning and significance to elements within the frame and setting them apart from what is outside the frame' (Buechler, 2000: 41). In multiparty domains, parties develop interpretations about the issues under consideration, about how and why they are interdependent and about how they are currently interacting and might interact in the future to deal with the domain issues.

In addition to being a sensemaking process that helps us to understand and interpret a set of issues, framing also enables us to locate ourselves with respect to those issues. Through framing, we place ourselves in relation to the issues or events thereby taking a stance with respect to them (Taylor, 2000) and placing ourselves in concert with or in opposition to other parties. This stance-taking process involves making attributions about how and why events have occurred (i.e. causality) and who is responsible (i.e. acknowledging or blaming). 'A frame reflects our interpretation of what is going on and how we see ourselves and others implicated in what is happening' (Gray, 2003: 12). With respect to their framing of each other, one party may view the other as extremely powerful in controlling vital resources that affect the ability of their organisation to meet its strategic objectives. Consequently they may frame the other as a potential supporter or blocker, depending on how they respond to actions initiated by the former. For example, Monsanto Corporation frames the introduction of genetically engineered soybeans into Europe as a legitimate business objective while French farmers and environmental advocates such as Greenpeace frame this action as a threat to their future economic viability and as a destroyer of biodiversity respectively. In the eyes of Monsanto, these other two groups are framed as blockers.

At the collective level of the domain, how parties frame the issues that link them to one another and how they frame each other's behaviour affects the ease with which they can construct a common interpretation of the domain around which to collaborate. Thus, framing contributes to whether there is conflict within the domain, why it occurs, and whether and how it can be settled (Lewicki et al., 2003) and whether the parties learn from each other (Bouwen and Taillieu, 2004).

Numerous definitions of frames have been provided by researchers in cognitive psychology, microsociology and sociolinguistics. Research on framing has been conducted at several different levels of analysis – on individual decision frames (e.g. Kahneman and Tversky, 1978), on negotiations between individuals (e.g. Donnellon and Gray, 1990; Pinkley and Northcraft, 1994), and on the intergroup and the societal level (e.g. Snow, Rockford, Benford and Worden, 1986; Schön and Rein, 1994; Taylor, 2000). Frame analysis is a common technique used by researchers studying public policy conflicts (Creed, Langstraat and Scully, 2002; Schön and Rein 1994; Lewicki et al., 2003) and social movements (Benford and Snow

2000).[1] I explore two distinctly different conceptions of frames here: a cognitive perspective and a sociolinguistic one.

Cognitive psychologists view frames as cognitive structures in our memory (Bartlett, 1932) that help us organise and interpret new experiences (Minsky, 1975). In this view, frames are relatively static entities; they are retrieved from memory to guide interpretation of new experiences. The choice of which frame to adopt in a given situation depends on the cues that others in an interaction send as well as on one's own repertoire of memories (Bateson, 1972; Van Dijk, 1977).

The sociolinguistic perspective on frames suggests that they are social constructions – that is, they represent agreed-upon 'ways to make sense of a situation' (Tannen, 1979). When two or more people define a situation the same way, we say they are socially constructing it. Most definitions of frames generally share the fundamental assumption that they are like road maps that help us organise our knowledge and to sort and predict the meaning of new information, events and experiences (ibid.). Sociolinguistics claim that frames are created when people engage in conversation (Dore and McDermott, 1982; Donnellon and Gray, 1990) and that disputants use conversations to test to see if one's interpretations are compatible with those of others. From the sociolinguistic perspective, frames reveal how speakers organise what is going on in the midst of an interaction and can be recreated through conversation (ibid.; Putnam and Holmer, 1992). Frames help us decipher what someone means at any point in a conversation as well as which points are important, which are not Gumperz (1982) and the extent of overlap in the parties' frames.

Framing is not only a sensemaking process (Weick, 1995) but also a discursive, or sensegiving one (Gioia and Chittipeddi, 1991). That is, social movement actors construct collective action frames to diagnose a problem as well as to articulate appropriate actions to remedy it (Benford and Snow, 2000). Framing is also used mobilise adherents (ibid.). Thus we use framing to try to persuade others to adopt the frames that make sense to us. This discursive use of framing influences how problems are constructed, how blame are injustice are attributed, and how stakeholders are recruited to take retributive action to right what they perceive as wrongs (ibid.).

FRAMING AFFECTS IN MULTIPARTY DOMAINS

Framing plays an important role in the creation, evolution and perpetuation of multiparty conflict and collaboration. Frames are used (a) to define issues; (b) to shape what action should be taken and by whom, (c) to protect one's self and characterise others, (d) to justify a stance we take on an issue, and (e) to mobilise people to take or refrain from action on issues (Gray, 2003). In this section, I describe the roles that frames play in domains and identify a number of specific types of frames that can shape domain dynamics.

Framing to Define Issues

Huxham and Vangen (2005) note that, despite agreements to try to collaborate, partners often differ on their aims for the collaboration. I argue that these differential aims stem from how the partners frame issues, and the extent of overlap in their framing determines whether or not the domain is seen as conflictual. One area in which these differences in framing abound is in how people view environmental hazards and whether or not they pose health risks for the community. Risk frames can influence the level of conflict in multiparty domains. For example, partners interested in energy use may frame the risks associated with the use of various energy sources differently (Otway, Maurer and Thomas, 1978; Vaughan and Siefert, 1992) and consequently, their preferred solutions also differ. Consider the following example (Gray, 2003: 12-13):

> In the year following the accident at the Three Mile Island nuclear power plant, technical experts from the utility and some citizens held different frames about the risks associated with cleaning up the reactor. The utility was eager to release the radioactive krypton gas remaining in the crippled reactor in order to reduce any threat of a further catastrophic accident. Local citizens, on the other hand, were worried about potential health effects from releasing the krypton into the atmosphere. Each framed the potential risk differently.

This data is consistent with previous research on the risks associated with nuclear power: people who favour nuclear power tend to frame the issues in terms of economic and technical benefits while opponents focus primarily on psychological risks (Otway et al., 1978). Technical and lay populations also frequently hold differential risk frames with the former stressing prediction and prevention of risks and the latter concerned about risk detection and repairing remediation (Elliott, 1988). Differential risk frames are at the heart of many environmental conflicts (c.f., Hanke, Rosenberg and Gray, 2003; Elliott, 2003) and can impede even well-intended motivations to search for collaborative solutions to these conflicts (Lewicki et al., 2003).

Perceptions of fairness also influence how partners' frame domain issues that translate into entitlement claims. That is, when disputants perceive they are deprived of something they deserve or are entitled to, they may evoke a justice frame to represent their grievance. Justice frames are evoked to redress perceptions of unfairness and/or to prevent injustice from occurring.

This can be seen in negotiations among international alliance partners who often run into roadblocks when agreeing on the extent of technology transfer that should accrue to foreign partners. Justice frames are often anchored in differing conceptions of rights (Ury, Brett and Goldberg, 1993) and conflicting legal tenants. For example, competing claims to water rights emanate from tribal versus state law making it difficult for parties to find common ground on how water rights should be allocated (Folk-Williams, 1988). Tribal law links water rights to aboriginal possession and preservation of tribal sovereignty whereas state laws often favour property rights. The environmental justice movement illustrates another example of entitlement claims rooted in fairness frames. Proponents of this movement seek redress for disproportionate exposure to toxic materials and their attendant negative health effects because many plants that produced these poisonous by-products were located in African American communities in the United States (Bullard and Wright, 1989; Bullard, 1990; Taylor, 2000). Justice frames are often linked to perceptions of fundamental rights as in the case of Native American water rights above. This often renders them intractable (Lewicki et al., 2003; Hilgartner, 1985) because disputes over 'rights' are more positional than disputes over 'interests' and are more likely to lead to escalation of conflict (Ury et al., 1993). Unless potential partners can accept and understand the importance of each other's frames to their sense of safety and identity, domain collaboration may be impossible.

Framing to Shape Actions

Closely associated with how parties frame the issues are their preferences for whether and how they prefer that the resultant conflict should be resolved (Merry and Silbey, 1984; Sheppard, Blumenfeld-Jones and Roth, 1989; Vaughan and Siefert, 1992). For example, as noted earlier, in conflicts over the risks associated with toxic pollution, if parties frame a problem from a technical perspective, they may prefer to develop an accurate cost/benefit analysis of technical alternatives before taking any action and then base their action on this analysis. In contrast, parties who frame the issue as a health risk may champion immediate protection from the risk no matter what the cost. Additionally, parties who frame issues in terms of zero tolerance for risk or refuse to frame life in terms of cost/benefit analyses may find it difficult to join a collaborative table seeking to define 'acceptable' risks (Hanke et al., 2003).

Table 10.1 Conflict management frames

Frame Type	Definition	Example
Avoidance/ Passivity	Statements that give a preference for doing nothing, letting the matter rest, inertia, no action	
Fact Finding	Recommendations for investigation, collecting more information and facts, conducting research on the problem.	But I think you need to know that we have presented the facts of this incineration project, the actual data we've collected. We have been very forthcoming and open with the entire community
Joint Problem Solving	Statements that prefer community or joint action, common ground, mediation, collaboration and collective processes	I'd really prefer to get everyone to sit down and talk this thing out. We're all reasonable people
Authority Decides Based on Expertise	Local authorities, agencies, or institutions or boards make the decision because they have the technical knowledge and expertise	As a matter of fact there are fights within EPA over some of these issues and then somebody has to decide. It's just like anything else. So, but then in the end, you have to weigh the pros and cans and all of the points of view
Adjudication	Statements that imply that a third party should decide, such as an arbitrator, the courts, judges, or judicial authority	The only chance we have...is the courts. And there's some of us that feel that the only way the issues will be resolved is through litigation
Appeal to Political Action	Recommendation to handle the problem through enacting, abolishing or laws and regulations. Addressing the conflict through lobbying, referendums, supporting candidates, and legislative actions. Appeals to state or federal agencies to enact, change or abolish laws	We used to write letters to everyone and now we know who to target. We know who has the power. The power starts at Congressman and ends at President. They're the only ones who are going to make any difference for us at this point. We don't waste our time very much any more with (name of State)
Appeal to Market Economy	Negotiation of water rights, market solutions, economic and system changes	We should develop an incentive system that would encourage some users to sell their water to others
Struggle, Sabotage & Violence	Statements that refer to continued fighting, civil disobedience, force, etc.	If necessary, we will engage in civil disobedience to get out point across
Other Conflict Management Modes	Statements that recommend decisions based on 'common sense', all other approaches that do not fit into the categories above	This conflict would have been solved years ago if they would have just used common sense

Source: Gray (2003).

Conflict management frames deal with parties' preferences for how the conflict should be managed or dealt with (Lewicki et al., 2003). Early work on conflict frames (Sheppard et al., 1989) classified four frames that informal third parties use to decide what strategy to use to address a dispute. Subsequently, other researchers coded disputants' frames as cooperative or competitive. More recently, Lewicki et al. (2003) suggested nine options that disputants in environmental and public policy conflicts considered. Like Keltner's (1994) struggle spectrum, Lewicki et al.'s conflict management frame types ranged along a spectrum from the least active (avoidance, passivity) to the most active (struggle, sabotage and violence). See Table 10.1 for the complete list of conflict management frames.

When several potential partners have *joint problem solving frames* this affords the greatest chance that collaboration will ensue. To initiate a collaborative forum a convener or at least one or more parties with a vision that collaboration is possible are needed to bring others to the table (Gray, 1989; Carlson, 1999). These visionaries initiate what Vickers (1965) calls the appreciative work within the domain – recognising and pointing out the interdependencies among the stakeholders and helping them to imagine the potential gains from exploring whether and how they could join forces (Gray, 2007).

When potential partners have different conflict management frames, without the help of a third party, it is more difficult for them to find a way to begin a collaborative process. For example, if one group prefers joint problem solving, while another prefers adjudication, it may be difficult for them to sit down to negotiate a resolution unless the latter temporarily suspends the litigation. If both prefer adjudication, however, or appeal to political action, the conflict is likely to simmer or even escalate depending on what happens in other decision-making arenas (e.g., the courts or the political arena).

Framing to Protect Core Identities

Another important dynamic that occurs frequently in inter-organisational domains relates to partners' identities. To the extent that parties cherish their memberships in particular groups, *identity framing* may either help or hinder the formation and success of collaborative initiatives. Social identity is the self-image that is created and maintained via social category membership (Tajfel and Turner, 1985; Hogg, Terry and White, 1995). Identities of social groups are constructed through social comparison processes with other groups and often in opposition to the identity of another group (Tajfel and Turner, 1985; Snow and Benford, 1992). Such intergroup comparisons highlight differences between the groups and similarities within one's own group and stimulate judgments of superiority about one's own group (Tajfel and Turner, 1985). Consequently, groups develop reflexive frames that typically convey positive views about themselves and projective identity frames that usually carry negative characterisations of other groups. Identities that become salient in multiparty contexts are associated with demographic characteristics, but also locations (e.g. where they are from or where they live or work), roles (e.g. as a carpenter or social reformer), institutions with which parties' associate (e.g. a federal government employee), or interests (e.g. whether they support capital punishment or not) (Kusel, Doak, Carpenter and Sturtevant, 1996).

When partners disagree with each other over substantive issues, these disagreements can easily bleed over to become identity conflicts when one group's stance poses a challenge to the legitimacy of another group's beliefs and values or right to act. And when groups perceive threats to their identity, conflicts intensify (Rothman, 1997). Social movement groups entice new members to join by heightening their awareness of injustices done to their identity group by other groups (Benford and Snow, 2000). Identity challenges call into question the legitimacy of how a group has defined itself and even its very right to exist (Kelman, 1999).

> Thus identity strength and identity salience may be crucial factors in heightening a dispute's intractability because they narrow their latitude of acceptance of alternatives (McAdam and Paulsen, 1993: 146). The more that one perceives a direct threat to an identity to which they are strongly committed, the more they are likely to resist compromise proposals (Gray, 2003: 23).

When parties believe that what are at stake are the essential beliefs and values that define who they are, they develop strong defensive reactions that fuel the conflict (Northrup, 1989; Rothman, 1997). For example, an attempt at collaboration over the future of a US national park was unsuccessful, in part, because many local residents believed that the environmental policies of the park threatened their livelihoods (from logging and resource extraction) and personal freedom to use land as they chose (Gray, 2004).

Just as differing identities can build walls among potential collaborators, similar identities can tear them down. An example of this occurred in a particularly intractable conflict between a large Canadian logging company (MacMillan Bloedell) and environmentalists who opposed the firm's logging practices. The dispute was stalemated until the two lead attorneys met unexpectedly while walking their babies in the park one day and discovered their common identity as young mothers. This common identity frame enabled them to revisit the conflict with less antagonism and eventually craft a mutually agreeable solution (Lawrence and Svendsen, 2002).

Framing to Justify Their Actions, Motivate Recruits and Blame Enemies

The role of framing in social movement formation has been considered extensively (e.g. in the environmental and social justice movements). Framing occurs in two ways. First, participants in social movements use framing in 'interpretive' ways to collectively formulate their grievance (Buechler, 2000: 41). In other words, framing plays a significant role in creating a common cause, mission or vision among participants, and a common perception of the enemy. Second, participants in social movements use framing in 'intentional' ways to 'ripen' movement issues so as influence others' actions with regard to the issues (Heifetz, 1994). Martin Luther King's famous 'I have a dream' speech, for example, framed a vision that gave meaning and action to members of the civil rights movement. It was also designed to ripen the issue of civil rights as a social justice issue in larger society. The speech was designed to increase the prospects for social change by mobilising actors, both inside and outside of the movement. The original 'Earth Day' celebration was intentionally designed to cement a vision for the environmental movement itself and as a way to heighten awareness of injustices against the environment.

The more an individual's social identity is framed as a group identity, the greater will be the motivation for parties to adopt stereotypical labels for members of other groups to which they do not belong (Tajfel and Turner, 1979). Consequently, parties adopt *characterisation frames*, typically derogatory ones, about how they understand other groups to be. 'Characterisations frames arise from the attributions of blame and causality that we make about our experiences and about what others have done to shape our experience' (Gray, 2003: 23). The 'fundamental attribution error accounts for this characterisation process because we justify our own behaviour as "correct" or "good" and tend to blame others, or situational factors, for our fate, while attributing others' failures to their agency (Ross, 1977).

Framing Who Has Power and Who Should Solve Domain Problems

Struggles for power are often at the root of intractable conflicts, particularly those involving multiple parties (Gray 1989; Hardy and Philips, 1998). Researchers studying collaboration point out that power differences among potential collaborators can inhibit successful collaboration (Gray, 1989; Huxham and Vangen, 2005; Menkel-Meadow, 2001). Adopting a discursive perspective on power, I argue that partners adopt power frames in which they construct themselves as more or less powerful vis-à-vis other partners. Depending on these constructions, they then enact strategies to influence, and hopefully, control the discourse within the domain (Philips and Hardy, 1998). Gray (2003) identified seven types of power frames in interviews with disputants they interviewed: gaining authority, voice, resources, or sympathy, or building a coalition, using force or moral authority (see Table 10.2). An analysis of four intractable natural resource disputes, showed that framing the dispute in terms of power (e.g.) was a dominant lens adopted by a wide array of disputants (Brummans, Putnam, Gray, Hanke, Lewicki and Wiethoff, 2005) and was particularly strong among environmentalists. Evidence from a case about Voyageurs National Park suggests that extensive use of power framing by many stakeholders within a domain mediates against finding collaborative solutions to domain problems.

> Disputants on all sides of the conflict resorted to political strategies. Park opponents forced federal Congressional hearings in an attempt to decommission the park and relied on numerous forms of social protest to oppose park decisions. The Park Service, allied with environmental groups, countered with coalition-building strategies of their own. Some park opponents even charged that the federal mediation effort (described above) was a political ploy initiated by Senator Paul Wellstone to prevent him from having to take a public stand on the Voyageurs case and another hotly contested conflict over the Boundary Waters Canoe Area (Gray, 2005: 207).

Social control frames represent a final frame type identified by Gray (2003). Based on an earlier conceptualisation of worldviews introduced by Wildavsky and Dake (1990), social control frames capture parties' expectations about how social decisions should be made. Parties adopt individualist frames when they expect to exert a high degree of ownership over decisions and believe they can act independently of others. In contrast to individualists who want the freedom to decide their own affairs, these are fatalists who believe they are victims of others' decisions and can exert little control over their own affairs. Parties who envision all groups as having a large measure of collective control over societal decisions are said to adopt egalitarian frames. This contrasts with the hierarchist frame – one that holds that those with technical expertise should be authorised to make decisions for other societal actors.

When potential partners all subscribe to egalitarian social control frames, organising a multi-stakeholder collaboration should be relatively easy because each group believes it should play a role in deciding the domain's future. Parties with hierarchist frames would push hard for government technocrats to handle domain decision-making, while individualists would be wary of collaborative processes that could curtail their freedom to act as they see fit, and fatalists would likely have opted out under the premise they had no influence from the start.

Table 10.2   Power frames

Frame Type	Definition	Example
Authority/ Positional	Actual ability to make decisions on the basis of formal role assignment, job title/description, or organisational position	I mean he had the power because he was the ranking member of the transportation committee. He had the power to basically just push through whatever he wanted
Resources	Have power because of resources (e.g., time, support staff, money) that others do not possess	It all comes down to the golden rule again. Those who got the gold make the rules
Expertise	Possess relevant or unique knowledge and experience that others do not have	He is influential because he knows a lot about the technical issues in the case
Personal	An individual's interpersonal style gives them credibility and power in interaction (e.g. charisma, competent communication skills, negotiation experience etc.)	I think that if we would have had somebody like Dave from the beginning it probably would have been really good, because Dave is a powerful and capable person
Coalitional/ Relational	Power comes from membership in and/or affiliation with a particular group of people who support that individual's point of view	They know how to rally the numbers just like the NRA Association can put their people, whether it's right or wrong
Sympathy/ Vulnerability	Power comes from the victim role because victims' situation is likely to be supported by others on an emotional level (e.g., children, endangered species)	They've used it to get their way, and after a while they either just did not come back to the table or they would come back and just be angry and mad for the rest of the day, like a small child would be, because they didn't get their way
Force/Threat	Power comes from coercion from a party's threat to use their Best Alternative to a Negotiated Agreement (e.g. to sue another)	When the government came in to possess the land ... There were some threats and some intimidations that were made
Moral/ Righteous	Have power because position is on the 'moral high ground' or believe themselves to be ethically or morally 'right'	He's usually not in big trouble when he runs for re-election. But, if he took on the moral high ground, he stands a terrible risk of really pissing off people who have very deeply held beliefs
Voice	Have power because they have a forum in which to be heard, a 'voice at the table' in this dispute. Power comes from participation, from having the ability to communicate one's own views	Whatever type of board that is set up, I want a seat at the table

Source: Gray (2003).

Framing Winning or Losing

A final type of frame that potential collaborators might adopt is what Gray (2003) refers to as *loss/gain frames*. In reflecting on the domain dynamics potential collaborators make assessments whether they are winning or losing in their interactions with other parties. If parties conclude they are profiting from the current organisation of the domain, they will have little motivation to respond favourably to a call for collaboration. On the other hand, those who frame the status quo in terms of a loss may view collaboration as a hopeful prospect. In situations known as hurting stalemates (Zartman, 1981), conflicting parties each frame their interactions negatively and believe that cessation of hostilities would be preferable to the status quo. While potential collaborators may not need to terminate hostility in order to join forces, framing this step as an improvement over current dynamics provides the best impetus for launching a collaborative initiative.

REFRAMING

When partners develop a new way of interpreting the issues in a domain or revise their appraisal of their partners, this is called reframing. Reframing requires some degree of perspective taking – that is, standing back, observing and reflecting on other ways to view the issues and either shifting to a new interpretation or at least entertaining an alternative one. I call the latter process 'enlarging one's framing' because it involves entertaining the idea that there may be more than one way to interpret the situation. As Schön and Rein (1994: 171) observe, reframing 'depends on the ability of at least some of the actors to inquire into the intentions and meanings of other actors involved with them in the controversy'.As long as parties believe that their own view is the only possible one to understand the issues in dispute, they cannot reframe. However, once they realise that one's own vantage point on a situation influences how it gets framed, they may be willing to entertain other possible frames and consider the merits of each.

It is important to note here that how one conceptualises reframing depends on whether you start with a cognitive or sociolinguistic approach to framing (Dewulf, Gray, Putnam, Aarts, Lewicki, Bouwen and Van Woerkum, 2004). Reframing in the cognitive tradition is analogous to replacing a lens or to changing the relationship between what is figure and what is ground in an image. Reframing is more like replacing one lens in the brain with another one in the face of discrepant information. For example, one's understanding of what the key issue is in a dispute can shift when new information is presented. One may shift from viewing the situation as an employment dispute to reframing it an interpersonal one. Here, the focus is on what changes in how a party is thinking about an issue (Putnam and Holmer, 1992). From a sociolinguistic perspective, the reframing can occur in a number of ways. Here the reframing focuses on the nature of how the parties are interacting through talk. The conversation may be reframed from an adversarial orientation in which the parties are making polarising statements to a problem solving one in which they are jointly looking for (ibid.: 2004). Thus, reframing can occur in both the content of one's sensemaking and in the process of how the parties are interacting (ibid.). We consider both possibilities further below.

When potential partners frames diverge, it is unusual for them to revise their interpretations of others or of the issues on their own without provocation although there are several good examples of conflicting parties 'seeing the light' about the need for collaboration after engaging in protracted conflict. This occurred when the Quincy Library group was formed in 1992 at the urging of three long-time adversaries, a township supervisor, a forester and an environmentalist who represented local government, the timber industry and an environmental group respectively. 'The three men were all concerned about effects on the local economy of sharp declines in timber harvests on the Plumas National Forest, which virtually surrounds the town of Quincy (CA)' (Bryan and Wondolleck, 2003: 64). In the interest of saving the local economy and promoting sustainable forestry, they proposed a collaborative roundtable discussion which eventually generated a new approach for timber harvesting. A similar case, the National Coal Policy Project, in which coal producers and environmentalists forged a collaborative agreement was also launched by two long-time adversaries (Gray and Hay, 1986).

When reframing induces parties to seek new avenues for improving their interaction, we see a shift from micro- to meso-level dynamics in organisations fields. Framing and reframing in a collaborative setting can be understood as providing a link between these two levels. Reframing is, on the one hand, an individual activity/process in which a party cognitively re-appreciates the context and their interaction with others and comes to see it in a new light. At the same time, framing and reframing are also promoted collectively. As parties begin to confronting their differing frames in a collaborative or a conflict setting, they are also constructing a meso or multiparty level interpretation of the situation (Dewulf, 2006). Further, as they interact with one another, their talk either continually reinforces or reshapes this meso-level framing.

While conflicting parties may be able to promote constructive reframing for themselves more frequently, reframing is fostered through the intervention of a third party neutral. According to the contact hypothesis (Amir, 1994), if groups in conflict interact in quality ways, they increase the possibility that parties will revise their negative stereotypes about each other. Explicit intervention by third parties can help structure collaborative dialogue in ways to promote quality interactions (Gray, 1989). Descriptions of the role of mediators, for example, explicitly describe their roles as framing the issues for the parties and helping the parties to reframe the issues in ways that facilitate resolution (Moore, 1986; Lam, Rifkin and Townley, 1989). Third parties help disputants reformulate their positional statements in terms of interests (Fisher, Ury and Patton, 1991) and try to de-emphasise blaming and encourage listening. They help parties to develop social accounts of the dispute that legitimise the framing of all involved (Gray, 2005). Several techniques used in negotiations, such as logrolling and finding a bridge solution, can also be used to construct integrative agreements (Lewicki, Saunders and Minton, 1999). Other approaches to reframing include interpreting a counterpart's tactic in a different light or directly renegotiating the rules of the game being played (Lewicki et al., 1999), searching for superordinate goals to which all parties can subscribe (Sherif, 1958), and narrowing of the issues so that the parties address only a subset of the issues under contention (Moore, 1986). For particularly intractable disputes in which parties are unwilling to attempt collaboration, however, interventions based on knowledge of frames may still prove useful, and third parties who function as conveners (Gray, 1989; Carlson, 1999) may be able to bring the requisite neutrality, credibility and clout to entice parties to try frame-based interventions when mediation is clearly premature. In the next section, I describe some of these interventions based on frame analysis.

FRAME-BASED INTERVENTIONS

Frame-based interventions offer some distinct advantages for increasing mutual understanding or improving parties' interactions short of launching a full-scale collaboration. First, using frame analysis, parties can improve their understanding of the where and why their views about the domain converge and diverge with others. Because of their tendencies for stereotyping and selective listening (Osgood, 1983), parties frequently have mistaken conceptions of how the others construe domain issues. Second, frame-based interventions designed to respect identity differences and acknowledge all disputants' voices may offer opportunities for a trial dialogue among them in which they learn about each other's frames without promising to forge a 'solution' to domain conflict. They simply create an opening in which parties can listen, explore and reconsider their own framing.

Frame-Based Conflict Assessment

The objectives of traditional conflict assessment processes used in anticipation of consensus-building, are to help third party neutrals to: (a) understand the history and background of the conflict, (b) determine the relevant parties and their power relationships, (c) glean the positions, and, more importantly, the interests and BATNAs of the parties, and (d) diagnose whether or not a consensus-building process is feasible (Gray, 2005). However, when parties are unwilling to agree to collaboration, they still may agree to be interviewed by a third party and attend a meeting in which the third party maps the frame conflicts that emerge from the interviews for all those concerned about the problem. This frame-based conflict assessment can offer all parties a different lens or lenses for construing the issues, each other and the barriers among them and help them to garner a more realistic view of other parties' than their own data collection provides. Other methods besides interviews and report out, such as a modified search conference (Emery and Purser, 1996) or cognitive mapping techniques (Bryson and Finn, 1995) might also be possible.

Interveners using frame-based assessment could focus on a few of the frame types described earlier, selecting those that seemed most salient for the situation. Depending on the nature of the dispute, there may also be other content-oriented frames (e.g. about nature, health, education, social service delivery, information technology) that are pertinent and critical to the specific domain. Frame-based conflict assessment should provide a richer understanding of the factors inhibiting the parties from collaborating and may motivate the potential partners to undertake other pre-collaboration steps to explore their differences. Interveners should try to map the patterns of frames held by parties, the overlaps among them, and to assess the tenacity with which they adhere to these frames. Although these approaches fall short of collaboration because the parties are not ready or willing to reframe their differences, they are intended to make more modest gains in improving relations among the parties. They create opportunities for the disputants to investigate, 'try on', and enlarge their own and others' frames about the conflict while honouring the disputants' own framing and not requiring them to abandon or reframe their existing interpretations. The latter point is important because minimising any threats or challenges to the disputants' own framing while inviting them to try on more expansive frames may introduce doubts about their convictions while building trust among the parties.

Table 10.3   Frame-based options for intervening

Type of Intervention	Level	Purpose(s)	Brief Description
Listening Dyads (Triads)	Intergroup	1. Teach Perspective-taking 2. Encourage participants to enlarge frames 3. Envision a joint future	1. Jot down your whole story frame (WSF) for the conflict 2. Pair up with someone you don't know 3. Spend 5 minutes sharing with them your WSF 4. Listen carefully to their WSF 5. Try not to convince the other that yours is 'right'. If the group seems ready, have them continue 6. Write a joint story that incorporates key concerns of each of you 7. Pair up with someone else 8. Tell them the joint story you created with your 1st partner
Getting Past Stereotypes	Individual	1. Reduce negative stereotyping 2. Develop appreciation of your own identity frames 3. Develop appreciation of others' identity frames	1. List the negative stereotypes other parties use to describe you (your group) 2. Think about what you value that is denigrated by these stereotypes 3. Rewrite the stereotype as an identity frame reflecting the core value you stand for 4. List your negative characterisations of other parties 5. Think about what the other party values 6. Re-write the characterisation as a positive statement reflecting what the other person might value
Reframing Yourself or Enlarging Your Own Identity	Individual or stakeholder group	1. Acknowledge your own multiple identities 2. To see yourself in terms of your memberships in wider communities	1. List the most important identities that you would use to describe yourself 2. List the most important identities that other disputants would use to describe themselves 3. Identify any identities that you have in common with the other disputants (e.g. parent, member of same community, religious organisation) 4. Think of 2 or more social contexts in which your different identities might emerge (e.g. home, work, church) 5. In what ways do you and the other disputants share common values (e.g. both like to fish, both appreciate solitude)

Table 10.3   Frame-based options for intervening (continued)

Type of Intervention	Level	Purpose(s)	Brief Description
Imaging (Self–Other Categorisation)	Intergroup	1. To acknowledge the negative characterisations we use 2. To share the impact of others' characterisations on your group and learn how yours affect others 3. To learn about others' core identities	1. Meet with your own stakeholder group 2. Each group makes a list of the negative characterisations that they use to describe the other disputants 3. Discuss what it feels like to be a victim of these characterisations 4. Discuss the implications of continuing to hold these negative stereotypes of each other
Mirroring	Intergroup	1. To acknowledge the negative characterisations we use 2. To share the impact of others' characterisations on your group and learn how yours affect others 3. To learn about others' core identities	1. Meet with your own stakeholder group 2. Each group makes 3 lists: a) the negative characterisations that they use to describe the other disputants; b) how they expect the other party to characterise them; c) the positive aspects of their relationship with the other party 3. Parties post their lists 4. Groups discuss their observations about the lists
Perspective–taking Exercise	Individual, group or intergroup	1. To gain a more in-depth appreciation of the other party's frames on the dispute 2. To develop empathy for how the another party makes sense of the dispute	1. Consider the frames that another disputant has about the dispute 2. Try to write out their whole story frame 3. Do they have any identity frames that are important to the dispute? 4. What conflict management frames do they prefer and why? 5. Which of their frames might be the most/least amenable to change? Why?

Table 10.3   Frame-based options for intervening (continued)

Type of Intervention	Level	Purpose(s)	Brief Description
Single-text Story	Individual, intergroup	1. To work towards consensus on whole story frame 2. To develop skills in enlarging frames	1. Collectively select one person (or subgroup) to initiate the most inclusive whole story frame that they can think of 2. Have that person (or group) write down the WSF in a one or two-page description 3. Pass the initial version to another person (or subgroup) and have them 'build on' the initial version. They cannot reject the WSF but must frame it more inclusively 4. Continue process until parties can agree on whole story
Conflict Management-Dynamics Exercise	Intergroup	1. To help disputants recognise common and divergent conflict management options and their relationship to conflict dynamics	1. Participants individually list all of the conflict management options that are acceptable to them in the present situation 2. Have group members identify and discuss the conflict dynamics that are present which make these options necessary or preferable 3. Have group members identify and discuss the conflict management options acceptable to them should the dynamics change in significant ways
Social Control-Dynamics Exercise	Intergroup	1. To help disputants appreciate the ways in which people operate within specific social control frameworks	1. Have group members identify their own social control frameworks using the 'EFC social control instrument' 2. Have group members provide examples or stories demonstrating their social control frameworks 3. Have group members discuss the flexibility of their frameworks and under what conditions their frameworks might shift or change

Table 10.3 introduces a range of frame-based interventions that can be used to promote frame enlargement and initiate civil dialogue among potential collaborators. Since some of the interventions are designed for within-group or individual reflection and some for across-group work, they are introduced below according to these distinctions.

Individual focus. The exercises in this section are designed to promote individual work on frame exploration. Two exercises, *reframing or enlarging your own identity and imaging*, each encourage participants to reflect on their own identity group memberships and to understand how their identity changes as they shift from membership in one group vs. another (e.g., church deacon vs. veteran). These reflections are intended to increase awareness about how one's own identity is comprised of multiple associations and note that what is important shifts as different memberships become salient. The *identifying stereotypes* exercise also invites participants to examine their own identity frames and to examine the stereotypes that others use to characterise those who hold this identity and the negative impact of these stereotypes. Then participants are asked to reverse the analysis and consider how their own stereotyping may affect members of other groups. Additionally, exploring stereotypes involves a counterintuitive appreciative process of finding value in that which a stereotype denigrates. *Perspective taking and single text story* (discussed below as intergroup exercises) can also be conducted as individual exercises.

Dyadic focus. These exercises are designed for pairs of participants from different groups. In *Listening dyads* participants work with their own and others' whole story frames. Each member of the dyad takes five minutes to share their whole story frame while the other participant listens. Then the second person tells their whole story frame. This kind of interchange allows participants to see their interaction through each other's eyes and encourages them, at least temporarily, to suspend judgement about the other's viewpoint. Through this exchange, for the first time parties may really understand how others view the situation and why.

Inter-group focus. The inter-group designs are intended to foster interaction across groups and to promote learning and increase perspective taking. Ideally, these exercises would allow parties to enlarge their repertoire of frames about the domain. In *mirroring* participants compare their beliefs about how others see them with others' actual descriptions of them. By exchanging these stereotypical perceptions, parties learn how they come across to others but also consider their own misconceptions of others. The *single text exercise* encourages parties to enlarge their individual whole story frames to construct a joint one that reflects more than one viewpoint. The *conflict management* and *social control dynamics* exercises invite analysis of each group's assumptions about how societal decisions (such as the domain issues they are facing) should be resolved and the best methods for trying to resolve the conflict(s) among the parties.

In general, frame-based interventions can be used to train parties who are in ritualistic, ideological, or historical conflict with each other (e.g. representatives of different federal agencies, pro-life versus pro-choice groups, racially divided groups, environmental proponents and opponents). Several of these approaches have demonstrated some potential for opening a dialogue among potential collaborators. A successful mirroring exercise was used by the author in work with members of the US Fish and Wildlife Service and the US Forest Service working in the same national forest who had been at odds with one another for years. The author also experimented with the use of dyadic listening exercises among parties concerned about Voyageurs National Park after an eighteen-month mediation failed to settle their conflict. Finally, the Public Conversations Project (PCP) utilises similar techniques to organise productive dialogues about reproductive freedom and other highly contentious topics. Psychologist Laura Chasin, PCP's founder, describes the purpose of a dialogue this way:

> We said that the only goal was mutual understanding. It would not be an opportunity to try to persuade, meaning we had some ground rules. Incendiary name-calling (such as 'baby killer' or 'religious fanatic') was forbidden, and questions had to convey genuine curiosity (no 'Don't you think your position is stupid?)
> http://www.oprah.com/omagazine/200511/omag_200511_understanding.jhtml

Even if reframing or frame enlargement is not accomplished though the use of frame-based interventions, at least the parties have engaged in good faith efforts to explore interests and hear each other's concerns which can often reduce tension and prevent escalation of disputes.

CONCLUSION

How parties in multi-organisational domains make sense of the dynamics in which they and other group's engage has considerable ramifications for whether or not they can successfully forge a collaborative partnership. Parties' interpretations or frames represent important antecedent characteristics that shape how they view the issues, each other and the actions needed for the future direction of the domain. Widely discrepant frames can prevent potential partners from even envisioning possibilities for collaboration, and, even if they search for collaborative solutions to domain problems, the extent to which parties view the domain through a variety of different lenses makes reaching agreement on a commonly accepted direction for the domain difficult and sometimes impossible (Lewicki et al., 2003).

In this chapter I have identified several key types of frames that have impeded potential partners from forging collaborative agreements in the past. In addition to specific types of frames, constellations of frames adopted by parties can predispose them towards collaborative solutions or lock them into intractable conflicts (Brummans et al., 2005). Consequently, by analysing parties' framing patterns, it is possible to gain insight into the fundamental disjunctures that fuel conflicts and make resolution elusive.

A second contribution of this chapter is preliminary development, a theory of intervention for conflicted domains. By analysing how potential partners frame domain problems, I build on this knowledge to generate a repertoire of different intervention techniques that can be used to foster collaboration (in tractable domains) or to promote civil dialogue among disputing parties in intractable ones. Whereas mediation as an intervention seeks to enable the parties to reframe their interpretations of their interactions so as to find a resolution of the dispute, framing interventions focus on frame enlargement rather than reframing (although the latter is not precluded). This approach to intervention promotes awareness, perspective-taking and reflection in the hope that the parties can begin to entertain others' views alongside of their own. While certainly not exhaustive, the nine frame-based interventions introduced here offer fruitful designs for encouraging parties to adopt broader views than merely their own regarding domain dynamics. Since these ideas are still largely theory-driven, their potential remains open to exploration. I hope that articulating the bases for these interventions will inspire others to experiment with this approach. Short of engaging in full-blown collaborations, through these interventions parties can begin to enlarge their own perspectives, increase understanding and trust, and promote civil dialogue instead of destructive conflict, which may eventually sow seeds for fruitful future collaboration.

NOTE

1. See Putnam and Holmer (1992) and DeWulf, Gray, Putnam, Lewicki, Aarts, Bouwen, and Van Woerkum (2005) for more extensive reviews of multiple approaches to the framing.

REFERENCES

Amir, Y. (1994), 'The Contact Hypothesis in Intergroup Relations', in W.J. Lonner and R.S. Malpass (eds), *Psychology and Culture*, Boston: Allyn and Bacon, pp. 231-237.

Barlett, F.C. (1932), *Remembering: A Study in Experimental and Social Psychology*, Cambridge: Cambridge University Press.

Bateson, G. (1972), *Steps to an Ecology of Mind*, New York: Ballantine Books.

Benford, R.D. and D.A. Snow (2000), 'Framing processes and social movements: An overview and assessment', *Annual Review of Sociology*, **26**, 611-639.

Bouwen, R., and T. Taillieu (2004), 'Multi-party collaboration as social learning for interdependence: Developing relational knowing for sustainable natural resource management', *Journal of Community and Applied Social Psychology*, **14** (3), 137-153.

Bouwen, R., M. Craps and E. Santos (1999), 'Multi-party collaboration: Building generative knowledge and developing relationships among "unequal" partners in local community projects in Ecuador', *Concepts and Transformation*, **4** (2), 133-151.

Brummans, B., L. Putnam, B. Gray, R. Hanke, R. Lewicki and C. Wiethoff (2005), 'Moving Beyond Stakeholder Groups: Profiles of Disputants Framing of Environmental Conflicts', Working paper, Center for Research in Conflict and Negotiation, Pennsylvania State University, University Park.

Bryan, T.A. and J.M. Wondolleck (2003), 'When Irresolvable Becomes Resolvable: The Quincy Library Group Conflict', in R. Lewkici, B. Gray and M. Elliott (eds), *Making Sense of Intractable Environmental Conflict: Concepts and Cases*, Washington, DC: Island Press, pp. 63-89.

Bryson, J.M. and C.B. Finn (1995), 'Creating the Future Together: Developing and Using Shared Strategy Maps', in A. Halachmi and G. Bouckaert (eds), *The Enduring Challenges in Public Management: Surviving and Excelling in a Changing World*, San Francisco: Jossey-Bass, pp. 247-280.

Buechler, S.M. (2000), *Social Movements in Advanced Capitalism*. New York: Oxford University Press.

Bullard, R.D. (1990), *Dumping in Dixie: Race, Class, and Environmental Quality*, Boulder: Westview Press.

Bullard, R.D. and B. Wright (1989), 'Toxic waste and the African-American community', *Urban League Review*, **13** (1-2), 67-75.

Carlson, C. (1999), 'Convening', in L. Susskind, S. McKearnen and J. Thomas-Larmer (eds), *The Consensus Building Handbook*, Thousand Oaks, CA: Sage, pp. 169-198.

Creed, W.E., J.A. Langstraat and M.A. Scully (2002), 'A picture of the frame: Frame analysis as technique and as politics', *Organizational Research Methods*, **5** (1), 34-55.

Dewulf, A. (2006), *Issue Framing in Multi-Actor Contexts*, Ph.D. Dissertation, Leuven, Belgium: Katholieke Universiteit Leuven.

Dewulf, A., B. Gray, L. Putnam, N. Aarts, R. Lewicki, R. Bouwen and C. van Woerkum (2004), *Disentangling Approaches to Framing: Mapping the Terrain*, Working paper, Center for Organizational and Personnel Psychology, Katholieke Universiteit Leuven, Leuven, Belgium and Center for Research in Conflict and Negotiation, Pennsylvania State University, University Park, PA.

Donnellon, A. and B. Gray (1990), *An Interactive Theory of Reframing in Negotiation*, Pennsylvania State University, University Park, PA: Center for Research in Conflict and Negotiation.

Dore, J. and R.P. McDermott (1982), 'Linguistic indeterminacy and social context in utterance interpretation', *Language*, **58** (2), 374-398.

Elliot, M. (1988), 'The Effect of Differing Assessments of Risk in Hazardous Waste Facility Siting Negotiations', Working paper, Georgia Institute of Technology, City and Regional Planning Program.

Elliot, M. (2003), 'When the Parents be Cancer-free: Community Voice, Toxics, and Environmental Justice in Chattanooga, Tennessee', in R. Lewicki, B. Gray and M. Elliott (eds), *Making Sense of Intractable Environmental Conflicts*, Washington, DC: Island Press, pp. 303-332.

Emery, M.R. and R.E. Purser (1996), *The Search Conference: A Powerful Method for Planned Organizational Change and Community Action*, San Francisco: Jossey-Bass.

Faulkner, M. and M. de Rond (2000), *Cooperative Strategy: Economic, Business and Organizational Issues,* New York: Oxford University Press.

Fisher, R., W. Ury and B. Patton (1991), *Getting to Yes*, New York: Penguin Books.

Folk-Williams, J.A. (1988), 'The use of negotiated agreements to resolve water disputes involving Indian rights', *Natural Resources Journal*, **28** (1), 63-103.

Gioia, D.A. and K. Chittipeddi (1991), 'Sensemaking and sensegiving in strategic change initiation', *Strategic Management Journal*, **12** (6), 433-448.

Goffman, E. (1974), *Frame Analysis: An Essay on the Organization of Experience,* New York: Harper and Row.

Gray, B. (1989), *Collaborating: Finding Common Ground for Multiparty Problems*, San Francisco: Jossey-Bass.

Gray, B. (1995), 'Obstacles to Success in Educational Collaborations', in M. Wang and L. Rigby (eds), *School/Community Connections: Exploring Issues for Research and Practice*, San Francisco: Jossey-Bass, pp. 71-100.

Gray, B. (2003), 'Framing of Environmental Disputes', in R. Lewicki, B. Gray and M. Elliott (eds), *Making Sense of Intractable Environment Conflict: Concepts and Cases*, Washington, DC: Island Press, pp. 11-34.

Gray, B. (2004), 'Strong opposition: Frame-based resistance to collaboration', *Journal of Community and Applied Psychology*, **14** (3), 166-176.

Gray, B. (2005), 'Framing in Mediation and Mediation as Framing', in M.S. Herrman (ed.), *Handbook of Mediation: Bridging Theory, Research and Practice*, Oxford, UK: Blackwell, pp. 193-216.

Gray, B. (2007), 'Interventions for Fostering Collaboration', in C. Huxham, C., M. Ebers, S. Cropper and P. Ring (eds), *Handbook of Collaboration*, New York: Oxford University Press.

Gray, B. and T.M. Hay (1986), 'Political limits to interorganizational consensus and change', *Journal of Applied Behavioral Science*, **22** (2), 95-112.

Gumperz, J.J. (1982), *Discourse Strategies*, Cambridge: Cambridge University Press.

Hanke R., A. Rosenberg and B. Gray (2003), 'The Story of Drake Chemical: A Burning Issue', in R. Lewicki, B. Gray and M. Elliott (eds), *Making Sense of Intractable Environmental Conflicts: Concepts and Cases*. Washington, DC: Island Press, pp. 275-302.

Hardy, C. and N. Phillips (1998), 'Strategies of engagement: lessons from the critical examination of collaboration and conflict in interorganizational domains', *Organization Science*, **9** (2), 217-230.

Heifetz, R.A. (1994), *Leadership without Any Answers*, Cambridge, MA: Belknap Press.

Hilgartner, S. (1985), 'The Political Language of Risk: Defining Occupational Health', in D. Nelkin (ed.), *The Language of Risk: Conflicting Perspectives on Occupational Health*, Beverly Hills, CA: Sage, pp. 25-62.

Hogg, M.A., D.J. Terry and K.M. White (1995), 'A tale of two theories: A critical comparison of identity theory with social identity theory', *Social Psychology Quarterly*, **58** (4), 255-269.

Huxham, C. and D. Macdonald (1992), 'Introducing collaborative advantage', *Management Decision*, **30** (3), 50-56.

Huxham, C. and S. Vangen (2005), *Managing to Collaborate*, New York and Oxon, UK: Routledge.

Jansen, R.J.G. and J. Knoben (2007), 'From Inter-organisation Conflict to Collaboration: The Case of the Music Recording Industry', this volume.

Kahneman, D. and A. Tversky (1978), 'Prospect theory: An analysis of decision under risk', *Econometrica*, **47** (2), 263-291.

Kelman, H.C. (1999), 'The Role of Social Identity in Conflict Resolution: Experiences from Israeli-Palestinian Problem-solving Workshops', Paper presented at the International Association of Conflict Management, San Sebastian, Spain, June 22.

Keltner, S.K. (1994), *The Management of Struggle: Elements of Dispute Resolution through Negotiation, Mediation, and Arbitration*, Cresskill: Hampton Press, Inc.

Kusel, J., S.C. Doak, S. Carpenter and V.E. Sturtevant (1996), 'The Role of the Public in Adaptive Ecosystem Management', Sierra Nevada Ecosystem Project: Final Report to Congress, Vol. II, Assessments and Scientific Basis for Management Options, Centers for Water and Wildland Resources, University of California-Davis.

Lam, J.A., J. Rifkin and A. Townley (1989), 'Reframing conflict: Implications for fairness in parent-adolescent mediation', *Mediation Quarterly*, **7** (1), 15-31.

Lawrence, A. and A. Svendsen (2002), *The Clayquot Controversy: A Stakeholder Dialogue Simulation*, CD available from the authors.

Laws, D. and M. Rein (2003), 'Reframing Practice', in M.A. Hajer and H. Wagenaar (eds), *Deliberative Policy Analysis: Understanding Governance in the Network Society*, Cambridge, UK: Cambridge University Press, pp. 172-206.

Lewicki, R., B. Gray and M. Elliott (2003), *Making Sense of Intractable Environmental Conflict: Concepts and Cases*, Washington, DC: Island Press.

Lewicki, R.J., D.M. Saunders and J.W. Minton (1999), *Negotiation*, Boston, MA: Irwin McGraw-Hill.

McAdam, D. and R. Paulsen (1993), 'Specifying the relationship between social ties and activism', *American Journal of Sociology*, **98** (3), 640-667.

Menkel-Meadow, C. (2001), 'Negotiating with lawyers, men and things: the contextual approach still matters', *Negotiation Journal*, **17** (3), 257-293.

Merry, S.E. and S. Silbey (1984), 'What do plaintiffs want? Re-examining the concept of dispute', *Justice System Journal*, **9** (2), 151-177.

Minsky, M. (1975), *A Framework for Representing Knowledge. The Psychology of Computer Visions*, New York: McGraw-Hill.

Moore, C.W. (1986), *The Meditation Process*, San Francisco: Jossey-Bass.

Northrup, T. (1989), 'The Dynamic of Identity in Personal and Social Conflict', in L. Kriesberg, T.A. Northrup and S.J. Thorson (eds),

Intractable Conflicts and their Transformation, Syracuse: Syracuse University Press, pp. 55-82.

Osgood, C. E. (1983), *Psycho-social Dynamics and the Prospects for Mankind*, Illinois: University of Illinois.

Otway, H.J., D. Maurer and K. Thomas (1978), 'Nuclear power: The question of public acceptance', *Futures*, **10** (2), 109-118.

Phillips, N. and C. Hardy (1998), 'Strategies of engagement in interorganizational domains', *Organization Science*, **9** (2), 217-230.

Pinkley, R.L. and G.B. Northcraft (1994), 'Conflict frames of reference: Implications for dispute processes and outcomes', *Academy of Management Journal*, **37** (1), 193-205.

Putnam, L. and M. Holmer (1992), 'Framing, Reframing and Disuse Development', in L. Putnam and M.E. Roloff (eds), *Communication and Negotiation*, Newbury Park: Sage, pp. 128-155.

Ross, L. (1977), 'The Intuitive Psychologist and his Shortcomings: Distortions in the Attribution Process', in I.L. Berkowitz (ed.), *Advances in Experimental Social Psychology*, Orlando: Academic Press, pp. 173-220.

Rothman, J. (1997), *Resolving Identity-based Conflict: In Organizations, Nations and Communities*, San Francisco: Jossey-Bass.

Schön, D.A. and M. Rein (1994), *Frame Reflection: Toward the Resolution of Intractable Policy Controversies*, New York: Basic Books.

Sherif, M. (1958), 'Superordinate goals in the reduction of intergroup conflicts', *American Journal of Sociology*, **63** (2), 349-358.

Sheppard, B., K. Blumenfeld-Jones and J. Roth (1989), 'Informal Thirdpartyship: Studies of Everyday Conflict Intervention', in K. Kressel, D.G. Pruitt and Associates (eds), *Mediation Research: The Process and Effectiveness of Third-Party Intervention*, San Francisco: Jossey-Bass: pp. 166-189.

Snow, D.A. and R.D. Benford (1992), 'Master Frames and Cycles of Protest', in A.D. Morris and C.M. Mueller (eds), *Frontiers in Social Movement Theory*, New Haven, CT: Yale University Press, pp. 133-155.

Snow, D.A., B. Rockford Jr., R.D. Benford and S.K. Worden (1986), 'Frame alignment processes, micro-mobilization and movement participation', *American Sociological Review*, **51** (4), 464-481.

Tajfel, H. and J.C. Turner (1979), 'An Integrative Theory of Intergroup Conflict', in W.G. Austin and S. Worchel (eds), *The Social Psychology of Intergroup Relations*, Monterey, CA: Brooks/Cole, pp. 33-47.

Tajfel, H. and J.C. Turner (1985), 'The Social Identity Theory of Intergroup Behavior', in S. Worchel and W.G. Austin (eds), *Psychology of Intergroup Relations*, Chicago, IL: Nelson-Hall Publishers, pp. 7-24.

Tannen, D. (1979), 'What's in a Frame? Surface Evidence of Underlying Expectations', in R. Freedle (ed.), *New Directions in Discourse Processes*, Norwood, NJ: Ablex, pp. 137-181.

Tannen, D. (1993), *Framing in Discourse*, New York: Oxford University.

Taylor, D. (2000), 'Advances in environmental justice: Research, theory and methodology', *American Behavioral Scientist*, **43** (4), 504-580.

Trist, E. (1983), 'Referent organizations and the development of inter-organizational domains', *Human Relations*, **35** (3), 269-284.

Ury, W., J.M. Brett and S. Goldberg (1993), *Getting Disputes Resolved: Designing Systems to Cut the Cost of Conflict*, San Francisco: Jossey-Bass Inc.

Van Dijk, T.A. (1977), *Text and Context*, London: Longmar Group Ltd.

Vaughan, E. and M. Seifert (1992), 'Variability in the framing of risk issues', *Journal of Social Issues*, **48** (4), 119-135.

Vickers, G. (1965), *The Art of Judgment*, London: Chapman and Hall.

Weick, K.E. (1995), *Sensemaking in Organizations*, Thousand Oaks, CA: Sage.

Wildavsky, A. and K. Dake (1990), 'Theories of risk perception: Who fears what and why?', *Daedalus*, **119** (4), 41-60.

Wondolleck, J.M. and S.L. Yaffee (2000), *Making Collaboration Work: Lessons from Innovation in Natural Resource Management*, Washington, DC: Island Press.

Zartman, I.W. (1981), 'Explaining Disengagement', in J.Z. Rubin (ed.), *Dynamics of Third-Party Intervention*, New York: Praeger, pp. 148-167.

11. From Inter-organisational Conflict to Collaboration: The Case of the Music Recording Industry

Rob Jansen and Joris Knoben

INTRODUCTION

In this chapter, the origination and development of conflicts in an inter-organisational domain (c.f. Gray's multiparty domains, this volume) is examined by focusing on the developments in the music recording industry. This chapter analyses the development that took place after the introduction of a new technology in this industry, which had a large impact on the composition of the industry as well as on its (internal) dynamics. After the entrance and subsequent spreading of the innovation, the industry was characterised by conflicts between organisations. Over time, however, collaboration between organisations started to emerge. These developments have raised the following research question: which factors play a part in the origination of inter-organisational conflict and its development towards inter-organisational collaboration?

Conflicts are defined in this chapter as 'the existence of tension, annoyance, and animosity between two or more separate organisations that are not necessarily involved in any collaborative activities' (adopted from Simons and Peterson, 2000). One of the core elements of this definition is that actors that are in conflict do not necessarily have to be involved in any collaborative activities. This element clearly distinguishes this research from many of the existing research on inter-organisational conflicts, which usually focuses solely on solving conflicts within collaborative settings. In contrast, an inter-organisational collaboration is defined as 'the relative enduring transaction, flow, and linkage between an organization and one or more organizations in its environment' (Oliver, 1990).

There are many examples of cases that involve numerous independent actors who are competing or having conflicts, but who would collectively gain by collaborating rather than competing on an issue (Faerman, McCaffrey and Van Slyke, 2001). The main underlying reasoning is that through the pooling of resources and expertise, collaboration can solve problems that cannot be solved by confrontation or competition (Trist, 1983). However, little research that deals with the development from conflict to collaboration on an inter-organisational level exists. The research that does exist usually focuses on the degeneration of collaboration into conflicts (e.g. Kumar and van Dissel, 1996; Park and Russo, 1996) or on the management of conflicts in intra-organisational settings (e.g. Alper, Tjosvold and Law, 2000). The aim of the research presented in this chapter is to shed some light on the development from conflict to collaboration in an inter-organisational domain. This research can provide new insights into the development of inter-organisational relationships over time, which is a highly relevant, but understudied, topic (c.f. Knoben, Oerlemans and Rutten, 2006). This chapter starts with an overview of the existing theoretical insights concerning the development of inter-organisational networks and inter-organisational conflicts. This overview is presented to provide a background against which the dynamics of our case have been researched. Second, a description of the music recording industry and its dynamics will be given. By describing the characteristics of the industry and, subsequently, the developments affecting these characteristics, the potential for inter-organisational conflict is presented. From this, the development from conflict to collaboration is sketched by explaining why the innovation initially launched those companies already populating the industry into conflict with new market entrants and how these 'older' companies then came back to embrace new entrants. This story has been constructed by using papers that describe the dynamics in the music recording industry. These papers have been gathered through citation analysis and by applying a snowball sampling method, making initial use of the ISI[1] and ABI Inform[2] databases. The papers have been searched for characteristics of, and processes occurring in and around the industry that provide indications for the origination and development of the inter-organisational setting. The characteristics and processes represent organisational- and industry-level factors. In the final sections of this chapter, the results of the analysis will be discussed and some directions for future research will be presented.

INTER-ORGANISATIONAL DYNAMICS

Network Change

Research into inter-organisational dynamics indicates that inter-organisational structures usually change incrementally over time, but that major restructurings are likely to happen after a large exogenous shock has taken place (Burkhardt and Brass, 1990). Such a shock is often called a critical event, which can be defined as 'an impulse that allows tension to be released from the network and allows the network to reconfigure or even break down' (Knoben et al., 2006: 298). The introduction of a radically new technology, defined as a novel, unique and successfully introduced technology (Dahlin and Behrens, 2005), is often argued to be such an event (e.g. Burkhardt and Brass, 1990; Madhavan, Koka and Prescott, 1998; Soh and Roberts, 2003), although many other examples exist as well, such as bankruptcies, the entry of new competitors, economic recessions, changes in consumer demands, and so on (Knoben et al., 2006). Although the innovation that spurs the dynamics of such a critical event may be of a technological nature, it affects not merely technological aspects of inter-organisational relationships and networks. The underlying reason for the major restructuring of the inter-organisational structure is the fact that a critical event leads to a sudden and dramatic increase in uncertainty. Attempts to cope with this uncertainty can lead to adjustments in the inter-organisational structure and power distribution in favour of those able to cope with the uncertainty relative to those who cannot. Therefore, it is possible that a critical event will result in changes in the inter-organisational structure, the power division, or both (Burkhardt and Brass, 1990; Tushman and Anderson, 1986).

It is, however, nearly impossible to state, ex-ante, which events will lead to large changes in the structure of inter-organisational settings (Maclaurin, 1954), as many events that may seem to induce large levels of uncertainty actually reinforce the existing inter-organisational structure. The latter can be explained by the fact that when the central and powerful actors in a network structure are most capable of dealing with the uncertainty resulting from the innovation, the existing structure is reinforced, rather than changed (Madhavan et al., 1998). Research has shown that this is often the case (Soh and Roberts, 2003; Gay and Dousset, 2005). As a result of this capability of the central and powerful actors, inter-organisational structures are subject to large inertial forces. Research by Kim, Ok and Swaminathan (2006) indicates that these inertial forces are the largest for old, large, previously inert inter-organisational structures.

It follows from the logic presented above that it is not the event that is critical, but the way that actors react to such an event (Halinen, Salmi and

Havila, 1999). Recent research by Koka, Madhavan and Prescott (2006) has identified several characteristics of an event that might help to predict which events lead to which kind of network change. They pose that uncertainty is a three-dimensional concept. The first dimension involves the uncertainty about the environment itself, the second dimension, the uncertainty about the behaviour of the actors in the environment, and the third dimension, the uncertainty about which approach is the best one to address the first two types of uncertainty. The impact of an event on an inter-organisational network depends on the number of dimensions of uncertainty that are heightened by the event (see Oerlemans, Gössling and Jansen, Chapter 9 in this volume for a more elaborate description).

This notion has several implications for the dynamics of inter-organisational relationships, and for the case of the music recording industry in particular, as we will discuss later.

Conflict Development

It has been noted earlier that most existing research in the field of inter-organizational conflicts focuses on the management of conflicts within collaborative settings (e.g. Gobeli, Koenig and Bechinger, 1998), or on the failure of inter-organisational collaborations (e.g. Arino and de la Torre, 1998). Nevertheless, there are also some studies that address the development from conflict to collaboration in cases where there were no prior collaborative activities between the organisations. One such study by Browning, Beyer and Shetler (1995) focuses on the building of cooperation in a competitive industry as a result of the emergence of strong foreign competition (a critical event in this case). Another study by Faerman et al. (2001) describes the emergence of collaboration in the highly institutionalised financial markets.

Browning et al. (1995) performed a qualitative analysis of the developments in the semiconductor industry in the US. For a long time, the firms active in this industry were not only very competitive, but were also involved in many long-drawn-out inter-organisational conflicts, most of which ended with long battles in court. Most of these conflicts arose around issues of proprietary standards. However, these colliding firms were forced to pool their resources in response to a sudden increase in foreign competition. The firms in the semiconductor industry tried to form one big collaborative organisation called SEMATECH in order to cope with the increase in foreign competition. Due to their long history of conflicts and collisions, doing so proved to be difficult. Browning et al. (1995) tried to identify the factors that were conducive or detrimental to this process. They found that high levels of equivocality and large differences in organisational culture between organisations hampered the move from inter-organisational conflict to collaboration. Moreover, they found that strong leadership, constructive conflicts, prior social ties, and concerns about the future are conducive to inter-organisational collaboration.

In a more or less comparable study in the financial markets, Faerman et al. (2001) identified the factors that were conducive to the formation of a regulatory institute, in which six large US banks were involved. Eventually, the process succeeded despite fierce competition among the actors involved and incentives for all actors to resort to adversarial lobbying and legal challenges. Faerman et al. (2001) find that the success of the collaboration despite the conflicting interests can be explained by looking at: (a) the initial dispositions towards collaboration, (b) the extant issues and incentives, (c) the leadership, and (d) the number and variety of organisations involved.

The findings mentioned above involve combinations of actor-, organisational- and industry-level aspects that play a role in the origination of conflict and the development from conflict to collaboration. After the following section concerning the specifics of the music recording industry, the afore-mentioned findings will be assessed in terms of their applicability to the characteristics and developments found in the particular case presented in this study. This assessment will then allow for some degree of generalisation.

THE ORIGINATION AND DEVELOPMENT OF CONFLICTS IN THE MUSIC RECORDING INDUSTRY

This section will describe how inter-organisational conflicts arose in the music recording industry and how they developed over time. The explanation developed here is based on an assessment of why it is likely that conflict arises from inter-organisational dynamics, in an industry where dramatic changes in characteristics can be referred to as part of the 'everyday-business' of the music recording industry (i.e. the destruction of routines), and where high levels of both technological as well as market uncertainty (i.e. the consequences of a critical event) resulted in the recognition of these uncertainties as being manifestations of two of the three dimensions of the uncertainty concept outlined by Koka et al. (2006). The first type of uncertainty was seen by the industry to be resulting from the environment, whereas the second was considered to be originating from the behaviour of other actors. We will begin the following section by describing the characteristics of the music recording industry and then look at the changes that took place from a historical perspective. After that, we will turn to the developments that these changes bestow upon the industry and its inter-organisational relations. This will set the stage for viewing the potential for conflicts. Finally, the industry dynamics and the consequential reconfiguration of inter-organisational relations are analysed to capture the development from conflict to collaboration.

Characteristics of the Music Recording Industry

The music recording industry is approximately one hundred years old (Alexander, 2002b) and has historically been structured as an oligopolistic market (Peterson and Berger, 1971; Lopes, 1992). This structure generally refers to a small number of large central market suppliers, with a number of peripheral suppliers. The central actors are leading in intra-industry behaviours. Generally speaking, oligopoly can result in constructive competition or in relative stagnation (Thorelli, 1986). Below, a number of important characteristics of the industry under study will be described. These characteristics were derived from the papers that were gathered by means of a citation analysis and a snowball sampling method described in the introductory section.

The first characteristic, the *core product*, is the main source of income and profit, and constitutes a great part of the *raison d'être* of the industry. The core product of the industry can be split up in two basic ingredients. One ingredient is the content of the product, i.e. the music that is recorded by artists. The second ingredient is the carrier of the product, i.e. the media through which the content is made available and made consumable to buyers. The first carriers of recorded music were wax rolls (Alexander, 1994b). The carriers developed through various media from these rolls to the current digitised media (for a description of this development and its different shapes: see ibid.). The 'composition' of this recorded music product has not been the same throughout the history of the industry (c.f. Peterson and Berger, 1975). In this context, composition refers to the number of songs on a single carrier. Changes in the composition of the product indicate a shift in what music recording companies will be producing and drawing their income and profit from. As Anand and Peterson (2000) state, historically, the multi-song 'album' format has replaced 45 rpm singles as the prime profit source for record labels. However, they also refer to the recent turnaround from the consumers' point of view, towards a focus on individual songs rather than on multi-song albums. The first ingredient will be dealt with when discussing the second characteristic, the innovation focus.

The combination of the carrier and the music are what can be seen as the core product. A carrier with higher capacity to contain music can hold multiple songs, whereas low capacity carriers can hold few songs to one song. Whereas wax rolls could hold one song and had limited reproduction possibilities, compact discs have a limit of 74 to 90 minutes (15-20 songs) and have, due to digitisation, unlimited reproduction possibilities. Thus, this core product has undergone physical changes in the way it was carried and has undergone changes in composition, i.e. format. The (technological) changes in carriers precede the change in format and, as will be laid out in the innovation focus described below, cause instability and consequently uncertainty for some actors.

A second important characteristic is the *innovation focus* within an industry, which refers to the main changeability and advancement focus of the activities of organisations within an industry. The music recording industry, because of its oligopolistic structure (Peterson and Berger, 1996), basically followed the pace and direction of the main actors within the industry. These main actors share a number of organisational characteristics (Peterson and Berger, 1971). Recording companies usually have three divisions, namely manufacturing, sales and promotion, and production (Peterson and Berger, 1971).[3] On the organisational level, innovation in the 'production' division in terms of new artists and music streams is the most sensitive to environmental turbulence, which is similar to the first dimension of uncertainty described by Koka et al. (2006). McPhee (in Peterson and Berger, 1971) notes that the marketing environment of this industry is characterised as being very near the turbulent extreme because it depends on the rapidly changing style preferences of millions of predominantly young buyers. It is the production division that is expected to focus on entrepreneurship in a 'Schumpeterian' sense, and thus, on innovation. The other two divisions are segregated from the turbulent environment to a high degree and are therefore not expected to display this kind of entrepreneurship. In other words, the pace and direction of innovation focused on the content of the product, i.e. renewal and change in the artists and styles of music produced. Moreover, the music recording companies typically preferred stability in functions other than innovation in production, i.e. content, as they did not perceive these functions to be their core activities (Lopes, 1992).

As a result of the focus taken by the large central actors in the music recording industry, a change in content is unlikely to act as a critical event from a network perspective, as the workings of the industry do not consequently change much as a result. The main actors in the industry are usually on top of such developments and, therefore, the inter-organisational position of the main actors in the industry is not affected. Innovation in carriers, however, can be considered a large exogenous shock, as these innovations are originally developed in other sectors. History shows (see below) that subsequent innovations in carriers launched the main actors and the workings of the industry in an array of re-adjustment and disequilibrium. This re-adjustment phenomenon can be explained by the fact that the main actors in the industry had a tendency to react slowly towards developments that did not touch upon the content of their product, as these did not touch upon their focus of innovation. It is worth noting that this slow reaction is in line with the predictions of Kim et al. (2006) discussed earlier and closely resembles the liability of both size and age. As a result of the hesitation of the central actors, peripheral actors and new entrants got the opportunity to take advantage of these (technological) developments to enter the industry. Most often, however, the large central actors were able to maintain their dominant positions by integrating the new technologies into their manufacturing systems at a later stage.

The above description provides grounds for Zimmerman's assertion (in Alexander, 2002b) that the firms in the music recording industry have traditionally preferred technological stability, although they have ultimately benefited from technological change because of the improved economies of scale and lower average cost per produced product that has resulted from it.

Anand and Peterson (2000) analysed music charts for their research on the constitution of organisational fields. Their research points out a third important characteristic of the industry, namely the importance of the *market information regime*. A market information regime is defined as the web of information about activities in the market, in this case in the music recording industry, through which cognition about markets is generated, distributed and interpreted in assessing market success. This market information regime, in their study referring to chart information, serves as 'a common coin' for making decisions in the industry. The chart information was used in particular for strategic decisions, which then can have 'dramatic' consequences for the organisations making the decision (Noorderhaven, 1995). The chart information was and remains one of the key inputs for the strategic orientation of organisations in the industry. In accordance with previous research (which was however conducted in other contexts), they found that organised actors in the music field increasingly based their interpretation of past performance – and created belief structures for future activity – on the readings of chart information. It can thus be concluded that an existing market information regime provides a primary source of information for the actors who are making strategic decisions in the music recording industry.

Bourreau (2005) describes another side of the 'common' coin of the market information regime, namely that it also is used to spread promotional information. Considering the above, a stable market information regime in the music recording industry could result in a degree of routinisation of the in- and outflow of information for strategic orientation purposes.

The fourth characteristic is the *degree of concentration* in this industry (Alexander, 1994b, 2002a). The concentration degree of the industry[4] shows large fluctuations over time (Peterson and Berger, 1975). The Hirschmann-Herfindahl Index (HHI), which measures the concentration rate of an industry,[5] indicates that the number of central market suppliers has remained constant, but that the number of other market actors has changed substantially throughout the years (see Figure 11.1).[6] These fluctuations coincide with innovations in the content ingredient of the product, i.e., new music styles are being produced in addition to the mainstay of production. Peterson and Berger (1996) claim that this is due to the control exercised by the main actors, who make use of vertical integration (controlling the production chain), thereby leaving ample space for new recording companies to enter but not enough space for them to obtain control over a 'large piece of the pie'. Put more directly, it is hard to gain a substantial foothold in the industry when manufacturing and distribution are continuously controlled by the central actors. A consequence of this is horizontal collaboration or integration. The main point to be made here is that previous innovations in the content or media ingredient did not lead to a loss of control of the central actors.

The final characteristic, developments in the *composition of the industry*, refers to the different organisations that populate the industry. Traditionally, the music recording industry was predominantly composed of content producers (a few large and a large number of small recording companies; see also concentration degree above), as well as the producers of the core product (mainly the recording companies) and the distributors of the core product (retailers that sell music products). This composition has remained fairly stable throughout the history of the industry, at least until the maturation of compression techniques for digital music (Alexander, 1994b). Alexander (1994a) describes three waves of new entry in the industry. These waves were technology-driven and eventually provided improvements in the mass production capabilities (and thus a lower cost per produced product) for the main industry actors, as well as for small start-ups. However, at the outset there was an advantage for the innovators, who tended to be the early adopters of the phonogram, magnetic tape and CD innovations. A large part of this success lies in the popularity of the innovation with consumers (ibid.). Similar to the developments in the degree of concentration of the industry described in the section above, these earlier waves of technological innovation with respect to the media carrying the content did not alter the structure of the industry because the controlling position of the central actors remained intact. This position was further stabilised by horizontal and vertical integration, following waves of new entry (c.f. ibid.) once the innovation was institutionalised.

Having described the main characteristics of the music recording industry and its development in the preceding section, we now turn our attention to changes in these characteristics and their consequences. Changes are possible breeding grounds for inter-organisational conflicts, defined above as the existence of tension, annoyance and animosity between two or more separate organisations that are not necessarily involved in any collaborative activities. In other words, we expect the changes in the characteristics described below to result in inter-organisational tension, annoyance and animosity, thereby increasing the potential for inter-organisational conflict.

Figure 11.1   Concentration in the music recording industry

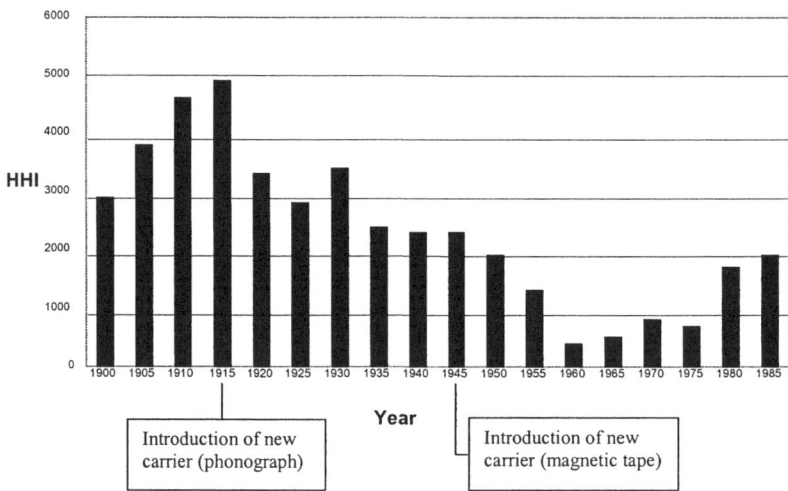

Source: Adopted from Alexander (1994b).

An analysis of this situation can allow us to describe and explain the origination of inter-organisational conflict and the subsequent development towards collaboration. From the description of the characteristics, it becomes clear that there are two main drivers for potential conflict, both of which can create the dynamics that may lead to higher levels of tension, annoyance and animosity. The first is a technological innovation (i.e., an innovation in media), and the second is a strong external shock that alters the way the controlling central actors bestride the industry.

Origination of Conflict

The issue around which the inter-organisational conflict in the music recording industry revolves is predominantly concerned with the question as to whether or not (illegal) distribution of music through the internet harms the industry's turnover and profit margin.

Box 11.1   Conflicts within the industry

I. In January 2000, MP3.com launched its My.MP3.com service, which allowed subscribers to play music over the Internet as long as they owned, borrowed, or purchased the CDs that contain the requested recordings. [...] Although MP3.com purchased licenses to perform the music, it did not own any licenses to reproduce the recordings. As a result, the major record companies and their artists brought suits against MP3.com, alleging copyright infringement. In its defence, MP3.com claimed that its service constituted fair use, contending that its service provided a transformative 'space shift' by allowing subscribers to enjoy the sound recordings they owned without carrying physical CDs around. The defendant also argued that the My.MP3.com service benefited, rather than harmed, the plaintiffs by enhancing sales, since the service required subscribers to demonstrate that they owned, borrowed, or purchased the CDs containing the requested recordings. In addition, MP3.com noted that its service did not compete directly with the plaintiffs in the digital downloading market and, instead, 'provide[d] a useful service to consumers that, in its absence, will be served by 'pirates.'' [...] MP3.com lost the lawsuits badly and was sold shortly afterwards to Vivendi Universal, which incorporated MP3.com into its subscription service and then sold the service to Roxio. (Yu, 2004: 913-914 and 915)

II. The Big Five (EMI, Universal, Sony, Time Warner, and BMG) focused their mounting concerns about piracy in all formats on the legal case against Napster,[...]. Napster functioned as a music search engine that linked participants to a huge and constantly updated library of user-provided MP3s. Its key architectural feature was an on-line database of song titles and performers, searchable by keyword. The Napster network's MusicShare client provided access to search indices and file lists of those using the service. Its brokered architecture effectively coordinated peers and increased search functionality, and its search and play interface was highly user-friendly.

III. [...]. From the Napster network's perspective, the larger the connected base of its peer-to-peer system, the greater the value of the network to creators, advertisers and consumers. [...] No sooner had Napster become a 'killer app' than legal woes beset the company. The Recording Industry Association of America (RIAA), a lobbying and trade group representing the Big Five's interests, filed suit against Napster on 7 December 1999, claiming that the free service cut into sales of CDs. Napster's enabling architecture became its legal vulnerability: when a computer with peer-to-peer software is connected to the Internet, it is configured to be both a receiver or client and a sender or server, and its user has become a publisher as well as a consumer. The legal case against Napster turned on the fact that although it did not generate revenue, the service supplied users with peer-to-peer software and provided a brokering service that managed a real-time index of available music files. This combination of marketed products and services, the RIAA argued, effectively turned Napster into a music piracy service. (McCourt and Burkart, 2003: 338-339)

The actors with vested interests argue that this is a prelude to the destruction of the core product and the *raison d'être* of the industry (see for a discussion: Liebowitz, 2005, but also Box 11.1 for a number of examples of conflict). In fact, example II in Box 11.1 illustrates the reaction of the main actors in the industry, who went to court to undertake legal action. The 'main actors versus Napster' is an example of the rising conflicts resulting from a new entry in the industry. The main argument put forward by the Recording Industry Association of America (RIAA), the industry's representative in the United States, follows the logic outlined above.

This party claims that internet-based distribution is harmful, whereas independent researchers find it can be both harmful and beneficial to the turnover and profit margins of the industry. An all-compassing explanation of these positive and negative effects has not yet been found, which leaves us and the industry floundering in the dark. However, it is unclear whether or not this is the single cause for inter-organisational conflict in the music recording industry, as exemplified by, for example, the case of the industry suing Napster (Burgunder, 2002).

The two drivers that could lead to inter-organisational conflict in the case of the music recording industry have already been identified above. Scherer (in Alexander, 1994b) states that turbulence-creating technology shapes many opportunities for innovative new entrants, and new entries can powerfully erode concentrated market structures and the power positions of incumbents. A technological innovation in the medium that carries the content and the upsetting of the institutionalised market structure could lead to intensified inter-organisational dynamics and conflicts, as well as to collaborative ventures. If we claim these two drivers to be the precursors of inter-organisational conflict in this industry, we need to be able to point to a turbulent technological change, which would drive the dynamics leading to conflict. This turbulent technological change is digitisation.

This change refers both to the digitisation of music and the digitisation of information. The former refers to the way music is stored on a carrier, whereas the latter concerns the spreading of information for promotional purposes and the acquisition of information for strategic orientation purposes. As Bourreau (2005: 431) puts it: 'Compared to the other crises that the recording industry went through, the "digital crisis" is peculiar because it is caused both by a major evolution of the music format and of the promotion process, while in the past, the industry always faced only one of these evolutions at a time.' It follows from this that earlier 'crises' were less radical than digitisation, thus perhaps not affecting all of the dimensions of Koka et al.'s (2006) uncertainty concept, or affecting these dimensions in a minor fashion. Cunningham, Alexander and Adilov (2004) state that the distribution of music in digital form was first facilitated by the introduction of compact discs in the 1980s. This fundamental shift in distribution from analogue carriers to carriers containing bits and bytes led to the exchangeability of carriers. This means that the reproduction of the content does not result in quality loss when it is transferred from one digital carrier to another. This principle shift in carrier sets the stage for turbulent times, as an innovation in the core of the supposedly non-sensitive divisions of manufacturing (from analogue to digital), as well as in sales and promotion (from solely physical to a combination of physical and digital distribution), has spurred dynamics in the music recording industry. Bourreau (2005) describes two consequences of digitisation for the use and sales of recordings. Due to digitisation, the physical carrier disappears (c.f. the description of the core product, where reproducibility is described) and the sound format changes, i.e. (compressed) computer file formats contain the music instead of a CD or a cassette tape. The disappearance of the formerly required physical carrier allowed for the sharing of music, the unbundling of the music product, infinite bundles of music, and high degrees of customization by consumers (i.e. prosumption by prosumers) (ibid.; Bandulet and Morasch, 2005). This means that the flexibility of a product or multiple products increased, in the sense that more combinations were possible, and reproduction and distribution became unlimited. As a result, consumers are able to produce their own music product, blurring the boundaries between traditional producers and end-users in the process.

A noticeable development stemming from digitisation is the introduction of the new compression routines for data and sound files (Cunningham et al., 2004). This introduction can also be characterised as a radical innovation, following the definition of Dahlin and Beerens (2005). The compression routines allow easy transfer of music content across the internet, without resources necessarily flowing back towards the music recording companies. These resources can be in currency or in information for strategic orientation, which emphasises yet another important consequence of digitisation. It also affected the information streams related to the product. Bourreau's (2005) discussion on the market information regime shows the importance of this regime for spreading information to promote sales. Anand and Peterson's (2000) discussion of this regime shows that it serves as a major input channel for strategic orientation and decision-making, i.e. which artists and music are hot, and which are not. The drivers for radical changes in the structure of the inter-organisational network were thus in place. The loss of control by the central actors in the industry as a consequence of the developments with compression and changes of the market information regime, provided fertile ground for conflict development, as the central actors were launched into uncertainty regarding orientation, promotion and product sales. In such cases, inter-organisational conflicts are more likely to arise than in stable situations

(Crabtree, Bower and Keogh, 1997) because (the network positions of) the 'traditional actors' are seriously threatened. The disposition of the traditional music recording companies towards the new compression routines created room for other firms and entrepreneurs to commercialise this invention, which can explain the high level of conflicts that arose afterwards. An example is the Napster case, which is extensively documented and described by Burgunder (2002). Alexander (2002b) states that MP3 technology (a type of compressed computer file format for music) made digital file distribution more efficient. However, the main actors of the recording music industry were not equipped to deal with the two drivers of innovation that are indirectly described by Cunningham et al. (2004), and which Bourreau (2005) terms the digital crisis. As new organisations burst into the industry scene (c.f. Alexander's, 1994b: third wave), the composition of the industry changed. Organisations providing services that enabled the distribution of the new file format through the internet rocked the stability of the industry by entering the industry, not as producers, but as successful distributors. This caused relatively uncertain, dynamic times for the industry and stimulated inter-organisational reconfiguration because the main actors were not able to handle it (c.f. Madhavan et al., 1998).

In essence, the oligopolistic control over the distribution of the core product, together with the basis for strategic orientation, waned. Pfeffer and Salancik (1978) argue that the need for reducing environmental uncertainty is a function of the industry structure. They state that uncertainty is greatest for organisations operating in industries of intermediate concentration, whereas high degrees of concentration reduce uncertainty because of the supposed increase in visibility of other actors' behaviour. Therefore, both the radical innovation, as well as the resulting new entries, changed the existing dependencies and control configuration within the industry, and thus, increased uncertainty levels. Since exerting control and lowering dependencies and uncertainties are main behavioural drivers, a struggle for control emerged, increasing the potential for conflict. This loss of control and increase in uncertainty due to the new entrants changed the business model of the music recording industry. With a changing business model, the need for strategic reorientation seems vital. As Teece puts it: 'Competition in the market gets displaced by competition for the market' (2000: 47).

Changes in the way information is gathered (Anand and Peterson, 2000) and spread (Bourreau, 2005) for orientation and promotion purposes in the music recording industry changes the way the market is understood. Thus, the two seeds for inter-organisational conflict were sown by the technological innovation of compression and the change in information streams. On the one hand, as has been argued above, changes in the composition of the industry occurred, and, on the other hand, the basis for strategic orientation shifted.

These resulted in loss of control and an increase in uncertainty on the business and the core product. However, the changes in these characteristics do not in themselves explain why conflict arose between the music recording industry's main actors and the new entrants that positioned themselves as an alternative distribution channel.

Box 11.2   Pros and cons – artists speaking

I. What record companies don't really understand is that Napster is just one illustration of the growing frustration over how much the record companies control what music people get to hear, over how the air waves, record labels and record stores, which are now all part of this 'system' that recording companies have pretty much succeeded in establishing, are becoming increasingly dominated by musical 'products' to the detriment of real music. Why should the record company have such control over how he, the music lover, wants to experience the music? From the point of view of the real music lover, what's currently going on can only be viewed as an exciting new development in the history of music. And, fortunately for him, there does not seem to be anything the old record companies can do about preventing this evolution from happening. (The Artist Formally Known As Prince; in Giesler and Pohlmann (2003: 94)).

II. Being the gatekeeper was the most profitable place to be, but now we're in a world half without gates. The Internet allows artists to communicate directly with their audiences; we don't have to depend solely on an inefficient system where the record company promotes our records to radio, press or retail and then sits back and hopes fans find out about our music. (Courtney Love; in Burkart, 2005: 489)

III. We are in the business of art. This is a walking contradiction if ever there was one. However, there is no denying it. On the artistic side, Metallica create music for ourselves first and our audience second. With each project, we go through a gruelling creative process to achieve music that we feel is representative of Metallica at that very moment in our lives. We take our craft – whether it be the music, the lyrics, or the photos and artwork – very seriously, as do most artists. It is therefore sickening to know that our art is being traded, sometimes with an audio quality that has been severely compromised, like a commodity rather than the art that it is. (Lars Ulrich; in Spitz and Hunter, 2005: 177)

Rather, it was the action taken in response to this challenge, which, according to Peitz and Waelbroeck (2004), involved reinforcing copyright laws, implementing technological protection, and enforcing legal protection through lawsuits against enablers of (uncontrolled) file-sharing. The real trigger of the inter-organisational conflicts was the fact that the music recording industry, represented by the RIAA, and individual artists (see for an example of Metallica: Albanese (2000); but also see Box 11.2 for some mixed opinions by artists who can all be considered successful) filed suit for a decrease in income and theft. This has not been limited to Napster, but has also involved other uncontrolled file exchange enablers, who have been under scrutiny, and are still under scrutiny. This is how inter-organisational conflict between the central actors and new entrants, who were eroding the existing workings of the industry, was created and continues to be created.

The artists, as can be derived from the examples I and II in Box 11.2, were not unanimous in their view of what was going on. Example I illustrates the loss of control incurred by the central actors as a consequence of the new entry. In the words of the Artist, 'there does not seem to be anything the old record companies can do about preventing this evolution from happening' (Giesler and Pohlmann, 2003: 94). Example II illustrates the change in the market information regime, which can be seen in Courtney Love's statement: '...we don't have to depend solely on an inefficient system where the record company promotes our records to radio, press or retail and then sits back and hopes fans find out about our music' (Burkart, 2005: 489).

For the case of the music recording industry, it can be concluded that the inter-organisational conflict that arose was caused by the unwelcome and radical changes in the industry's characteristics, resulting from technological innovation and leading to an increase in uncertainty and loss of control. The entry of new organisations that followed spurred the industry into a kind of uncertainty it had not witnessed before. The central actors lost control and had to cope with this uncertainty.

Development to Inter-organisational Collaboration

Although firms in the music recording industry traditionally resist but eventually benefit from innovation, the transition from resisting to benefiting takes time and adaptation. The technological innovation resulted in uncertainty and loss for control by the central actors. The threat posed 'has provided all record labels (i.e. music recording companies) with motivation to engage in learning and capability development in order to mitigate potential damage from this disruptive technology'. (Easly, Michel and Devaraj, 2003: 93). Easly, Michel and Devaraj continue by stating that this is particularly valid for record labels that have the greatest (potential) threat of internet piracy, which corresponds to the (uncontrolled) file-sharing mentioned above. In this case, the greatest potential threat exists for the central actors in the industry, i.e. they are the owners of most of the content (music) that is out there. The inter-organisational conflict with the original distribution agents could thus be resolved if learning and capability development would take place. In this case, where actors are tied to the technological innovation of the compression routines and the central actors are in a state of shock because they have to change their way of doing business, the following learning and capability development points could be explored:

- Internalisation of distribution methods: consumers apparently favour the way file-sharing allows them to enjoy the product, as can be concluded from the research of Liebowitz (2005) and Oberholzer and Strumpf (2004). The digitised music is separated from physical carriers. Fitting distribution channels thus need to be established to allow for this type of distribution.
- Adaptation of product form: consumers apparently also favour the way compression allows them to bundle and unbundle music in a variety of ways, as they see fit (Bourreau, 2005). This demands flexibility in order for consumers to be able to enjoy music by creating a self-chosen combination of songs.
- Establish profitable business models: claims that file-sharing decreases turnover and profits (Liebowitz, 2005) are abundant but also contradictory to one another. The development of the new business model demands an adjustment, by means of learning and capability development, to the dynamics imposed on the industry by the two drivers of technical innovation and by the erosion of the current market structure regarding the previous two bullets in this list (please refer to Box 11.3 for some examples of manifestations of these new business models).

Example I in Box 11.3 stresses the developmental nature of business models in this industry. If one looks back at Box 11.2, the same artist condemns (uncontrolled) file-sharing, but does eventually recognise the potential of the digitisation of their product, and makes a distribution channel. In other words, the initial conflicting situations that artists and central actors in the industry had with the first wave of entrants has developed into collaboration with later entrants. Also, examples II and III show a degree of collaboration arising because of guarantees by the software builders that they would only condone file-sharing in legal ways. By displaying this behaviour and intention, the collaboration materialises with both first entrants as well as later entrants, the former illustrated by example II and the latter by example III in Box 11.3.

The first two items in Box 11.3 touch upon the interface of the companies with its consumers. As discussed with the characteristics of innovation focus, McPhee (in Peterson and Berger, 1971) notes that the marketing environment of this industry is characterised as near the turbulent extreme because it depends on rapidly changing style preferences of many predominantly young buyers (also see Scott, 1999). This seems to touch on what Bourreau (2005) calls the quality improvement of the product, which is split up in sound quality and portability. Sound quality refers to the possibility for the consumers to choose the quality in which they want to enjoy the music, as this can be set at the 'manufacturing' stage. Thus, the way and quality of consuming the product is determined by the consumer. A clear link with the process of prosumption that has arisen in many industries is present here. Prosumption refers to high levels of customisation through a combination of production and consumption by so-called prosumers (Tapscott, 1996; Toffler, 1980). In other sectors, the process of prosumption has led to large productivity gains and is often seen as one of the main pillars of the contemporary economy (Tapscott, 1996). Therefore, the arrival of this phenomenon in the music recording industry is likely to provide big opportunities for both new entrants and existing actors.

Box 11.3   Development towards collaboration between former conflicting actors

> I. It is a case of musical Darwinism. When your career spans decades, it is inevitable that you have adapted to the times in order to survive. Such is the case with Metallica and Pearl Jam who both have made major strides in adapting to the use of the Internet for digitally distributing their music. Metallica – notorious in certain circles for coming down hard on music pirates – has led various efforts to decrease the amount of pirated music available and inflict harsher penalties on those who steal content. But not wanting to leave fans out to dry digitally, Metallica recently unveiled MetallicaVault.com, a Web site devoted to freely distributing bootlegs in MP3 format. [...] Metallica created the site with the help of Speakeasy and thePlatform. According to thePlatform's VP of marketing, Andrew Olson, the group is not inherently opposed to digital distribution, but this format allows, 'fans to get first crack at it' (Levack, 2003: 9).
>
> II. John Kennedy, chairman and CEO of IFPI said: 'Kazaa ('s software, ed.) was an international engine of copyright theft which damaged the whole music sector and hampered our industry's efforts to grow a legitimate digital business. It has paid a heavy price for its past activities. At the same time Kazaa will now be making a transition to a legal model and converting a powerful distribution technology to legitimate use. This is the best possible outcome for the music industry and consumers. Our industry will have a new business partner and consumers will experience new ways of enjoying music online, with more choice. This is a win-win scenario.' (RIAA, 2006)
>
> III. In April 2003, Apple Computer unveiled a new online music service, the iTunes Music Store, offering low-priced music downloads from the five major record labels. In October, a few months after Apple introduced iTunes, Roxio relaunched Napster as a subscription-based music service. [...] From the industry's standpoint, both iTunes and Napster provide an exciting opportunity. While these services offer legal alternatives to KaZaA, Grokster, Morpheus, and other allegedly illegal file-sharing networks, they also help students and computer users develop habits that the industry hopes will continue. As Napster's former President Michael Bebel proclaimed, [t]his deal encourages a new generation to try a legitimate service, enjoy and adopt it, and later when they have more time and money, continue it. So far, customers seem to be generally satisfied with these services. (Yu, 2004: 922)

Portability refers to the reduction in file sizes, which enhances the number of songs that can be taken along. These reduced sizes enhance flexibility in numbers but also in possible combinations. The third item in Box 11.3 would appear to be the newly stabilised structure of the industry, in which the central actors have regained a sufficient amount of control to make the degrees of uncertainty surrounding them acceptable. In order to 'reach' this bullet, a gain in control and uncertainty reduction needs to take place, at least from the central actors' perspective.

As has been stated earlier, the traditional actors in the music recording industry are not famous for quick adaptation to innovations lying outside of the production function (i.e. new music styles or artists) of the central actors. Historically, central actors needed time to re-establish their control over the market (see Figure 11.1) after each innovation that impacted functions, other than production. By having a firm grasp on the vertical aspects of the industry (i.e. manufacturing and supply chain), innovations were eventually absorbed by these central actors by means of vertical and horizontal integration, as the structure in the oligopolistic market did not erode in full. Each historical innovation either provided a shift in medium or a shift in strategic orientation. Digitisation and its subsequent developments, however, provided a dual innovation, in the medium as well as in the basis for strategic orientation (i.e. a changing market information regime). The medium change facilitated a parallel (illegal) distribution channel for music through file-sharing on the internet. The shift in strategic orientation was comprised of the demise of the inflow structure regarding information needed, for example, to catch up with music fads, as well as the establishment of new channels for informational and promotional activities.

This state of turmoil provided the basis for the origination of inter-organisational conflict discussed above. As the central actors of the industry did not have the learning skills or capability development to establish the know-how to tackle the developments directly from within their own companies, they set out to collaborate with the entrants stepping in after the first wave, and remained in conflict with the initial entrants. Of course, the skills and capability may have been present, but the time needed to wait for intra-organisational or traditional intra-industry development might have been scarce. The first entrants were perceived as a threat in a broad sense, mainly as a threat to the control possessed by the central actors, but the second and third ones were not. The initial increase in the threat to the degree of control in the hands of the central actors can be linked to an increasing degree of uncertainty in the industry caused by the new entrants. Pfeffer and Salancik (1978) hypothesised that inter-organisational behaviour with regard to tie formation can be partially explained by the inclination of organisations to reduce uncertainty. Moreover, they argue that there is an association between the degree of concentration in an industry (i.e. industry structure) and the level of uncertainty for actors in that industry. Therefore, the initial increase and subsequent decrease in uncertainty as a consequence of changes in industry structure (ibid.) can explain the inter-organisational behaviour of actors, which in turn appears to play a role in the development of conflict to collaboration. In other words, the behaviour concerning the formation of inter-organisational links was triggered by the organizational inclination to reduce uncertainty levels, which could not be sufficiently reduced through conflicts but instead required collaboration with subsequent entrants. This point will be pursued further below.

The conflicts between the original actors populating the industry and the first wave of entrants as a consequence of digitisation taught second and third wave entrants what was acceptable to both the legal system as well as the industry. The initial positionings and interactions of these later entrants were likely to have been received quite differently from the first ones. Thus, in terms of finding ways to tackle the problems, these new entrants could now serve as possible collaborative partners, as can be seen in the recent success of ITunes.[7] The vehicle to develop collaboration with these latter waves appears to be what Yu (2004) terms battle strategy number 5, licensing (e.g. example III in Box 11.3). Licensing is the business model on which the agreement between actors in the industry and a digitised distribution channel is built. It is essential to facilitate the collaborative relation, as without the 'right' to sell the content originally produced by artists and their record companies, there would be seeds for conflict. However, merely having permission does not suffice, as it should also be difficult or otherwise unattractive to spread this product for free. The licensing model, following Yu (2004), is aimed at providing copy-protected files for a low price. With this approach, the companies make money and the consumer gets the content desired in a manner that is acceptable (i.e. flexibly used, low price, and so on). The licensing business model thus constitutes the end state, the collaboration. These findings are largely in line with the earlier findings of Browning et al. (1995) and Faerman et al. (2001), which indicate that such developments are not bound to a single sector or case but are present in similar cases in different sectors as well.

The central actors in the music recording industry needed to learn and develop capabilities to be able to deal with the uncertainty that was created by the changes, so the development towards collaboration is driven by an attempt to nullify these deficiencies. The business model of licensing brought the opportunity for collaboration. The conflict and confrontation can be seen as a first reaction, more a coping mechanism to deal with the tension, annoyance and animosity resulting from the upset of the workings of the industry. The collaboration can be seen as a recognition of the perceived threat to the main actors and an attempt to establish stability in order to access the new distribution channel and to get a grip again on strategic developments.[8] The repositioning of the entrants in the network thus showed different paths for first entrants and for later entrants. The first entrants got caught in conflicting situations, as they were changing a relatively inert industry overnight. However, as example II in Box 11.3 shows, even some of these initial entrants developed collaborative relations. The later entrants (see example III)[9] were able to develop collaborative relations without first going through the conflict stage. From the relationship between industry structure, level of uncertainty, and inter-organisational linking behaviours, as posed by Pfeffer and Salancik (1978), it can be derived that the development of collaboration out of conflict is a consequence of consecutive developments of the industry structure and the accompanying levels of uncertainty. The level of uncertainty is coped with by inter-organisational linking behaviour, which is driven, in the case of the music recording industry, by the need for learning skills and capability development (i.e. the establishment of a new market information regime). In this sense, the central actors in the music recording industry appear to have dealt with the uncertainty that emerged and have successfully regained control over the industry.

CONCLUSION AND DISCUSSION

This chapter began with the following question: 'Which factors play a part in the origination of inter-organisational conflict and its development towards inter-organisational collaboration?' In order to find an answer to this question, the case of the music recording industry was explored and existing theoretical insights were used to uncover the relevant factors. The selected case was researched by analysing previous research. Two 'drivers' were found that account for the origination of inter-organisational conflict and its development towards collaboration within the music recording industry, namely technological innovation (i.e., an innovation in media), and a strong shock that alters the way the controlling central actors can function in the industry. More specifically, the digitisation of the product content (music) and digitisation of the information streams to and from the central actors caused upheaval. It seems plausible that this upheaval was caused by the fact that the developments described in the above impacted on different types of uncertainty at once, whereas previous developments usually impacted only on a single type of uncertainty.

From the historical analysis of the case, it can be concluded that the introduction of a new technology is by no means always reason for inter-organisational structures to reconfigure. It appears that an inter-organisational reconfiguration seems likely only when a new introduction fundamentally upsets the core characteristics of the industry (such as the market information regime and the innovation focus of organisations in an industry) and that this is due to the changing levels of uncertainty. Since these characteristics are different for many sectors and industries, a general definition of what kind of shocks will lead to inter-organisational change is hard to formulate. Instead, researchers should always look at the core characteristics of the context (i.e. the industry) in which a shock takes place. Doing so would allow more insight into which kind of events can trigger changes in inter-organisational settings.

In this particular case, the large external shock led to a loss of control and a loss of strategic orientation for the central actors, as compression routines for music files enabled uncontrolled exchange of music. The reaction of the central actors can be characterised as slow (relative to the spread of digitisation) and the market can be termed a relatively stagnated one, following Thorelli's (1986) terms, or inertial, following Kim et al. (2006). The uncertainty brought on by the combination of the two drivers provided the base for the origination of inter-organisational conflict in the industry between the central actors and new entrants. Unfortunately, in this case, the studied materials were not rich enough in detail to determine the relative share of the different dimensions of Koka et al.'s (2006) uncertainty concept in shaping dynamics. Richer data is thus needed for further explication. However, there are hints of the environmental uncertainty and behavioural uncertainty in the papers that have been included in this research. This research thus points to the factors related to the degree of radical change an industry goes through. In line with conventional wisdom, derangements of historically or traditionally stable core characteristics of an industry are facilitators of inter-organisational conflict. However, when the upset does not ebb away, a need for coping with the new situation needs to be devised by the actors within the industry. It has been argued in this research that learning and the development of capabilities by the actors within the industry are the key developmental factors needed to foster inter-organisational collaboration, because the actors involved may lack the skills or the time to learn and develop know-how all by themselves, which has been tied to industry structure and accompanying levels of uncertainty in the above. This reasoning is in line with the resource deficit argument from resource dependence theory, which states that organisations need to obtain resources in order to function but cannot be expected to possess all the necessary resources themselves. In this case, the need to learn and develop capabilities can be considered a knowledge resource that the central actors in the industry did not possess. However, this learning and capability development seems to be an ego-centred approach as it is only the focal organisation that needs to undertake it. From our research, learning and capability development have not been demonstrated; rather they were reasoned to be accommodated in a collaborative relationship. The development of new business models through licensing appears to be the vehicle through which collaboration will eventually arise. Building on resource dependence theory, the initial relational setting of the central actors in the industry and the new entrants was possibly a result of the desire of the former to keep up their degree of autonomy. However, this appeared impossible and the traditional market players were confronted with a high degree of dependence on the new entrants. This degree of dependence is connected to the central actors' lack in learning skills and capability development. It can be concluded from this that the autonomy/dependence dilemma for a focal organisation in this industry has evolved over time. In essence, then, this calls for a consideration of the dilemma in longitudinal or processual terms to be able to tie it directly to development in or of inter-organisational relations.

This research presents three essential (inter-)organisational processes as a linear development. This could be considered a linearity imposed by the researchers. First, a loss of control by the central actors gave rise to inter-organisational conflict. To put it boldly, the central actors did not know how to handle these changes. This conflict evolved and lasted, but the recognition that consumers actually appreciated the new way of consuming and prosuming the core product led to a necessity on the part of the central actors to further develop their knowledge and capability. This might in itself be considered learning by the industry and individual organisations (the second process), in addition to the learning and capability development that is needed to cope with the developments. The search for a constructive way of handling the problems led to collaboration with other entrants (the third process), which was a different strategy than the one the central actors of the industry pursued with the entrants they were originally in conflict with. By accommodating the learning and capability development in a collaborative relation, the central actors re-established a desirable degree of vertical control, i.e. the parallel uncontrolled distribution channel is internalised. The imposed linearity of course simplifies the interaction of the processes taking place. As argued earlier, however, this reasoning is sound only when this strong assumption is taken on. If this assumption is relaxed, thus letting go of the imposed linearity, the interaction of the processes throughout the studied timeframe becomes presumably more important in order to grasp the origination and development. To be able to conduct such research, more data is needed in the sense of gathering specific longitudinal dyadic data next to the data used in the analysis above.

From this, it can be concluded that, in turbulent times, different coping strategies can be deployed by organisations or even industries. In this case, the industry has an oligopolistic structure in which a few actors are relatively dominant. Seeking confrontation and conflict as a coping strategy appears unsuccessful in situations where the core of the industry is upset. Seeking to learn and develop capabilities in order to cope with uncertainty seems sensible, but the ability of organisations to do so is limited when time is scarce, and is dependent on the presence of the necessary skills. The final coping strategy is seeking collaboration in order to learn and develop capability, i.e. obtaining the resource you need. Whether or not licensing as described above really contains this learning and capability development remains a question for further empirical research.

NOTES

1. http://www.isiknowledge.com.
2. http://proquest.umi.com/login.
3. The distinction between 'manufacturing' and 'production' is found in the mass reproduction of the product versus the creation process of the content of the product. 'Manufacturing' refers to mass reproduction and production to the content creation process.
4. The papers that were used to write this section build mainly on data gathered in European- and United States-based markets and describe dynamics undergone by organisations that are active in these geographic spheres. This limits the generalisation of the paper.
5. The Hirschmann-Herfindahl-index is the sum of the squared market shares of all firms in the industry. Therefore, it fluctuates between 10.000 (for an industry with only 1 monopolistic firm) and 0 (for an industry with almost infinite amounts of small firms) (Corbey and Van Hulst, 1999).
6. It has to be noted that the concentration degree refers to music recording companies here.
7. According to the annual report of recording label EMI, ITunes continued to drive the market development of controlled online music distribution (EMI, 2005). The international recording industry representative (IFPI) heralds the growth of digital music retailing, of which ITunes is estimated to have a 70 per cent share of single track downloads on the United States market (IFPI, 2006). The central actors all utilise ITunes as one of the digital distribution methods.
8. This refers, for example, to the number of downloads. Which artists, styles and types of songs are popular? What kind of content innovation do we need to strive for?
9. The name Napster was used for two different actors that joined the inter-organisational setting at two different times. The first actor was one of the first entrants that facilitated the exchange of music in digital ways. This shook up the industry as it was considered illegal and lead to the central actors incurring loss of control. The second actor was a later entrant that simply bought the name

Napster for reputation effects, but was and is legitimately selling music in digital formats. It follows that Napster as a name cannot be considered to be an example of initial conflict and subsequent development to collaboration.

REFERENCES

Albanese, A. (2000), 'Napster case forges ahead', *Library Journal*, **125** (10), 18.

Alexander, P.J. (1994a), 'Entry barriers, release behaviour, and multi-product firms in the music recording industry', *Review of Industrial Organization*, **9** (1), 85-98.

Alexander, P.J. (1994b), 'New technology and market structure: Evidence from the music recording industry', *Journal of Cultural Economics*, **18** (2), 113-124.

Alexander, P.J. (2002a), 'Market structure of the domestic music recording industry', *Historical Methods*, **35** (3), 129-132.

Alexander, P.J. (2002b), 'Peer-to-peer file sharing: The case of the music recording industry', *Review of Industrial Organization*, **20** (2), 151-161.

Alper, S., D. Tjosvold and K.S. Law (2000), 'Conflict management, efficacy, and performance in organizational teams', *Personnel Psychology*, **53** (3), 625-642.

Anand, N. and R.A. Peterson (2000), 'When market information constitutes fields: Sensemaking of markets in the commercial music industry', *Organization Science*, **11** (3), 270-284.

Arino, A. and J. de la Torre (1998), 'Learning from failure: Towards an evolutionary model of collaborative ventures', *Organization Science*, **9** (3), 306-325.

Bandulet, M. and K. Morasch (2005), 'Would you like to be a prosumer? Information revelation, personalization and price discrimination in electronic markets', *International Journal of Economics and Business,* **12** (2), 251-271.

Bourreau, M. (2005), 'A comment on Peitz and Waelbroeck', *Economic Studies*, **51** (2/3), 429-433.

Browning, L.D., J.M. Beyer and J.C. Shetler (1995), 'Building cooperation in a competitive industry: Sematech and the semiconductor industry', *Academy of Management Journal*, **38** (1), 113-151.

Burgunder, L.B. (2002), 'Reflections on Napster: The ninth circuit takes a walk on the wild side', *American Business Law Journal*, **39** (4), 683-707.

Burkart, P. (2005), 'Loose integration in the popular music industry', *Popular Music and Society*, **28** (4), 489-500.

Burkhardt, M.E. and D.J. Brass (1990), 'Changing patterns or patterns of change: The effect of a change in technology on social network structure and power', *Administrative Science Quarterly*, **35** (1), 104-127.

Corbey, M. and W. van Hulst (1999), *Bedrijfseconomie,* Schoonhoven: Academic Service Economie en Bedrijfskunde.

Crabtree, E., D.J. Bower and W. Keogh (1997), 'Conflict or collaboration: The changing nature of inter-firm relationships in the UK oil and gas industry', *Technology Analysis & Strategic Management*, **9** (2), 179-191.

Cunningham, B.M., P.J. Alexander and N. Adilov (2004), 'Peer-to-peer file sharing communities', *Information Economics and Policy*, **16** (2), 197-213.

Dahlin, K.B. and D.M. Behrens (2005), 'When is an invention really radical? Defining and measuring technological radicalness', *Research Policy*, **34** (5), 717-737.

Easly, R.F., J.G. Michel and S. Devaraj (2003), 'The mp3 open standard and the music industry's response to internet piracy', *Communications of the Association for Computing Machinery*, **46** (11), 90-96.

EMI (2005), 'Connect: Annual report 2005', http://www.emigroup.com/ Financial/Default.htm.

Faerman, S.R., D.P. McCaffrey and D.M. van Slyke (2001), 'Understanding interorganizational cooperation: Public-private collaboration in regulating financial market innovation', *Organization Science*, **12** (3), 372-388.

Gay, B. and B. Dousset (2005), 'Innovation and network structural dynamics: Study of the alliance network of a major sector of the biotechnology industry', *Research Policy,* **34** (10), 1457-1475.

Giesler, M. and M. Pohlmann (2003), 'The social form of Napster: Cultivating the paradox of consumer emancipation', *Advances in Consumer Research*, **30**, 94-100.

Gobeli, D.H., H.F. Koenig and I. Bechinger (1998), 'Managing conflict in software development teams: A multilevel analysis', *Journal of Product Innovation Management*, **15** (5), 423-435.

Halinen, A., A. Salmi and V. Havila (1999), 'From dyadic change to changing business networks: An analytical framework', *Journal of Management Studies*, **36** (6), 779-794.

IFPI (2006), 'Ifpi:06 digital music report', http://www.ifpi.org/site-content/publications/publications.html.

Kim, T.-Y., H. Ok and A. Swaminathan (2006), 'Framing interorganizational network change: A network inertia perspective', *Academy of Management Review,* **31** (3), 704-720.

Knoben, J., L.A.G. Oerlemans and R.P.J.H. Rutten (2006), 'Radical changes in inter-organizational network structure: The longitudinal gap?', *Technological Forecasting and Social Change*, **73** (4), 390-404.

Koka, B.R., R. Madhavan and J.E. Prescott (2006), 'The evolution of interfirm networks: Environmental effects on patterns of network change', *Academy of Management Review,* **31** (3), 721-737.

Kumar, K. and H.G. van Dissel (1996), 'Sustainable collaboration: Managing conflict and cooperation in interorganizational systems', *MIS Quarterly,* **20** (3), 279-300.

Levack, K. (2003), 'Veteran rockers to head to the front lines of digital distribution', *Econtent,* **26** (8-9), 9-11.

Liebowitz, S.J. (2005), 'Pitfalls in measuring the impact of file-sharing on the sound recording market', *Economic Studies,* **51** (2/3), 435-473.

Lopes, P.D. (1992), 'Innovation and diversity in the popular music industry, 1969 to 1990', *American Sociological Review,* **57** (1), 56-71.

Maclaurin, W.R. (1954), 'Technological progress in some American industries', *American Economic Review,* **44** (2), 178-189.

Madhavan, R., B.R. Koka and J.E. Prescott (1998), 'Networks in transition: How industry events (re)shape interfirm relationships', *Strategic Management Journal,* **19** (5), 439-459.

McCourt, T. and P. Burkart (2003), 'When creators, corporations, and consumers collide: Napster and the development of on-line music distribution', *Media, Culture & Society,* **25** (3), 333-350.

Noorderhaven, N.G. (1995), *Strategic Decision Making,* Wokingham: Addison-Wesley.

Oberholzer, F. and K. Strumpf (2004), 'The effect of file sharing on record sales: An empirical analysis', http://www.unc.edu/~cigar/papers/ FileSharing_March2004.pdf.

Oliver, C. (1990), 'Determinants of interorganizational relationships: integration and future directions', *Academy of Management Review,* **15** (2), 241-265.

Park, S.H. and M.V. Russo (1996), 'When competition eclipses cooperation: An event history analysis of joint venture failure', *Management Science,* **42** (6), 875-889.

Peitz, M. and P. Waelbroeck (2004), 'The effect of internet piracy on music sales: Cross-section evidence', *Review of Economic Research on Copyright Issues,* **1** (2), 71-79.

Peterson, R.A. and D.G. Berger (1971), 'Entrepreneurship in organizations: Evidence from the popular music industry', *Administrative Science Quarterly,* **16** (1), 97-106.

Peterson, R.A. and D.G. Berger (1975), Cycles in symbol production: The case of popular music', *American Sociological Review,* **40** (2), 158-173.

Peterson, R.A. and D.G. Berger (1996), 'Measuring industry concentration, diversity, and innovation in popular music', *American Sociological Review,* **61** (1), 175-178.

Pfeffer, J. and G.R. Salancik (1978), *The External Control of Organizations: A Resource Dependence Perspective*, New York: Harper and Row.

RIAA (2006), 'Kazaa settles with record industry and goes legitimate', press release 27 July 2006, http://www.riaa.com/news/newsletter/072706.asp

Scott, A.J. (1999), 'The US recorded music industry: On the relations between organization, location, and creativity in the cultural economy', *Environment and Planning A*, **31** (11), 1965-1984.

Simons, T. L. and R. S. Peterson (2000). 'Task conflict and relationship-conflict in top management teams: The pivotal role of intragroup trust', *Journal of Applied Psychology*, **85** (1), 102-111.

Soh, P.H. and E.B. Roberts (2003), 'Networks of innovators: A longitudinal perspective', *Research Policy*, **32** (9), 1569-1588.

Spitz, D. and S.D. Hunter (2005), 'Contested codes: The social construction of Napster', *The Information Society*, **21** (3), 169-180.

Tapscott, D. (1996), *The Digital Economy: Promises and Peril in the Age of Networked Intelligence,* New York: McGraw-Hill.

Teece, D.J. (2000), 'Strategies for managing knowledge assets: The role of firm structure and industrial context', *Long Range Planning*, **33** (1), 35-54.

Thorelli, H.B. (1986), 'Networks: Between markets and hierarchies', *Strategic Management Journal*, **7** (1), 37-51.

Toffler, A. (1980), *The Third Wave,* New York: Morrow.

Trist, E. (1983), 'Referent organizations and the development of inter-organizational domains', *Human Relations*, **36** (3), 269-284.

Tushman, M.L. and P. Anderson (1986), 'Technological discontinuities and organizational environments', *Administrative Science Quarterly*, **31** (3), 439-465.

Yu, P.K. (2004), 'The escalating copyright wars', *Hofstra Law Review*, **32** (3), 907-951.

PART IV

Conclusions

12. Conclusions: Questions for Future Research

Leon Oerlemans, Tobias Gössling and Rob Jansen

INTRODUCTION

The aim of this book is to advance our understanding of processes in multi-organisational partnerships, alliances and networks. In order to meet this aim, the book needed to respond to a frequently heard criticism on network research, namely that it is predominantly of a 'structuralistic' nature and does not pay sufficient attention to (dynamics of) network processes. By taking an interactionist approach on collaboration, control, learning, conflict in- and failure of inter-organisational relationships and networks, the book attempts to deal with this criticism and add to an existing gap in the literature.

The overviews in the previous chapters present a variety of literature relevant for studying processes in inter-organisational relationships and networks. They also pose and answer many research questions, address a variety of topics, present reviews, develop concepts, definitions, theories, hypotheses and methodologies, and offer empirical evidence. Moreover, several chapters use original empirical data to support or highlight theoretical findings and assumptions. At the same time, the chapters here have developed new research questions and topics, some of which have been studied, others not, indicating that the authors have uncovered research gaps in their respective fields. Various contributors to this book have already identified a number of these gaps in their chapters.

This concluding chapter aggregates, identifies and organises the most relevant questions that need, in our view, the further attention of scholars. We do not have the ambition to be complete, because the field is too diverse, unexplored and complex. We were therefore forced to restrict ourselves and select what we believe to be the most demanding of future study.

To structure our questions for future research, we applied two interconnected guidelines. First, we applied a thesis – antithesis – synthesis approach. We began the book with the observation that the structural account dominates the field (thesis) and that there is a need for a relational account of inter-organisational relationships and networks (antithesis). This plea for a relational account harbours the danger of substituting one myopic view for another. The chapters in this book showed that a relational account can provide added value for network studies and in this sense, the book made its point. However, it would be unwise to totally neglect the contributions made by the structural account, as it has convincingly showed that, for example, bridging ties, structural holes and structural embeddedness have important individual and collective outcomes. This concluding chapter is consequently guided by the idea that the structural and relational accounts of inter-organisational relationships and networks are complementary (synthesis) and can help us to further study and understand the link between structure and action (Ibarra, Kilduff and Tsai, 2005), which is one of the most important research themes in social science. The second guideline we applied, which is connected to the first, helped us to structure the findings of this book and search for the open research questions. We found that the relationship between network structures and interaction between network actors is one that can be interpreted as a variation on how to link the macro and micro. This link has several dimensions, which can be seen in the following questions: to what extent and in which ways do network structures impact on processes in relationships and the other way around? To what extent and in which ways do network structures and processes in relationships co-evolve? These combinations of level of analyses, on the one hand, and assumed causal directions, on the other, will direct what will follow below.

The remainder of this chapter is structured as follows. In line with the structure of the book, we will discuss important findings and directions for future research for each of the themes (i.e., control, learning, conflict and failure). Where possible and relevant, we will connect these themes.

MONITORING AND CONTROL IN PARTNERSHIPS AND NETWORKS: POSSIBLE DIRECTIONS FOR FUTURE RESEARCH

Control of networks is crucial in order to be able to coordinate tasks and manage the rationing of surpluses (Dekker, 2004). Furthermore, control appears to be a critical factor for the success of networks (Park, 1996). The characteristics of inter-organisational relationships, however, suggest that classical management instruments of control are not appropriate (Mouritsen and Thrane, 2006). This is due to the fact that these control mechanisms imply hierarchical settings. Yet it is the absence of complete hierarchies that is a constituent element of inter-organisational relations. In other words, partners of inter-organisational relationships cannot make use of their managerial fiat (c.f. Park, 1996; Williamson, 1991). The purpose of control in inter-organisational relations is to provide incentives and action conditions that make partners stick to the purpose of the collaboration (Dekker, 2004 with reference to Fisher, 1995).

In this context, Dekker (2004) argued that the field of network control is to a large extent underexplored. That is to say, little is known about the actual coordination mechanisms of networks. Mechanisms, however, are more process than structure characteristics. Hence, by emphasising mechanisms, Dekker's view concerning research on the relationship between control and networks is a processual one. He proposes a categorisation of control mechanisms that could be at work in inter-organisational relationships and networks. Table 12.1 shows this categorisation.

Table 12.1   Formal and informal control mechanisms in inter-organisational relationships

Outcome Control	Behaviour Control	Social Control
Ex-ante mechanisms		
Goal setting	Structural specifications:	Partner selection
Incentive systems/reward	Planning	Trust (goodwill/capability)
structures	Procedures	Interaction
	Rules and regulations	Reputation
		Social networks
Ex-post mechanisms		
Performance monitoring and	Behaviour monitoring and	Trust building
rewarding	rewarding	Risk taking
		Joint decision-making
		Partner development

Source: Dekker (2004: 32).

Network control has outcome, behavioural and social aspects. The control mechanisms in use are *ex-ante* and *ex-post* mechanisms. The mechanisms contain incentive systems, monitoring, rules, trust building, etc.

Control is related to power. Power is a central precondition for control, in so far as possessing power in a relationship with another actor is necessary for being able to control him (see Clegg, 1989). Networking has partially to do with managerial interdependencies. Power can be defined as the observation of dependency (Astley and Zajak, 1991). Exchange dependencies generate power relations between actors (ibid.; Pfeffer and Salancik, 1977). Empirical research in the structural tradition on networks shows, for example, that the centrality of an actor has a positive influence on his power (Mizruchi, 1982; Mintz and Schwartz, 1985; c.f. Bonacich, 1987). However, even though there is a strong emphasis on structural accounts in network research, scholars are more likely to relate network control to mechanisms, interaction and processes. This is remarkable, especially given the research output relating structural features of networks with network outcomes. The question concerning control as a consequence of centrality and density remains unanswered. Given the impact of network characteristics on power and the fact that power is a precondition for control, we assume that structural network characteristics will impact on the possibility of controlling partners. The assumption is that both structural characteristics are positively related to control.

The contributions of the first part of this book apply foremost to relational approaches towards control in networks. Gössling (Chapter 2) proposes that institutions play a crucial role in influencing actors' behaviour in inter-organisational relationships and networks. Institutions matter because and if contravention becomes sanctioned. Sanctioning is interaction. This means that an actor's behaviour is not influenced by a myopic social construct but rather by the normative expectations and interaction power of other actors. However, the possibility of imposing normative expectations on others depends on factors such as spatial and organisational distance and the (non)existence of ties between actors. In this sense, structural aspects of the relationship between actors play a crucial role in the application of institutional mechanisms. In other words, structures provide the framework for control whereas interaction provides the content.

Van Nuenen (Chapter 3) focuses on the underlying normative structures (belief structures) that are central to processes of inclusion and exclusion. Her research is of importance because the majority of research in this field has focussed on economic or strategic and dependence factors for explaining tie formation (Gulati, 1998), whereas she points at cognitive processes that influence tie formation. Her findings indicate that inclusion and exclusion follow from iterative social interactions. In other words, social networks underlie organisational networks. Her findings therefore suggest that social networks influence interaction in organisation networks. Control takes the form of social control in social networks. Hence, if social networks underlie organisation networks, then the locus of control refers to the control exercised within the boundaries of the inter-organisational setting. Relational aspects that are central to social networks determine the structure of professional networks via inclusion/exclusion mechanisms. These mechanisms therefore depend on both relational (micro) and structural (macro) characteristics. Research that aims at understanding these mechanisms and their consequences should consequently focus on these two dimensions.

Sullivan, Barnes and Matka (Chapter 4) present a case that is consistent with the two aforementioned conclusions: The locus of control in the cases in their chapter shifted from the formal to the informal. In this context, the collaborative capacities of the respective parties determine the possibilities for collaborative control. Their research identifies factors that affect partnership capacity. These are legitimacy, power, the capacity to contribute to the network, the perception of the status of the network and the development of collaborative relationships between partners. Whereas most of these factors refer to relational aspects, structural aspects play a role in the latter. Furthermore, the authors stress the meaning of power in this context, which is also related to structural characteristics of actors. Power partly depends on the centrality of an actor in a network (Gomez, Gonzalez-Aranguena, Manuel, Owen, Del Pozo and Tejada, 2003). Hence, in order to understand the determinants of collaborative control, an analysis of the structural aspects of networks (density and centrality), as well as the interactional ones (relational characteristics, such as the content of relational ties, and resource dependencies) is needed.

Purdue (Chapter 5) refers to the capacities of network partners when focusing on the learning of network partners and networks. In describing the role of facilitators and mediators for community organisations, Purdue provides a vivid illustration of what actually flows through conduits in networks. His reference to trust and informal aspects of relations and social control highlights the importance of qualitative aspects of relationships, as opposed to structural ones. Trust, however, also is related to the structural characteristics of a network actor (Buskens, 1998; Gössling, 2004). Purdue highlights this phenomenon in the cases presented in his chapter: The governmental organisation as an actor with a high degree of centrality tries to steer network processes with formal control. This effort is doomed to fail as a consequence of a lack of trust, which is a type of informal control. The case description also implies a low degree of density between the authority and the community activists.

The chapters in the first part of the book maintain the assumption that control in inter-organisational relationships contains formal and informal elements. This assumption is not, as such, ground-breaking. However, it stresses the importance of connectionist aspects of network relations, as opposed to structural aspects. It clearly brings to light the interaction between collaboration partners and the underlying social networks. Furthermore, it exemplifies the process-oriented aspects of network relations. However, our discussion shows that relational and process-oriented aspects matter in combination with structural aspects. Control is interaction within a structural framework. Hence, the chapters of the first part of this book support Park's (1996) suggestion that the appropriateness of control mechanisms depends on structural network characteristics. We propose to approach network control issues by taking both perspectives – structural as well as relational – into account. We have already made a suggestion for future research, namely that the control consequences of structural network assets need to be investigated. In the above, we argued that control and power in networks are related. To a certain extent, control can even be considered a way to exert power in inter-organisational relations. This issue obviously is linked to the choice of governance and brings us to the intricate relationship between different forms of control and the governance of inter-organisational relationships. Proponents of transaction cost theory, who dominate the field of the study of governance choice, emphasise the importance of formal control. However, due to the fact that the theory takes a static approach, the co-evolution of control mechanisms over time is not taken into consideration. An interesting avenue of research could be to find out the extent to which formal contracting gives way (or not) to more flexible practices as partners become increasingly embedded in networks due to ongoing interaction processes and trust-building. Another avenue of future research could focus on the co-evolution of firm development and network configuration and how this process is related to different types of control. In a longitudinal analysis of six new biotechnology firms, Maurer and Ebers (2006) find that firms can realise performance benefits when their members adapt their network configurations to changing resource needs, whereas inertia turns an organisation's network into a liability. They suggest that both formal and informal control could generate relational lock-in leading to inertia, which is to say, that the (social) network is not adapting quickly enough (ibid.: 276). Because their inertia model is developed on the basis of only a few cases, a survey-based approach could allow for further empirical generalisation.

The chapters in the first part of the book explicitly or implicitly pose additional questions for further research. Gössling mentions the necessity for more in-depth research on the nature and consequences of institutions in inter-organisational collaboration. In this context, the question arises to what extent density and centrality matter for imposing institutional pressure and sanctioning interaction partners.

Van Nuenen researches choices for exchange partners in a particular field. Thus, ultimately, her research focuses on causes of network structures rather than on their consequences. A question that arises from her research is the following: to what extent do interaction processes constitute different control mechanisms, which are moderated by the emergent structure, resulting from these processes? Van Nuenen's research deals with relational embeddedness in one field. However, actors are involved in multiple networks. The interesting question therefore arises to the extent to which processes of in- and exclusion are influenced by this multiple embeddedness and the extent to which multiple embeddedness gives rise to conflicting belief systems, which could in turn impact on in- and exclusion processes.

Sullivan, Barnes and Matka (Chapter 4) analyse the control consequences of collaborative capacities. However, they do so in a specific network. We assume that the network structure could have a moderating effect on this relation and therefore propose to research this effect.

Purdue (Chapter 5) describes the change of the role model of a government organisation (on a superior hierarchical level) to a partner (on the same hierarchical level). This implies a change of the network structure. We suggest further research concerning the extent to which this shift matters for the actor's ability to exert control.

LEARNING IN PARTNERSHIPS AND NETWORKS: POSSIBLE DIRECTIONS FOR FUTURE RESEARCH

As was stated in the introduction of this book, during the last decades, the subject of learning in organisational contexts has become very popular. Most scholars describe organisational learning or the learning organisation in positive and normative terms, an approach that one could label a learning bias, as it implies that organisations 'must' learn and that learning is a 'good' activity in and of itself. A comparable observation could be made for the field of network studies (network bias: networking is a desirable activity in and of itself), as only few studies exist in which the downsides of networking are researched (see for example: Raab and Milward, 2003). Recently, studies have emerged in which learning in networks or network learning has been the focus. Many of these studies do indeed take a rather normative approach to learning, assuming that organisations, organisations in networks and organisational networks should learn in order to be competitive and to survive in the market place. In this following section of this concluding chapter, we will take a critical stance towards such reasoning.

In a review of the literature on organisational learning, Örtenblad (2002) observes that the main perspective on organisational learning is functionalistic. The main characteristics of this functionalistic perspective on organisational learning are that individuals learn as agents for the organisation. It also means that, although the shared understanding of (the goals of) the organisation guides the learning effort it is the individual who learns. The organisational form is supposed to facilitate a positive climate for the learning of individuals. The structure of the organisational form is preferably of a flexible nature, as such a structure makes it possible to deal with the ever-changing demands of external actors, such as customers or suppliers. The external environment, which is also viewed as a source of learning, can be objectively known. The question 'how do organisations learn?' is answered by referring to organisational memory. This memory consists of shared understandings, routines, procedures and documents, and thereby envisions the organisation to be a knowledge storage device. Interestingly, only very few authors comment on one of the problems of knowledge transfer, namely that documents, reports, routines and so on, have to be interpreted by a receiving actor. Instead, it is mostly assumed that it is possible to transfer knowledge without changing it in the process.

Örtenblad (ibid.: 90) points out that the functionalistic theory of organisational learning is developing towards a so-called interpretive approach. This approach has the following characteristics:

- Reality is no longer objective, but subjective.
- Knowledge cannot be unambiguously described since it is context dependent.
- Learning is situated and localised.
- Learning entities are not individuals as cognitive individuals.
- Learning is a social practice and starts in relationships.
- The community (of practice) learns.
- Learning is not confined to the formal organisation.

The chapters in the 'learning' part of this volume, written by Hibbert and Huxham (Chapter 6) , DeFillippi, Arthur and Lindsay (Chapter 7), and Knight and Pye (Chapter 8), clearly fall in the realm of this interpretive approach. This is evidenced, for instance, by the definitions of learning that are used by these authors. Knight and Pye, for example, define learning as a social, political and non-linear process, whereas Hubbert and Huxham see learning as a flow of reflective moments organised around trajectories of participation. Thus, both emphasise the social and relational aspects of learning.

In order to distil relevant avenues of future research on inter-organisational and network learning from these chapters, we will organise our discussion around a number of issues, namely: *entities of learning; control, power and learning; conditions and structures for learning; learning processes, and learning outcomes*. Where possible and necessary, we will make links with the topics discussed in other parts of this book.

As Knight and Pye observe in Chapter 8, there are several and diverse conceptualisations of organisational learning, ranging from learning as information processing to learning as a social process involving individuals, groups of individuals, organisations, groups of organisations, and networks. Knight and Pye argue that greater conceptual clarity can be achieved by distinguishing the context of learning from the agent that learns. Both DeFillippi et al. and Hibbert and Huxham share this view. DeFillippi et al. argue that varying levels of brokerage and closure can impact on the potential to maximise community social capital, whereas the review by Hibbert and Huxham points at what they call 'situation characteristics', such as partner complexity and organisational form, both elements that refer to the context of learning. Although this is certainly a relevant distinction, it still leaves the question unanswered concerning the entity that is actually learning. Most authors, including those in this volume, do likely agree that individuals are involved in organisational learning to some extent. So, in as far as organisations or networks are able to learn, the learning is always connected to individual agents. But how is individual and organisational learning related? To answer this question, many scholars in this volume refer (in)directly to cognitive models of shared knowledge. DeFillippi et al., for example, refer to the concept of a knowledge work community in which actors have a joint enterprise, a shared repertoire, and are mutually engaged. But how are these two concepts actually related in theory and practice? Where does individual learning stop and (how) is it transformed in a shared model on an organisational or network level?

A topic related to the previous one is the relationship between power and control on the one hand, and organisational learning, on the other. Knight and Pye state that organisational learning is not only a social, but also a political process. When one thinks about the implications of this statement, an interesting research avenue emerges. Most studies on organisational learning seem to have the implicit assumption that learning is a kind of power-neutral process and that the outcomes of learning are beneficial to all participants. We will deal with the latter issue below. But is organisational learning actually a power-neutral process? Here, we advocate it is not. After all, when one asks the question 'who steers the learning process?', an obvious answer would be 'managers' or 'more powerful organisations inside networks'. Future research could investigate how power relations in inter-organisational networks influence the learning process, for example by researching the goal-setting process (whose learning goals dominate in the network collaboration?).

In Chapter 2, Gössling argues that institutions influence individual and organisational behaviour, such as learning. An interesting research question concerns the institutions or institutional arrangements that have an impact on specific learning behaviours. For example, which institutions stimulate the learning behaviour that results in new knowledge creation, and which institutions are beneficial for the behaviour leading to the implementation of new knowledge? Since these are two different processes, it is plausible that different institutions could be at work. Moreover, such a question is highly relevant, as the organisational learning literature focuses more on knowledge transfer and creation than on the implementation of the transferred or created knowledge.

DeFillippi et al. describe different scenarios of brokerage and closure that influence the potential of realising community social capital. In particular, the case of low closure and low brokerage is detrimental for the generation of community social capital. Hibbert and Huxham analyse combinations of different learning attitudes and knowledge outcomes and deduce that inter-organisational relations in which one of the partners has a selfish learning attitude will likely produce the transfer of existing knowledge and not the creation of new knowledge. An interesting research question that arises from these analyses is which factors affect the trajectories from one scenario to another (e.g. from 'selfish learning attitude' to 'shared learning attitude' or from 'low brokerage and closure levels' to 'high brokerage and closure levels') or which factors affect the likelihood that an inter-organisational relation will be in a particular scenario. More specifically, the question concerning which institutions are of particular importance for these movements needs to be asked.

Some inter-organisational and network structures seem to be more beneficial for generating knowledge outcomes than others. Purdue shows that, in a highly centralised inter-organisational network, where a governmental agency is the central actor, trust-building is hindered, leading to a network's poor (learning) performance. Moreover, both Hibbert and Huxham, and DeFillippi et al., point at the importance of balancing brokerage and closure, or to use the words of Hibbert and Huxham: there is a need for tightly structured (helping to generate desirable outcomes) and open network structures (linking distant communities and knowledge bodies that provide novel knowledge and information). These valuable insights help us to formulate a number of research questions focusing on the issue of the perception of networks, and aid in the further investigation of network dynamics.

The chapters on learning presented in this book all go beyond the dyad as the unit of analysis, which is actually the focus in the majority of network research (Gulati, 1998). They tend to discuss and study larger networks, such as communities of practice. But how do actors (micro) operate in these larger network (macro) structures in order to maximise both their individual as well as community social capital? Or, to put the question more precisely, how and to what extent do actors know that they are part of larger organisational structures that can help them to accomplish individual and common learning goals? This brings us basically to the issue of network perception. As Ibarra et al. (2005) observed, in the 1990s, organisational network research took a cognitive turn: organisations and their environments were re-conceptualised as cognitions in the minds of the participating actors. The cognitive approach of networks draws our attention to the fact that different actors perceive very different networks, even when looking at the same network structure, an issue that in a certain sense was also studied in the chapter by Van Nuenen. Here, we try to explore new research directions by linking the cognitive approach to organisational learning issues. To do so, two reciprocal processes have to be taken into account: (a) the impact of network structure on cognition; and (b) the impact of cognition on network structure.

As Iberra et al. (2005: 365) observe, the positions of individuals in social networks can bias their perceptions of the environment to the relative exclusion of more objective outside views, probably resulting in the reinforcement of similar perceptions within clusters of actors. Network interaction seems to affect perceptions through two different processes: a proximity effect due to local interaction and a systemic power effect due to centrality in networks (Ibarra and Andrews, 1993). When applied to organisational learning issues, the former process could lead to research that investigates how the network of inter-organisational ties within and across clusters of collaborating actors affect the cognitive construction of strategic learning opportunities. The latter process implies that network structure impacts on environmental cognitions. Walker (1985) showed, for example, that the perceptions of social equals with little previous interaction tended towards similar images of environmental change. In other words, equals learned from each other, creating new perceptions. In contrast, in dyads between more and less powerful actors, the former actors adopted the perception of the latter actors. The implication of these findings is that knowledge creation, as opposed to knowledge transfer, is more likely to occur between social equal actors from different social networks than between dyads in which substantial differences in power exist. It would be interesting to find out whether these patterns can be reproduced for actors in inter-organisational networks.

All chapters in the learning part of this book point at the reciprocal relationship between inter-organisational settings and structures, on the one hand, and learning, on the other. Since inter-organisational relationships and networks are used by actors for channelling resource flows, these chapters maintain the assumption that these settings or structures are, to a certain extent, known to actors, and are valued and structured by them. Research (Freeman, 1992; Kumbasar, Romney and Batchelder, 1994) has shown that cognitive biases influence perceptions of social structure. It was found that actors are likely to strive to maintain a perspective of a just world, in which their relations are ordered appropriately and in which they value themselves as more important than they are valued by others. If we want to study how perception structures networks, a number of relevant questions emerge related to the accuracy, schemas and cognitive ties between actors. For example, under which circumstances (networking for resource acquisition or for learning) does it matter whether actors have accurate cognitions as to who is connected to whom?

All authors in this book writing about the relationship between learning and inter-organisational networks view learning as a process. Hibbert and Huxman, for example, view learning as the development of knowledge through and within social practices. They agree with the view of Knight and Pye by stressing that knowledge development is a more relevant process than knowledge transfer. By focusing on knowledge development and creation, the process of creativity and its possible relationship to organisational and social structure comes to mind. Creativity, which can be defined as a process that leads to the generation of novel and appropriate ideas, processes, or solutions (Amabile, 1988), is at the very heart of the learning process, as its outcomes can help organisations in their efforts to establish or maintain competitive advantage. By unpacking the learning process in several sub-processes, scholars could investigate the impact of social and organisational structures on these processes. An interesting example of such an approach can be found in Perry-Smith and Shalley (2003). In their theoretical contribution, they argue that weaker ties are generally not always beneficial for creativity. Moreover, they hypothesise a curvilinear association between centrality and creativity, where actors occupying a peripheral position in a network with a large number of outside connections will have the highest creativity levels, leading over time to a more central position in the network. This nice example of a combination of a structural and relational account of networks impacting on a process (here: on the levels of creativity) in a longitudinal framework clearly deserves empirical exploration.

As to learning outcomes, we would like to recommend two avenues of future research. Hibbert and Huxham stated in their chapter that there is a distinction between 'learned from each other', which is a result of the transfer of knowledge, and 'learned with each other', which is the result of the joint development of knowledge. The latter form could be labelled cooperative learning. An interesting question is what incentives impact on the outcomes of cooperative learning (see also: Chapman, 2002). Are there differences between incentives that reward individual contributions to the joint outcomes and incentives, and ones that reward the joint outcome only? A second future research direction builds on the work of DeFillippi et al. in this volume. In their chapter, they stress the importance of virtual knowledge work communities in current organisational life. An interesting research question related to these virtual communities is to what extent the learning outcomes of these communities differ from outcomes generated in more traditional collaborations (e.g. with no performance feedback). Research in an educational context (Halttunen and Jarvelin, 2005) showed that students working in collaboration with IT-generated performance feedback outperformed their peers in the traditional collaboration. Whether this finding also holds for organisational virtual communities warrants further research.

CONFLICTS IN AND FAILURE OF PARTNERSHIPS AND NETWORKS: POSSIBLE DIRECTIONS FOR FUTURE RESEARCH

Inter-organisational relationships and networks are potential breeding grounds for conflicts that might even lead to the dissolution of the collaborative relationship. The truth of this statement results from the absence of formal structures and hierarchy. Moreover, joint objectives, which are introduced within a company by a higher level of hierarchy, are often subject to negotiation. These differences are a result of the features of inter-organisational collaboration, such as the coexistence of collective and individual goals without a clear formal hierarchy, a polycentric and often temporary allocation of power without formal power sources, and the interdependence of network actors (see also: Huxham and Vangen, 2000).

The importance of studying conflicts in inter-organisational relationships is exemplified by the chapters presented in this part of the book. The literature review in Chapter 9 concerning the factors affecting tie failure, by Oerlemans, Gössling and Jansen, revealed that scholars (a) use different definitions of tie failure; (b) propose a wide variety of possible failure factors, which can be categorised into three main groups (environmental, organisational and relational); (c) see relational features of inter-organisational relationships and networks as dominant factors causing tie failure. The possible directions for future research that can be derived from their chapter are rather straightforward. First, since this field of study is dominated by (empirical) applications of transaction cost theory, the question was raised as to whether this theory is really sufficient to model and explain the failure of ties. Given its static nature and its lack of attention to the impact of social structure, the addition of a more dynamic dimension to the transaction cost framework was recommended.

Second, a more detailed analysis of failures in inter-organisational relationships, especially with regard to the question concerning how different constellations of habitual and relational behaviour collide, was proposed. In line with the ideas put forward in Chapter 2 by Gössling, research could focus on the influence of norms of exchange on the likelihood of tie failure. In this context, norms of exchange are expectations about behaviour that are at least partially shared by a group of decision-makers. Following Kemp (1999), relevant dimensions of this concept are flexibility (a bilateral expectation of a willingness to make adaptations as circumstances change), information exchange (a bilateral expectation that parties will proactively and voluntary offer information useful for the partner), and solidarity (a bilateral expectation that there is a common interest and a feeling that a high value is being placed on the relationship). Using these aspects, one could posit that the level of norms, defined as expectations about behaviour like flexibility, information exchange and solidarity, has a negative effect on the intensity and frequency of conflict in an inter-organisational relationship. In other words, high norms of exchange will result in a low level of conflict. In this way, a theoretical connection is established between a specification of informal institutions and the probability of tie conflict and failure.

Third, a fruitful extension of tie failure research would be to study the impact of the social or organisational network in which the partnering firms are embedded on the relative performance of their alliances. Here, one can distinguish two avenues of future research. The first one focuses on relational embeddedness. An interesting question is whether inter-organisational ties, such as alliances, that are embedded to a greater or lesser degree in various networks have a higher or lower likelihood of failure. One can assume that ties which are more strongly embedded in networks benefit from higher trust and confidence levels and more intense flows of information and knowledge. These characteristics could lower the likelihood of tie failure. A second avenue could be to study the consequences of structural embeddedness. Organisations in networks characterised by high centrality levels do not only have to manage their individual inter-organisational ties, but are basically confronted with the management of a portfolio of ties, which could have different strategic scopes. This raises a 'span of control' question: to what extent can ties that are part of a highly centralised network be managed by participating partners? Overstretching the network management capabilities of organisations in such networks could impact negatively on relative tie performance. A third avenue of future research is a combination of relational and structural embeddedness. An interesting question could be the extent to which a different likelihood of tie failure of comparable ties in different networks exists.

Although Chapters 10 and 11 by Gray and by Jansen and Knoben focus on different levels of analysis, on a higher level of abstraction, they share an interesting communality, namely the transformation of conflict. Gray suggests that framing, which is defined as the process of constructing and representing actors' interpretations of the world around them, plays an important role in the creation, evolution and perpetuation of multiparty conflict and collaboration. Frames are used by actors to define issues, to shape what action should be taken and by whom, to protect themselves and characterise others, to justify a stance taken on an issue, and to mobilise people to take or refrain from action on issues. In particular, it is the power of framing to shape actions intended to solve conflicts that attracts our attention.

In their case study of the music recording industry, Jansen and Knoben focused on factors that play a part in the origination of inter-organisational conflict and its development towards inter-organisational collaboration. Concerning the triggers of inter-organisational conflict, two main drivers were identified: technological innovation and a severe shock that significantly changed the way central actors in the industry behave. As a result of the fact that turbulence in the industry did not vaporise, the initial state of conflict transformed into an emerging need for inter-organisational collaboration. This transformation was fuelled by a need for learning and the development of skills by the actors within the industry in order to reduce uncertainties.

It can be concluded that both chapters point at the importance of coping strategies to transform conflicts into solutions. To extend this research, a number of future research directions can be proposed. First, one could investigate the conditions under which coping strategies *are* or *are not* effective. This line of research might be informed by the work done by Raes, Heijltjes, Glunk and Roe (2006) on the evolution of intra-team conflict. In a longitudinal study involving 41 teams, these researchers found two distinct temporal process patterns emerge. The first process pattern developed in a stable manner and is characterised by high trust levels and relatively low levels of task and relational conflict. The second process pattern turned out to be unstable and was characterised by deteriorating trust levels and high, amplifying levels of conflict. Moreover, intra-organisational teams with stable patterns outperformed teams with unstable patterns. This research stresses that trust levels are conditional for patterns of conflict levels and over time lead to differing levels of stability and effectiveness. It would be interesting to apply this research model to an inter-organisational context in which trust might be even more important in the relative absence of hierarchical control.

Gray provides an extensive overview of frame-based interventions that could promote understanding in inter-organisational conflicts. Her research could be extended by systematically linking interventions and types of conflicts. Winkler (2006), for example, argues that conflicts between individual and common goals in inter-organisational partnerships and networks are frequent. In an attempt to systematically link types of conflict and interventions, he develops several proposals in which formal (e.g. the establishment of a network coordinator or the introduction of rules for joint decision-making) and informal interventions (e.g. shared understandings) are used to resolve conflicts. Further research on the interrelatedness of different interventions and different and other types of conflicts is needed.

CONCLUSION

There are systematic reasons for the division of network research into structural and relational approaches. The research methodology for these two approaches differs significantly. Structural accounts prefer the use of large-scale quantitative research methods; relational accounts apply quantitative in-depth methods and case studies. Furthermore, structural approaches often focus on networks as research units, whereas relational accounts more likely focus on dyads or ties and the characteristics of the network partners involved. However, as Jones, Hesterly and Borgatti (1997) stated, structural embeddedness is a foundation for social mechanisms. This means that research has to take the two different discussions into account in order to understand the network action, which was the guiding theme in this concluding chapter.

REFERENCES

Amabile, T.M. (1988), 'A model of creativity and innovation in organizations', *Research in Organizational Behavior,* **10**, 123-167.
Astley, W.G. and E.J. Zajak (1991), 'Intraorganizational power and organizational design: Reconciling rational and coalitional models of organization', *Organization Science*, **2** (4), 399-411.
Bonacich, P. (1987), 'Power and centrality: A family of measures', *American Journal of Sociology*, **92** (5), 1170-1182.
Buskens, V. (1998), 'The social structure of trust', *Social Networks*, **20** (3), 265-289.
Chapman, E. (2002), 'Effects of social cohesiveness and cooperative incentives on small group learning outcomes', *Current Research in Social Psychology*, **7** (17), 293-311.
Clegg, S. (1989), *Frameworks of Power*, London: Sage.
Dekker, H.C. (2004), 'Control of inter-organisational relationships: Evidence on appropriation concerns and coordination requirements', *Accounting, Organisations and Society*, **29** (1), 27-49.

Fisher, J. (1995), 'Contingency-based research in management control systems: Categorization by level of complexity', *Journal of Accounting Literature*, **14** (24), 24-53.

Freeman, L.C. (1992), 'Filling in the blanks: A theory of cognitive categories and the structure of social affiliation', *Social Psychology Quarterly*, **55** (2), 118-127.

Gomez, D., E. Gonzalez-Aranguena, C. Manuel, G. Owen, M. del Pozo and J. Tejada (2003), 'Centrality and power in social networks: A game theoretic approach', *Mathematical Social Sciences*, **46** (1), 27-54.

Gössling, T. (2004), 'Proximity, trust and morality in networks', *European Planning Studies*, **12** (5), 675-689.

Gulati, R. (1998), 'Alliances and networks', *Strategic Management Journal*, **19** (4), 293-317.

Halttunen, K. and K. Jarvelin (2005), 'Assessing learning outcomes in two information retrieval learning environments', *Information Processing & Management*, **41** (4), 949-972.

Huxham, C. and S. Vangen (2000), 'Ambiguity, complexity and dynamics in the membership of collaboration', *Human Relations*, **53** (6), 771-806.

Ibarra, H. and S. Andrews (1993), 'Power, social influence and sense making: Effects of network centrality and proximity on employee perceptions', *Administrative Science Quarterly*, **38** (2), 277-303.

Ibarra, H., M. Kilduff and W. Tsai (2005), 'Zooming in and out: Connecting individuals and collectives at the frontiers of organizational network research', *Organization Science*, **16** (4), 359-371.

Jones, C., W.S. Hesterly and S.P. Borgatti (1997), 'A general theory of network governance: Exchange conditions and social mechanisms,' *Academy of Management Review*, **22** (4), 911-945.

Kemp, R. (1999), 'Cooperation and conflict in international joint venture relationships', *SOM Research Report 99B33*, Groningen: University of Groningen.

Kumbasar, E.A., K. Romney and W.H. Batchelder (1994), 'Systematic biases in social perception', *American Journal of Sociology*, **100** (2), 477-505.

Maurer, I. and M. Ebers (2006), 'Dynamics of social capital and their performance implications: Lessons from biotechnology start-ups', *Administrative Science Quarterly*, **51** (2), 262-292.

Mintz, B. and M. Schwartz (1985), *The Power Structure of American Business*, Chicago: University of Chicago Press.

Mizruchi, M.S. (1982), *The American Corporate Network: 1904-1974*, Beverly Hills, CA: Sage.

Mouritsen, J. and S. Thrane (2006), 'Accounting, network complementarities and the development of inter-organisational relations', *Accounting, Organizations and Society*, **31** (3), 241-275.

Örtenblad, A. (2002), 'Organizational learning: A radical perspective', *International Journal of Management Reviews*, **4** (1), 87-100.

Park, S.H. (1996) 'Managing an interorganizational network: A framework of the institutional mechanism for network control', *Organization Studies*, **17** (5), 795-824.

Perry-Smith, J.E. and C.E. Shalley (2003), 'The social side of creativity: A static and dynamic social network perspective', *Academy of Management Review*, **28** (1), 89-106.

Pfeffer, J. and G.R. Salancik (1977), 'Organization design: The case for a coalitional model of organizations', *Organizational Dynamics*, **6** (2), 15-29.

Raab, J. and H. Brinton Milward (2003), 'Dark networks as problems', *Journal of Public Administration Research and Theory*, **13** (4), 413-439.

Raes, A., M. Heijltjes, U. Glunk and R. Roe (2006), 'Conflict, trust, and effectiveness in teams performing complex tasks: A study of temporal patterns, *METEOR Research Memorandum 7*, Maastricht: Maastricht University.

Walker, G. (1985), 'Network position and cognition in a computer software firm', *Administrative Science Quarterly*, **30** (1), 103-130.

Williamson, O.E. (1991), 'Comparative economic organization: The analysis of discrete structural alternatives', *Administrative Science Quarterly*, **36** (2), 269-296.

Winkler, I. (2006), 'Network governance between individual and collective goals: Qualitative evidence from six networks', *Journal of Leadership & Organizational Studies*, **12** (3), 119-134.

Index